Two Hundred
Good Restaurants

Two Hundred Good Restaurants

A Guide to Eating in San Francisco & the Bay Area

by
Russell S. Riera
and
Chris Smith

Illustrated by
Jim Parkinson
and
Frank Ansley

Moss Publications

California

Revised Second Printing, 1979 Edition

Library of Congress Catalog Card Number: 79:83832

ISBN 0-930870-01-8

Acknowledgement: We would like to thank Robert Hendrickson for the use of information from his book, *Lewd Food,* The Complete Guide to Aphrodisiac Edibles. Copyright © 1974 by Robert Hendrickson. With permission of the publisher, Chilton Book Co., Radnor, Pennsylvania.

Typography by Robert Sibley
Book design by R. S. Riera
Production by Nasrin Greene

Printed in the United States of America by
Griffin Printing and Lithograph Co., Inc., Glendale, California

To
Mimi Moss, Pearl Riera, Sam Moss,
Valerie Riera,
Emily Biddle, Sydney Dodge, Neny and James Firth

Introduction

Our search for good food began many years ago, and in a way it was a small Italian restaurant that started us down this path. One night, we were looking around for a place to eat and decided to try this mama-and-papa restaurant in North Beach. It was the right choice. They served us a Six Month Dinner—six months later we were still thinking about how good it was. That meal convinced us. We decided to keep looking for places to eat. Regularly.

We've both been Bay Area residents all our lives, and we've had the opportunity and the time to discover many different kinds of restaurants. Variety is what we have to offer you.

In this guide to San Francisco and the Bay Area, you'll find . . .

- Italian restaurants. Seafood houses. Chinese restaurants.
- Old-time establishments serving big, old-fashioned dinners.
- The best of the Bay Area's inexpensive restaurants.
- Small romantic restaurants. Ocean side cafes. Old World-style inns. Candlelit bistros.
- An around-the-world variety of restaurants: German, Indonesian, Moroccan, Swiss, Greek, Bolivian, and more.
- Places that specialize in: thick steaks, homemade pasta, oak-barbecued meats and oven-fresh pies, hand-spun pizza, crab cioppino feeds, homecooked breakfasts. Even the world's best hot dog stand.
- Everything from tree-shaded dinner houses in Bay Area neighborhoods to restaurants serving the kind of moderately priced feasts that San Francisco is famous for.

And more . . .

Of course, just discovering a restaurant isn't enough. What's more important is getting to know a restaurant. And we do. The menus of every restaurant in this book were explored for the best each place has to offer. And then these dishes are described under the section ''Menu Specialties'' in each restaurant's article. We want you to know exactly what you're getting. There's one last thing we'd like to mention—we've tried to make this a restaurant guide that's fun to read.

Contents

Restaurants by Type

The Popular Seven

Italian
Little Joe's	18
North Beach Restaurant	27
Gold Mirror	33
New Pisa	41
Vanessi's	54
U.S. Restaurant	56
Basta Pasta	57
Angelo's	63
Orsi's	67
La Pantera	78
Swiss Louis	84
Gold Spike	89
Guido's	95
Iron Pot	102
Lorenzo's	125
Giovanni's	130
Marcello's	137
Loreto's	142
Banchero's	144
Canzona's	156
Galli's	168
Galano's	187
Tino's	202
Old Spaghetti Factory	210
Raffaello	223
Depot Hotel	234
Union Hotel	241
Buscaglia's	249

Chinese
Mike's	19
Szechwan	35
Hunan	49
Sun Hung Heung	60
Harbin	77
North China	86
Sam Wo	101
Yenching	103
Tung Fong	110
Mandarin Village	140
The Royal Mandarin	172
Wah Yen	181
China First	191
Peking Duck	200
Foo-Loo-Soo	209
China House	211

Seafood
Sam's Grill	17
La Rocca's	30
Scott's	44
Tadich Grill	64
Pacific Cafe	69
Atlantis	104
South Pacific Grotto	105
Swan Oyster Depot	109
Broiler Fish House	145
Yankee Lobsterman	170
Monti's	186
Fisherman's Village	206
Jerry's Farmhouse	216
The Shore Bird	218

French
Le Rhone	31
Le St. Tropez	38
Jack's	42
La Croisette	48
Rue Lepic	70
Adriatic	85
La Quiche	110
Beau Rivage	120
Narsai's	126
Au Coquelet	127
Chez Daniel	134
Le Marquis	136
La Marmite	166
La Bonne Auberge	182
Le Pot-Au-Feu	199

Around-the-World

Spanish
Spanish Pavillion   25

Czech
Europa   45

Salvadorian
Coatepeque   76

Japanese
Otafuku Tei   24
Kichihei   99
Fugetsu   133
Genji   212

Filipino
Love's Pagan Den   128

Thai
Bangkok Cafe   98
Siamese House   98

Indonesian
Sari's   73
Rice Table   160

Tunisian
Carthage   74

West Indian
Connie's   74

Vietnamese
Saigon   80

Korean
Korea House   73

Mediterranean
Vasilis   47

Back Home

American
Butcher Shop   20
Blanche's   46
Beginning   79
Walker's   124
The Great American   135
Cranberry House   207
Jerry's Farmhouse   216
Nepenthe   222
Elk Cove Inn   229
Greenwood Cafe   230
Vast's   242
Paul's Boarding House   248

Prime Rib
House of Prime Rib   29
Sun Wah Kue   92
Juanita's   146

Fried Chicken
Estrada's   197

Barbecues
Station No. 1   88
Emil Villa's   132
Rod's Hickory Pit   132
Barbacoa   141
Zachary's   219
The Round Up   232
Poor Red's   250

Hamburgers
Original Joe's   54
Balboa Cafe   107
Fat Albert's   148
The Red Onion   153

Hot Dogs
Noble Frankfurter   106
Chris'   152
The Royal Frankfurter   178

Varied Interests

Specialists

Price Code

The purpose of our price code is simple — it is designed to give you a quick, clear picture of a restaurant's prices. The price categories represent what it will realistically cost a person for a complete dinner at the restaurant. For example, if the restaurant's prices are "inexpensive," your check for dinner will be $6.00 or less, not counting wine and tip. *The Categories:* Inexpensive, $1 to $6; medium, $7 to $10; a step above medium, $11 to $13; expensive, $14 and over. But it's the first and second categories that were used the most. In this book, 87% of the restaurants offer dinners in either the inexpensive or medium range.

Two Hundred
Good Restaurants

SAN FRANCISCO

Included in This Section

Page 18
Modestly priced Italian saute dishes prepared in
an open kitchen by a skillet showman.

Page 19
The place where many local residents go when they
want some of the best Chinese food in town.

Page 31
A family-run French restaurant offering Rhone Valley
specialties and six kinds of homemade dessert.

Page 62
A North Beach restaurant that serves traditional
5-course Basque meals for $5.00.

Obrero Hotel: San Francisco
Basque/5-course dinners including wine, $5.25

We've had many dinners at the Obrero, but like so many things, you always remember the first time.

Our first time was a warm Friday night, seven summers ago. A friend had told us about the place. She had also given us some vague directions and a few basic facts: dinner is served once a night. At 6:30. You get 5 courses. You pay $3 (today it's $5.25). And that includes wine!

This was a bargain worth looking for. And we were looking hard. Finally we spotted the Obrero across from a row of Oriental markets. It was a sturdy, three-story building of 1906 vintage. A small sign in front simply read "Obrero." Most signs tend to flirt with you. This one seemed to be hiding something.

The only entrance to the building was a little red door—locked. We noticed a doorbell off to one side and rang it. A second later there was a buzzzzzzz and the door opened by itself. Our friend had told us beforehand that the hotel was run by a tireless Basque mother of five. And the woman who greeted us at the top of the stairs couldn't have been anyone else. She led us down a long hallway into a plain, well-lit dining room, and disappeared into the kitchen. In the dining room were four large tables; all offered boarding house seating, and all were filled with a happy variety of people. Old. Young. Suits. Workshirts. It was as if you were having dinner with a Gallup poll.

At exactly 6:30, the wine was poured, and the food started to arrive. During the next hour, there were tureens of split pea soup, ocean-fresh rex sole, platters of roast lamb, French fries the size of baseball bats, salad, and fresh fruit. It was one hour of eating, talking, reaching, and laughing. By the end of the meal, there were no strangers at the table.

During that visit, a young doctor at the table kept telling us, "Don't tell anybody about this place." Sorry, Doc.

The Menu: A Basque dinner at the Obrero begins with a bottle of burgundy, crusty sourdough, and a tureen of soup (usually hearty split pea or vegetable.) Next come huge platters containing the second course (Fri.—fresh rex sole; Sat.—spicy oxtail stew; Sun.—chorizo sausage and beans.) Now, it's time for the Main Event (Fri.—roast lamb; Sat.—roast beef; Sun.—Basque style chicken) served with homemade mashed potatoes or hand-cut fries. According to Basque custom, a large bowl of salad is served along with this course. And to end the meal, there's apples, Gruyere cheese, and coffee. Finally, you get a check that reads . . . $5.25. For everything! A miracle, Basque style.

Local Color: At your table you may find some Basque sheepherders from Nevada. They visit the Obrero Hotel during the off-season. Maybe you'd like to know what they're saying to you. If a Basque sheepherder says "Agur," it means "Hello." If he says "Nola zira," it means "How are you." If he says "Baa," it means he's been around his sheep too long. **Prices:** Inexpensive. **Basics:** 1208 Stockton St. (near Pacific), San Francisco. Tel: 986-9850. Hours: Dinner is served at 6:30 pm daily. Reservations necessary. No cards. Wine and beer. Public parking (60¢ per hour) available at the Vallejo St. Garage, 766 Vallejo St. (near Powell).

Sam's Grill: San Francisco
Seafood/The same menu for over 100 years

Okay, let's go back. Way back. The year is 1867. Sam's opens. Time goes by. Then, somewhere along the line, it's noticed. They realize, "We're an institution," and never again touch a thing. The place still has saloon doors. Mahogany walls lined with rows of brass coat hooks. Veteran waiters in George Raft tuxedos. Tables covered with reams of starchy white linen. You could walk in and go snow-blind.

After 112 years of business, traditions are still firmly maintained. They close Saturday and Sunday. The menus are printed *daily*—after Sam's finds out what the fisherman and the farmer have to offer. This isn't a place that takes the word "fresh" lightly. At Sam's, they shop for fresh seafood and produce at 6 a.m., and the menu is printed at 10 a.m.—with the current date in the right-hand corner.

At Sam's, they treat their seafood with all the care it deserves. Take their sand dabs and rex sole, for example. These small, flavorful Pacific fish are fried whole and they're so delicate that twenty seconds too long in a frying pan can ruin them. So Sam's has one chef who pan-fries fish. Period. This man spends his entire evening making sure that each order of fish leaves the pan at its finest moment. Then the sand dabs and rex sole are boned—by an expert. Sam's has another man in the kitchen who does nothing but bone fish.

Some of Sam's specialties have been on the menu from the start. Dishes like Sam's deviled crab and clams Elizabeth have built up such a reputation over the last century, that this restaurant can honestly claim to have edible legends in residence. Yes, there are a number of valid reasons why some people call this place "the best seafood restaurant in the City."

Boston has the Union Oyster House. New Orleans has Galatoire's. So what? We have Sam's Grill.

Menu Specialties: ☐ Boned Sand Dabs a la Sam (a sand dab is a small fish that swims right outside the Golden Gate. Its meat is glistening white, moist and tender, with a mild, seductive flavor. You're served six beautifully fresh, pan-fried filets anointed with a drizzle of lemon butter.) ☐ Boned Rex Sole a la Sam (another one of San Francisco's prized local swimmers. A rex sole is a small, finely textured whitefish. You're served five pan-fried filets lounging in a pool of lemon butter.) ☐ Prawns Creole (large, moist prawns in a classic, deeply-flavored Creole tomato sauce.)

☐ Broiled Salmon (shipped in fresh from Astoria, Oregon. And then carefully cooked on Sam's fine old charcoal broiler.) ☐ Deviled Crab a la Sam (crab meat baked in a buttery, sherry-laced cream sauce that's as yellow as a sailor's sunrise, as fresh as a Pacific trade wind, and as spicy as a bosun's language.) ☐ Clams Elizabeth (live Little Neck clams from Puget Sound, Washington. Opened per order and baked with sherry, butter, lemon, paprika, and bread crumbs.)

Starters: Sam's has 21 different salads . . . including romaine with red beans, hearts of artichokes with anchovies, and a mixed vegetable salad made with green beans, zucchini, asparagus, and carrots. But all of these salads have one thing in common—their freshness. Soups: Turtle Soup (a rich, dark red chowder lightly spiced with cloves); Clam Chowder (made with live Washington Little Necks.) **Prices:** Medium. **Basics:** 374 Bush St. (near Kearny), San Francisco. Tel: 421-0594. Hours: 11 am-8:15 pm Mon.-Fri. Closed Sat., Sun. Cards: MC, V. Full bar.

Little Joe's: San Francisco
Italian/Modest prices and a skillet-show

Franco Montarello could have become a tightrope walker, a fire-eater, a juggler, or an acrobat. Instead, he became a short-order Italian saute chef. What a choice! Out of all those jobs, he picked the one that's the most difficult.

Franco's work area is a big problem in itself: it's a rectangular room not much wider or longer than a hallway. A lunch counter runs down the middle of the room. On one side there's Franco and a bank of stoves; on the other side sit twenty hungry diners with a full view of the kitchen. Behind these twenty prized stools there's always a lip-smacking group waiting to get into position.

Meanwhile, Franco is moving around the kitchen like a determined tornado. He juggles six cast-iron skillets almost at the same time. Hands seem to come out of nowhere—making petrale sole flip over in the pan, balancing a can of Bertolli olive oil over some broccoli, giving the sizzling veal parmigiana a shot of homemade tomato sauce, and eventually adding a squirt of sauterne to almost everything. When Franco makes this last move with the wine, it sends up such a wall of flame, people at the counter can feel the heat.

During this process, Franco finds time to wheel around and send a plate of just-cooked food spinning in a diner's direction. Sooner or later, we hope you're at the receiving end of such a throw. There are a lot of advantages in being part of Franco's counter culture.

Menu Specialties: □ Filet of Sole (Pacific-fresh sole sauteed in butter, chablis wine, and lemon juice.) □ Veal Parmigiana (breaded with sourdough crumbs, topped with Monterey Jack cheese and homemade tomato sauce, and sauteed in white wine.) □ Veal Scaloppine (sauteed in sauterne wine and Bertolli olive oil with fresh mushrooms.) And since the counter arrangement shortens the pan-to-mouth ratio, each dish has the added flavor of being tasted seconds after its finished. To improve on this set-up, Franco would have to serve people while they sat on the stove.

Dishes include rigatoni in a meaty Bolognese sauce, or sauteed Italian vegetables—a mix of fresh broccoli, cauliflower, and zucchini. **Prices:** Inexpensive. **Basics:** 325 Columbus Ave. (near Broadway), San Francisco. Tel: 982-7639. Hours: 11 am-7:30 pm Mon.-Sat. Closed Sun. No cards. Wine and beer. Public parking (60¢ per hour) available at the Vallejo St. Garage, 766 Vallejo St. (near Powell).

Mike's: San Francisco
Chinese/The Cantonese say "One of the best"

The Canton area of China is known for its mildly seasoned, subtly-flavored dishes. The Cantonese believe in letting the natural flavors of foods take center stage. And this is the kind of cooking you'll find at Mike's—a small, chef-owned restaurant located on Geary Boulevard, far from Chinatown. But that hasn't stopped this place from being discovered. Many of the Cantonese people we've talked to have referred to Mike's as "one of the best Cantonese restaurants in San Francisco."

We agree.

Chef Mike Lum Won has the ability to handle his dishes in a way that quietly elevates them above the ordinary. It's the mark of a Cantonese cooking master. Chef Won's skill shows in the beautiful moistness of his Crystal shrimp; in the delicate balance of ingredients in his chicken with Chinese vegetables and cashew nuts; in the subtle richness of his beef tenderloin with imported straw mushrooms; and in the exciting interplay of flavors in his sweet & sour pork deluxe. This may be the City's best sweet & sour dish—a combination of golden-crusted nuggets of moist pork in an intriguing ruby red sauce laced with dates, kumquats, Chinese melon, cherries, and lichee nuts. It's so good, you'll want to enjoy it slowly, possibly a molecule at a time.

Menu Specialties: □ Sweet & Sour Pork Deluxe (be sure to order the "Deluxe" version.) □ Crystal Shrimp (the ginger-and-sherry flavored shrimp are kept beautifully moist by quickly stir-frying them over a very high flame. The main ingredient in this dish is timing. Ten seconds too long in the wok means disaster. But don't worry. Chef Won keeps better time than a Bulova.) □ Boned Chicken with Cashew Nuts

(pieces of chicken breast toss-cooked with snow peas, bamboo shoots, whole buttom mushrooms, and cashew nuts. You may notice that the chicken in this dish has a fresh, high quality taste. And it's no accident. Every morning, chef Won conducts a one-man raid on Chinatown's poultry shops. His objective? Get the best.)

☐ Beef Tenderloin with Chinese Straw Mushrooms (the beef is marinated for 6 hours in sesame oil, ginger and onions. Then, it's stir-fried in a flavor-loaded Chinese brown sauce that's dotted with imported Taiwanese straw mushrooms.) ☐ Paper Wrapped Chicken (in each packet you'll find a moist piece of richly-sauced chicken breast that's bursting with flavor and mystery.) ☐ Wor Won Ton Soup (homemade won ton dumplings stuffed with shrimp and abalone, and served in a fresh chicken broth that's laced with slices of barbecued pork and cloud ear mushrooms.) ☐ Barbecued Spareribs (marinated for half a day in wine and spices, then roasted in a special Chinese oven.)

The Open Door Policy: Chef Mike Lum Won is a man with nothing to hide. During slow periods, customers are graciously allowed to go back to the kitchen and watch chef Won work his magic. **Prices:** Inexpensive to medium. **Decor:** The walls may be plain, but the white tablecloths, the gleaming white Chinese porcelain plates, and the excellent service all say, "We Care." **Basics:** 5145 Geary Blvd. (near 16th Ave.), San Francisco. Tel: 752-0120. Hours: 4:30-10 pm Mon., Wed.-Sun. Closed Tues. Cards: MC, V. Full bar.

Butcher Shop: San Francisco
American/Steaks, daily specials, and homemade desserts

Chef-owner Rick Salinas has done everything in the restaurant business except cater the Last Supper. Chef Salinas started his kitchen career 28 years ago as a dishwasher in New York. Since then, he's been a chef at the award-winning Scandia restaurant in Los Angeles, ran the kitchen at author Barnaby Conrad's restaurant, and prepared a birthday dinner for the producer of *Hello, Dolly!*, and a victory dinner for Senator John Tunney.

For his latest venture, chef Salinas has chosen to center his operation around some basic pleasures—thick steaks, homemade desserts, and reasonable prices. For those who may not feel like a steak, chef Salinas offers two daily specials. As soon as you're seated at a candlelit table in the Butcher Shop's small, attractively decorated dining room, host Alex Brashier, chef Salinas' partner, will point at an antique blackboard in the room where the specials are listed and describe each one to you. On that board there could be anything from chicken in champagne sauce to leg of lamb stuffed with spinach.

The blackboard is also used to announce the Butcher Shop's homemade desserts—items like Florida Key lime pie and Chocolate Cloud. But when it comes to desserts, don't ask Alex any questions.

The Butcher Shop's desserts are so rich, you'll gain half a pound just hearing Alex describe them.

As we've said, the prices at the Butcher Shop are reasonable. On a 3-course dinner, the specials are around $6.25, and a 16-ounce sirloin steak is $8.50. These prices really seem fair when compared to what's being charged at some restaurants in San Francisco. Recently, we were at a place where the prices weren't just high, they were out and out frightening. After a glance at the menu, we both looked like the guy in a science fiction movie who's the first one to see The Creature.

Menu Specialties: □ The 16-ounce Top Sirloin Steak □ The 16-ounce New York Steak (chef Salinas visits his meat supplier three times a week and personally selects the steaks for his restaurant. And when chef Salinas broils a steak, his experience shows. He's been cooking steaks for 28 years, and as they say, "practice makes perfect.") □ The Blackboard Specials (maybe prawns stuffed with crab meat, veal Savoyard, apple-stuffed loin of pork in an orange glaze, or beef Bavarian braised in dark beer.) □ The Butcher Shop Hamburger Steak (the Cadillac of hamburgers. A half-pound patty of well-trimmed prime sirloin that's ground fresh daily. The patty is first put in a red wine marinade, then broiled and topped with sauteed mushrooms.)

Dinner includes . . . 3 courses: Soup (maybe old-fashioned potato-leek or tomato corn chowder), tossed green salad (we suggest you try their Russian dressing laced with capers), and main course with a fresh vegetable and chef Salinas' original potato puff (the inside of a baked potato is mixed with sour cream, nutmeg and chives, then rolled into a large ball, coated with bread crumbs, and deep fried. Excellent.)

Dessert: It changes daily—maybe homemade peach cobbler or apple crunch pie. **Prices:** Inexpensive to medium. **Decor:** A small, relaxing dining room with New England-style cross-pane windows, white walls decorated with colorful paintings, and tables topped with crisp white linen, a candle, and a single yellow tulip. **Basics:** 2348 Polk St. (near Union), San Francisco. Tel: 771-5544. Hours: 11 am-3 pm, 6-10:30 pm Mon.-Sat. Closed Sun. Reservations suggested on weekends. Cards: MC, V. Wine and beer.

Luzern: San Francisco
Swiss-French/4-course dinners, gentle prices

San Francisco is lucky to have a large number of European chefs that have been cooking so long, they may have prepared their own baby food. One of these experienced chefs is Rolf Tschudi, but a look at Rolf's menu will tell you that he has yet to master something some of his uptown competitors do very well: Rolf never learned to multiply. So dinner uptown costs twice as much as it does at Rolf's neighborhood bistro. Most of Rolf's dinners are $5.95 to $6.95.

Rolf may not know how to multiply, but he does know how to add, so his dinners include 4 courses: a rich potato-leek soup, a salad with an interesting house dressing, a main course with two fresh vegetables for escorts, and cream caramel for dessert. For the main course you can choose anything from salmon Nantua with shrimp sauce to veal with mushrooms. And the mushrooms Rolf uses are the rare Morilles. Although these mushrooms are usually found only in expensive restaurants, Rolf can offer them because he's developed a special supply channel—his mother. Rolf's mother sends him the Morilles from her home in Switzerland. In fact, last August, she sent him four pounds of mushrooms as a birthday gift.

The parking situation at Luzern is just as satisfying as the food. Rolf's restaurant is located in the Sunset District, where the parking is plentiful enough to give your car a one-night exemption from the process of joining the big-city fleet of dentmobiles.

Menu Specialties: □ Veal aux Morilles (butter-sauteed veal scallops in a velvet-smooth, brandy cream sauce that contains a fortune in "Mama-sent" Morille mushrooms.) □ Salmon Nantua (fresh filet poached in a court bouillon that sings with herbs. Then topped with a cream-rich sauce.) □ Chicken Saute Grand Mere (chicken in a spicy red wine sauce laced with fresh mushrooms, bacon, and pearl onions.) □ Medallions of Beef Luzern (choice, tender beef filets in a golden sauce of butter and herbs.)
Dinner includes . . . 4 courses: Freshly made potato-leek soup, butter lettuce salad with a basil & tarragon-spiked dressing, main course with two fresh vegetables, and cream caramel for dessert. **Prices:** Inexpensive to medium. **Decor:** A small, 11-table bistro. Gold tablecloths, fresh carnations, and a huge photo-mural of the Swiss city of Luzern. **Basics:** 1431 Noriega St. (near 21st Ave.), San Francisco. Tel: 664-2353. Hours: 5-10 pm Wed.-Sat.; 4-9 pm Sun. Closed Mon., Tues. Reservations necessary on weekends. No cards. Wine and beer. Street parking usually available.

Agadir: San Francisco
Moroccan/Feast of a sheik, tent included

Dinner at the Agadir can be described in two words—an experience.

Shortly after you enter the Agadir's billowly, tent-style dining room and lay back on a low, gold velvet Moroccan couch, a waiter appears at your table. Suddenly, he drops to his knees. Then, in a soft voice, he asks you to extend your arms in a sleepwalker's position over a silver basin. Silently, he pours a warm cascade of water over your fingers and then gives you a towel. Once this ceremony is completed, you're ready to eat like they do in Morocco—with your fingers.

At the Agadir, your fingers will let you travel through an exotic 5-course feast. Among the caravan of dishes you'll taste are a spicy Charba soup, four kinds of Moroccan vegetable salad, and a multi-layered chicken B'stilla pie that takes five hours to make.

For the main course chef Jamal Alaoui gives you eleven dishes to choose from. Two of his most popular specialties are cornish hen Souri seasoned with Moroccan saffron and turmeric, and lamb Mouzia—flavored with honey and Rass el Hanoute, which means "head of the spice store," a magical, imported Moroccan mix of 17 spices. And since Moroccans consider this a very important item, chef Jamal has arranged to have direct shipments of this mixture sent to him regularly from a special source in Casablanca.

Agadir has a decor for lovers—the decor is sort of an aphrodisiac for the imagination. As you recline on a low velvet couch in a sea of ruby-red Persian rugs, you begin to feel like you're in Morocco. Scents of orange and spice drift through the air as you sit before a sheik's table of inlaid hand-carved wood. During the tea ceremony, a fez-capped waiter in balloon pants silently pours sweet mint tea into your glass from a height of four feet. And soft Moroccan music fills the room; it's as if they have a band of Berber musicians hidden behind the beaded curtains.

A night at the Agadir. Short of having a catered dinner on Alcatraz, this could be the most unusual dining experience you'll have in the Bay Area.

The Agadir Dinner: We will describe Agadir's dinner from start to finish. But first a word on . . . fingers. You've had them a long time. You shouldn't be afraid to use them. So start by picking up your bowl of Charba and, with the help of a long, wooden, ladle-like spoon, begin sipping it. *Charba* (a hearty soup with an aroma of saffron and mystery.) Next, your fingers will get to explore four kinds of *Moroccan salad* (one of chopped tomatoes and green peppers accented with cumin; a cucumber salad flavored with oregano and lemon juice; Zaalouk eggplant salad, a specialty created in the city of Rabat; and carrots cooked in a couscous pot with herbs and then chilled.) To help you eat the salads, the Agadir bakes crusty loaves of *Khobz bread*—edible scoops.

Now your fingers can tear into the masterwork of Moroccan cooking—B'stilla (a hot, oven-fresh pie made with layers of leaf-thin pastry, chicken, ground almonds, and a multitude of spices. The finished product is an Eastern bazaar of flavors. Delicious. In Morocco, B'stilla is sometimes even flavored with hashish.)

After the B'stilla comes the main course. With fingers ready, you could order *Cornish Hen Souri, Lamb Mouzia,* or *Cornish Hen Mqualli* (a whole cornish hen in a light lemon sauce with a fascinating, subtle flavor.) Finally, your fingers can grip a glass of *Fresh Mint Tea* and wrap themselves around some *Briouat,* a honey-glazed pastry with an almond filling. At the end of dinner your fingers are washed with orange flower water.

Are your fingers all through for the night? Good question. Let's look in on a typical couple after a romantic Agadir dinner. There they are. Twenty fingers. Two owners. One couch. Sitting motionless. Their energy drained by the Agadir's sensual feast. Wait! Five of his fingers are reaching for her shoulder. Look! Five of her fingers are squeezing his knee like it was Moroccan Khobz bread. Gee! Now fingers are flying everywhere . . . Oh, well . . . someday this couple will have another Moroccan dinner, and those fingers can always use the practice. **Prices:** A step above medium. **Basics:** 746 Broadway (near Stockton), San Francisco. Tel: 397-6305. Hours: 6-11 pm daily. Reservations necessary on weekends. Cards: MC, V. Wine and beer. Public parking (60¢ per hour) available at the Vallejo St. Garage, 766 Vallejo St. (near Powell).

Otafuku Tei: San Francisco
Japanese/Easy-to-take prices since 1921

Hitoshi Marumoto owns the Otafuku, the oldest Japanese restaurant in San Francisco. Hitoshi's aunt, Iye Izumi, opened the Otafuku in 1921, and ran the place until she was 90 years old. When aunt Izumi retired, she let her nephew become the caretaker of her recipes. And Hitoshi has done just that. At the Otafuku, aunt Izumi's original dishes are still being served.

The only liberties that Hitoshi has taken are with the decor. By installing large amounts of orange Formica, he's given the restaurant some cosmic Ginza flash. This bright appearance has had an effect on us. The Otafuku reminds us of the kind of place where a secret agent might meet his contact. It's probably just the result of seeing too many James Bond movies, but we always expect to walk into the Otafuku and spot some guy trying to develop a roll of microfilm in his teacup.

Throughout the years, the Otafuku has remained a place where the prices are humanitarian: the tempura is a decent $4.25; the stuffed Gyoza dumplings are a humane $3.10; and the sliced ginger beef

Shogayaki is a fair $4.35. The Otafuku's food and prices are something to be thankful for, and you just may get the chance. While you're eating, you may notice a Japanese man looking at you from the kitchen. This is Hitoshi. If you want to make him happy, just point at your beef Shogayaki and hold your chopsticks in a "V" for victory position.

Menu Specialties: □ Gyoza (the Japanese version of ravioli. The large crescent-shaped pasta dumplings are filled with an almost seam-bursting stuffing of seasoned pork.) □ Beef Shogayaki (thinly sliced strips of sirloin dipped in a light sauce based on soy, fresh ginger, and Japanese mirin wine, and grilled.) □ Tempura (deep-fried shrimp and fresh vegetables. If tempura is cooked correctly, the coating will be (A) air-light (B) greaseless (C) perfectly crisp. And at the Otafuku, they know their ABC's.)

Items above include rice, tsukemono pickles, green tea, and a soybean soup. Fact: In the 16th century, the soybean was considered so essential to Japanese life, it became part of the salary paid to military officers of the Japanese Imperial Court. Hmm, how do you endorse a soybean? **Prices:** Inexpensive. **Basics:** 1737 Buchanan St. (betw. Post and Sutter, across from the Japanese Cultural Center), San Francisco. Tel: 931-1578. Hours: 11 am-2 pm, 5-10 pm Mon.-Sat. Closed Sun. No cards. Sake and beer.

Spanish Pavillion: San Francisco
Spanish/Transplanted Madrid cafe, modest prices

Spanish food is a travelog of ancient cultures. It's a cuisine that's been influenced by the Phoenicians, Carthaginians, Moors, Goths, and, to a large extent, by Spain's contact with the New World. Tomatoes, corn, green peppers, and potatoes were unknown in Europe until Balboa and other Spanish explorers discovered them in the Americas and brought them back to their homeland. This was an act of courage. Imagine the Queen of Spain asking you if you've discovered any temples of gold in the New World, and you pull out a tomato.

The end result of history's effect on Spanish food can be tasted at the Spanish Pavillion. At this modest, 12-table restaurant, the initial mood is set by the decor: the place looks like a street cafe in Madrid. Then the food takes over. At the Pavillion, your exploration party can discover new worlds—such as the marinated Chuletas lamb, paella Valenciana, or one of the restaurant's seafood specialties. The people of Madrid eat 17 million pounds of fish per year, and the Pavillion is helping to raise San Francisco's consumption level by offering eight different seafood dishes, including prawns Enchilados, and clams en Salsa. And it doesn't cost a lot of money to discover these "new worlds"—the Chuletas lamb is $5.50, the paella is $6.25, and the seafood dishes range from $4.25 to $5.75.

Since Spanish dishes are not flavored with fiery spices, you'll discover that the Pavillion's food registers a lower temperature on the Fahrenheit scale than Mexican food. Perhaps this is why a Mexican friend of ours complained that the Pavillion's food was "too bland." But our friend would probably say the same thing if you popped a hot coal into his mouth.

Menu Specialties: □ The Moors brought saffron to Spain . . . the Spanish used it to flavor Paella Valenciana (the flavors of crab, whitefish, and prawns are carefully balanced against the flavors of chicken, ham, and chorizo sausage. Baked on a moist cushion of saffroned rice.) □ The Phoenicians brought the olive tree to Spain . . . the Spanish used the olive's oil to flavor Chuletas de Carnero Amarinadas (three lamb chops marinated 48 hours in olive oil spiked with lemon peel, fresh garlic and Peruvian port wine, then charcoal broiled.) □ The conquistadores came back from the Americas with red and green peppers . . . the Spanish used them to flavor Prawns Enchilados, and Clams en Salsa (both shellfish are simmered in a full-bodied sauce containing red and green peppers, Spanish paprika, tomatoes, white wine, cilantro, and laurel.)

Items above include a salad, rice, and Spanish bolillos bread. Starters: Papa Rellena (stuffed potato . . . a mixture of ground meat, hard-boiled eggs, and olives rolled into a ball and wrapped with a thick coat of mashed potatoes. Then it's baked until golden brown.) Potato Lovers: When Balboa brought the potato back to Spain in 1534, it was thought to be an aphrodisiac. During the next few years, potatoes sold for over $1,000 a pound. Imagine . . . the sign . . . at a Spanish market: "Potatoes—No down payment! 36 months to pay! E-Z credit!" **Prices:** Inexpensive. **Basics:** 3115 22nd St. (near South Van Ness), San Francisco. Tel: 285-0690. Hours: 5-midnight Mon., Wed., Thurs.; 5-1 am Fri., Sat.; 5-11 pm Sun. Closed Tues. (On Fri. and Sat., a flamenco guitarist plays from 8-11 pm.) Cards: MC, V. Wine and beer. Parking lot next door.

North Beach Restaurant: San Francisco
Italian/Handsome softly-lit setting and Bruno in the kitchen

Throughout history chefs have been considered important people. How important? In ancient Greece, a chef who created an especially fine dish was crowned before the public; in the 1870s, during San Francisco's wild Barbary Coast days, restaurant owner Stuart M. Lamont walked his 75-year-old chef home every night to prevent him from getting mugged; and in 1925, Rudolph Valentino had a chef brought in from Italy just to make the lasagna for one of his Hollywood parties.

There was a reason why these chefs were considered so important. They had something special to offer. And so does Bruno Orsi, the owner of the North Beach Restaurant. In fact, chef Orsi has a number of special things to offer.

To start with, Bruno makes his own pasta. He's imported a special machine from Lucca, Italy, and with it he prepares fresh tagliatelle and lasagna noodles. And Bruno is one of the few chefs left around who still makes his own ravioli. In our opinion, it's the best ravioli in San Francisco.

Bruno also cures his own prosciutto ham—a process that takes nine months. But again, the work produces results. The creamy prosciutto sauce that cloaks his pasta Pelosi is one of the most unusual pasta sauces in the City. Even the sauce on his chicken saute Toscana is a little different. And there's a good reason. Into the sauce of fresh tomatoes, mushrooms, and artichoke hearts, Bruno adds rosemary from his own garden and green olives that he cures himself.

Let's review: Bruno makes his own pasta, prosciutto . . . and even cures his own olives. No question—the only thing on the table that Bruno doesn't make is the silverware. And besides being a maker, Bruno is also a creator. There are some dishes on his menu that you just won't find in any Italian cookbook. Like his veal Portafoglio—a thick piece of veal cut like a wallet, stuffed with fontina cheese and prosciutto, and finished with a sauce that's a masterful blend of six herbs, sweet butter, white wine, cream, and a touch of Grand Marnier liqueur.

It's apparent that Bruno has a lot to do. But he has help. In the small, handsome, softly-lit dining areas of the restaurant, there's a staff of fourteen waiters led by Bruno's partner, Lorenzo Petroni, and in the kitchen, there are five chefs at Bruno's side. Of course, the man himself can usually be found behind skillet number one. It's something to see.

Once his hands are on a saute pan, Bruno is a man of emotion, care, and concentration. As his friend once told us, "When Bruno is cooking, it's like he's making love."

Menu Specialties: □ Chicken Saute Toscana □ Veal Portafoglio □ Petrale Portofino (fresh sauteed petrale sole layered with shrimp and baby clams, and served with a flavor-loaded white wine-butter sauce with a lemon accent.) □ Breast of Capon Valdostana (the capon is boned when they get your order, sauteed in olive oil, christened with a nutmeg-spiked cream sauce and Monterey Jack cheese, and baked.) □ Veal Scallopine alla Bruno (scallops of milk-fed Wisconsin veal in a rich brown sauce laced with Italian pine nuts and a fortune in fresh mushrooms.) Dishes include fresh vegetable.

If it's pasta you want: □ Ravioli Toscana □ Lasagna (made with fresh pasta, imported cheese, and two sauces—a long-simmered Bolognese sauce, and a rich supreme sauce.) □ Tagliatelle Verde (thin, freshly-made spinach noodles in a sauce of olive oil, fresh basil, and grated Pecorino cheese imported from Rome.) □ Pasta Pelosi (the sweet butter and cream in the sauce make it rich, the fresh tomato bits and mushrooms make it interesting, and Bruno's prosciutto ham makes it great.)

Comments of a Prosciutto Curer, "—Censored—": There's a reason why Bruno's one of the few chefs who still cures his own prosciutto. The process takes nine months. And the ham must be taken down every twenty-five days and rubbed with seasonings. Very carefully. The slightest bruise can result in the entire ham spoiling. When that happens, Bruno yells out a swear word. That's heard in Fresno.

The Complete Dinner: All of Bruno's a la carte entrees are available on the "truly complete" dinner—which includes 5 courses: A seven-item antipasto tray and a romaine salad tossed in Bruno's Italian dressing, a fine bean-thickened minestrone soup, Occhi di Lupo pasta with prosciutto sauce, main course with fresh vegetable, coffee, and for dessert, Semifreddo (an Italian cake layered with zabaglione cream, and flavored with a mixture of expresso coffee, sherry, rum, brandy, and liqueurs—Sambuca, Tuaca and Strega. The cake's sort of an edible saloon.) **Prices:** Medium to a step above medium. **Basics:** 1512 Stockton St. (near Columbus), San Francisco. Tel: 392-1700. Hours: 11:30 am-11:45 pm daily. Reservations necessary on weekends. All major cards. Full bar.

House of Prime Rib: San Francisco
See a Specialist/A one-item menu since 1949

The way most restaurants prepare their prime rib, it suffers more abuse than a pay telephone—the beef is overcooked, sliced before it's needed, and then robbed of its moisture under a heating lamp. But, beefeaters, there is some good news. We know a place that treats beef with respect—the House of Prime Rib. They're specialists. Prime rib has been the only item on their menu since 1949.

The House of Prime Rib does things the right way. To begin with, this restaurant pays a retired cowpuncher in Denver to personally select their beef and ship it to California. About 70 restaurants across the United States use this man's services. But the quality control doesn't stop here. When the beef arrives in San Francisco, it's aged a full 4 weeks in the House's meat locker. When the beef is ready to be cooked, it's jacketed in rock salt. This process locks in the meat's flavorful juices as the beef slowly roasts. After it's pulled from the oven, the beef is kept moist in a domed cart that looks like an Airstream trailer for a midget. Finally, the cart is wheeled to your table where a chef in starched whites slices you a thick cut of prime rib. And, if you like, you can have seconds on the rib. *No extra charge.*

But there's more. Every prime rib dinner includes a three-nation's breadbasket, rich creamed spinach, Yorkshire pudding, and . . . the Salad Ceremony. The waitress brings you a huge bowl of romaine generously laced with shredded hard-boiled eggs. The bowl is resting on ice. The waitress spins it. Faster. And faster. With her other hand, she slowly pours on the House's unusual, 8-spice, sherry-cream dressing. When the bowl reaches about 400 r.p.m., it's stopped. The lettuce is cold and dizzy. And the dressing is thoroughly mixed in.

The Menu: □ The Prime Rib Dinner (you'll be served a very juicy, very tender slice of beef in a rich, dark brown "au jus." To make the base of this au jus, beef bones and aromatic vegetables are simmered together for 24 hours.) When it comes to cooking beef, the House of Prime Rib tries hard. But they don't try as hard as Ulysses. According to legend, Ulysses roasted beef over an open fire with his bare hands. Flashback . . . at the barbecue, 1200 B.C.—Helen of Troy: "Oh, strong, wondrous Greek, is it hard mastering such a feat?" Ulysses: "Well, for the first few weeks, I used to scream a lot."

Dinner includes: The Salad Ceremony, a three-nation's breadbasket filled with German rye, French bread, and Siberian soldier's bread, main course with rich creamed spinach, fresh mashed potatoes, and Yorkshire pudding (a small pie made with popover dough. Baked to order. Perfect for sopping up the "au jus."), and coffee. Dessert: Pecan Pie (without-a-doubt homemade.) **Prices:** Medium. **Decor:** Soft lights, and large cocoa-colored tufted booths. You almost feel as if this is the Brown Derby on the Sunset Strip and it's 1930. **Basics:** 1906 Van Ness

Ave. (near Washington), San Francisco. Tel: 885-4605. Hours: 5:15-11 pm Mon.-Sat.; 4-10 pm Sun. Cards: AE, MC, V. Full bar. Validated parking at Shell Station, Van Ness Ave. at Washington.

La Rocca's: San Francisco
Seafood/A small place owned by a former fisherman

Fisherman's Wharf seems to have a strangle hold on some people whenever they want seafood—as if the Wharf held an exclusive contract with the Pacific Ocean. Author Riera's grandfather, Carmelo Riera, was partly responsible for giving Fisherman's Wharf this image. Carmelo was a Sicilian fisherman. Starting in 1912, when Carmelo and other fishermen hauled in their last net, they'd aim for the Wharf. They knew that every dockside restaurant owner would have a man there, ready to buy the day's catch right on the spot. So naturally, Wharf restaurants had the freshest seafood around.

But times have changed. Modern transportation methods have adjusted that situation. Today, any restaurant that makes an honest effort can get ocean-fresh seafood.

La Rocca's on California Street is such a place. As it happens, Pasquale La Rocca is the son of a Sicilian fisherman, and in 1929, at the age of nine, Pasquale himself started fishing for his uncle, who was known around San Francisco as "A. La Rocca, the Crab King." Pasquale's forty year career in the fish business has instilled him with a genuine pride in his profession.

And it shows. About the only thing that's frozen in Pasquale's kitchen are the ice cubes. He gets his rex sole, sand dabs and spring king salmon from local fishermen who operate small boats; each batch of clam chowder is made with ten pounds of freshly-shucked Little Necks; and he only buys live Dungeness crabs. According to Pasquale, Dungeness crabs aren't allowed in his kitchen unless they can "walk in by themselves."

After a number of visits to La Rocca's we're convinced that there's only one thing to do if you want your fish any fresher: buy a black fur wetsuit, learn to hold your breath underwater for long periods, and go live on Seal Rock.

Menu Specialties: □ Rex Sole □ Sand Dabs (both fish are grilled in butter. The kitchen will bone them for you on request.) □ Petrale Milanese (petrale sole in a golden crust that's made with sourdough crumbs and parmesan cheese.) □ Spring King Salmon □ Steelhead Salmon □ Ocean Sea Bass □ Swordfish (when it comes to cooking these four fish, you make the decisions. You can have them grilled or broiled, and, if you ask, while they cook the kitchen will baste them with a Sicilian mixture of olive oil and garlic. We suggest you ask.)

☐ Crab Louie (a meal-sized salad made with the meat of about one whole Dungeness crab.) Items include a shrimp salad and sauteed Italian green beans (except the Crab Louie).

Starters: Boston clam chowder. A big bowl. But there are places where you can get an even bigger bowl. Fact: along Australia's Great Barrier Reef, you'll find the Tridacna clam. They're easy to spot. The Tridacna clam weighs over 500 pounds. The Tridacna clam is so large, the aborigine natives who live near the Barrier Reef use the clam's shell as a bathtub for their children. **Prices:** Inexpensive to medium. **Decor:** Inside, there's little booths with wood-slat seats that look like cable car benches, and a counter where you can have dinner while watching two white-clad men crack crabs and shuck clams. **Basics:** 3519 California St. (near Laurel), San Francisco. Tel: 387-4100. Hours: 8 am-8 pm Mon.-Sat. (on Sun., only salads and seafood cocktails are served, no grilled or broiled items). No cards. Wine and beer.

Le Rhone: San Francisco
French/Husband in the kitchen, wife in the dining room

Chef-owner George Chalaye was raised on a 300-year-old Rhone Valley farm in Provence—an area food writer Waverly Root once called "the most magical of all the provinces of France." But Chalaye didn't stay down on the farm for long. When he turned 14, he signed on as an apprentice at Chez Pic—a celebrated restaurant 12 miles from his parents' farm.

Since then, he's cooked at the famous Plaza-Athenee in Paris and many other well known restaurants. In total, he's been a chef for 30 years. Think about it: at 8 hours a day, 5 days a week, that translates out to about 60,000 hours in the kitchen. Like a pilot with flight time, Chalaye is a man with a lot of "stove time" to his credit.

Of course, it takes more than experience to be a good chef. It takes talent. And that's not something a chef can order from a wholesaler or look up in a cookbook. With talent, a chef either has it or he doesn't. Chef Chalaye has it.

Chalaye's talent shows in the fresh, haunting taste of his cream of artichoke soup, in the classic richness of the bearnaise sauce covering his three-inch-thick filet mignon, and in the deep flavor of the wine sauce crowning his chicken Gigondas. Chalaye's talent also shows in his desserts. He makes six different homemade desserts each day, including strawberry tarts, black currant liqueur cake, floating island, mocha genoise cake, fresh apricot tarts, and Rhone Valley pogne buttercake. You can be sure that when the dessert cart rolls by, conversations stop.

The small dining room is the domain of Mrs. Chalaye—a very friendly lady with an almost musical French accent. Mrs. Chalaye looks after customers with a motherly concern. She's the kind of woman who always seems to worry that something may go wrong, although it never does. Mrs. Chalaye, don't worry. Everything at your restaurant is just fine.

Menu Specialties: □ Noisette of Beef Mousquetaire (a three-inch-thick filet mignon purchased from Marcel and Henri, quality French butchers in San Francisco. Served with Chalaye's golden bearnaise sauce.) □ Chicken Gigondas (chicken in a rich sauce made with Provencale herbs and an imported red wine from Gigondas—a sun-drenched French village near the Rhone River.) □ Mignon of Veal du Basilic (two butter-sauteed, inch-thick medallions of white Eastern veal in a dark brown sauce fragrant with fresh chopped basil.) □ Duckling du Pays aux Cerises (Long Island duckling with moist, tender meat that tells of careful roasting. Served with a gently sweet, crimson-colored sauce flavored with Grand Marnier liqueur and dotted with whole black cherries.)

Dinner includes . . . 3 courses: Soup (maybe cream of spinach or soupe des pecheurs—a Provencale-style seafood soup), salad (butter lettuce and tomatoes in a light house dressing made with French red wine vinegar and herbs from Chalaye's own garden), and main course with two fresh vegetables (at Le Rhone the vegetables are brought to the table in little earthenware pots or casserole dishes and everyone helps themselves. It feels like you're having dinner in a Frenchman's home. Some of the vegetables featured: an authentic Provencale ratatouille, carrots in a buttery cream sauce laced with fresh herbs, and a specialty of the Rhone Valley—potatoes dauphinoise gratinéed with Gruyere cheese.)

Dessert: Besides the other desserts we've mentioned, chef Chalaye also makes his own ice cream. If you're there when Chalaye's hazelnut ice cream is offered, consider yourself lucky. **Decor:** The restaurant has been made to look like a country inn in the Rhone Valley. There are two small dining rooms. The front room is set up like the courtyard of the inn. There's even a white fountain filled with potted plants in the middle of the room. The other room is decorated like the interior of the inn, with light yellow wallpaper, pictures of the Rhone Valley, and a polished grandfather clock. **Prices:** Medium to a step above medium. **Basics:** 3614 Balboa St. (near 37th Ave.), San Francisco. Tel: 387-4559. Hours: 5:30-10 pm Tues.-Sun. Closed Mon. Reservations suggested on weekends. Cards: MC, V. Wine and beer.

Gold Mirror: San Francisco
Italian/6-course dinners, Venetian decor

Your get-slim-quick grapefruit diet is hurting our country. America is supposed to be the best fed nation in the world. What are you trying to do, make us look bad? Come on, get patriotic and have a 6-course dinner at the Gold Mirror. By the time you finish the appetizers, the huge salad, the bean-thickened minestrone, and the richly-sauced ravioli, you're going to feel like a better citizen.

But the parade of dishes doesn't stop here. Like the first kiss after the lights go out . . . it's just the beginning. Save some appetite for the main course: arriving next may be chef DiGrande's veal saltimbocca, quilted with cheese and prosciutto ham; or his wine and lemon baptized prawns, stuffed with crab. The flavor of these prawns testifies that DiGrande remembers his father's words—"Always treat seafood with respect." And he isn't likely to forget these words, either. Papa DiGrande usually can be found within ten feet of his son's saute pan. After 55 years at sea, Papa DiGrande left the deck of a Sicilian fishing boat to work at his son's restaurant.

But food isn't the Gold Mirror's only asset. This is a "total package" restaurant. The decor, the service, and the parking are all good. As part of the decor, one wall is staged to look like the front of a Venetian Renaissance villa; the service is handled by friendly waitresses who treat you as though you really exist; and since the Gold Mirror is located in the Sunset District, there's usually an open space to dock your car. This combination, plus chef DiGrande's 6-course dinners, has people coming back here often—but not too often. You tend to get a little self-conscious when you're built like a planet.

Menu Specialties: ☐ Veal Saltimbocca ☐ Prawns Stuffed with Crab ☐ Chicken Cacciatora (butter-sauteed chicken that wears a wardrobe of artichoke hearts, fresh mushrooms, olives, Italian peppers, and tomatoes . . . a well-dressed chicken.) ☐ Medallions of Beef (tender medallions of steak are sauteed with Marsala wine, bay leaves, brandy, and capers until DiGrande hears a bell. From inside. Like with all fine chefs, God has installed a little internal clock in DiGrande that rings at the exact moment something should be removed from the fire.) ☐ Veal Scallopine (moist, tender scallops are sauteed in sauterne with fresh mushroons and 15 spices . . . 3 of which chef DiGrande grows himself.)

Dinner includes . . . 6 courses: A revolving tray of appetizers (including salami, marinated garbanzo beans, mortadella sausage, green onions, Greek olives, marinated artichoke hearts, and mushrooms vinaigrette), salad with a well-herbed olive oil and vinegar dressing, a vegetable-packed minestrone soup, homemade ravioli, main course with fresh vegetable, coffee, and a baseball-sized scoop of spumoni ice cream. **Prices:** Medium. **Basics:** 800 Taraval St. (near 19th Ave.), San

Francisco. Tel: 564-0401. Hours: 11:30 am-3 pm, 5-11 pm Mon.-Fri.;
5:30-11 pm Sat., Sun. Reservations suggested on weekends. All major
cards. Full bar. Street parking usually available.

Tycoon: San Francisco
Middle Eastern/4-course dinners, moderate prices

Plain meats and timid sauces have driven many people to the Tycoon's door. Tycoon is a Middle Eastern restaurant run by three young
Armenians . . . and their food is different enough to keep the dining
room filled with escapees from the cage of convention. Tycoon treats
escapees well. The small, architect-designed dining room, with its soft
lights and thick, burgundy rugs, was built around the idea of making
you feel comfortable. And to put you in the mood for dinner, gentle
Armenian music floats through the room.

Now you should be ready to weave your way through one of
Tycoon's 4-course dinners. It's a moderately priced trip that includes a
Middle Eastern appetizer plate, baked-this-afternoon Arab pitta bread,
spicy red lentil soup, fresh broccoli with Tahini sesame sauce, and
Bourma pastry filled with ground walnuts and honey.

For the main course, there are eight different dishes to choose
from—all of them sauced and marinated in a distinct Middle Eastern
way. One of the most popular dishes is beef Kawarma in a smooth
brown sauce. To make this dish, the beef is soaked for two days in a
wine marinade that's Tycoon's closely guarded secret. But one thing is
obvious—that marinade gives the meat flavor even the meat didn't
know it had.

Menu Specialties: □ Beef Kawarma □ Baby Lamb Shank Izmir (a
tender, well-trimmed lamb shank draped with a spicy Turkish tomato
sauce.) □ Chicken Sevan (a half chicken marinated for one day, then
broiled and served with a light, fragrant Armenian garlic sauce.) □
Lamb Shashlik Armenian Style (skewered lamb, tender and juicy with
marinade. Shish kebab done right. And if an Armenian can't do it right,
who can?)

Dinner includes . . . 4 courses: Phoenicia appetizers (Greek
olives, peppers, Hummus garbanzo & sesame dip, a lemony-flavored
Tabbouleh dip laced with fresh mint, and some Arab pitta bread
"scoops"), red lentil soup, main course with Tahini-sauced broccoli,
coffee, and Bourma pastry. **Prices:** Medium. **Basics:** 4012 Geary Blvd.
(near 4th Ave.), San Francisco. Tel: 387-9600. Hours: 5:30-9:30 pm
Mon., Wed.-Sat.; 5-9 pm Sun. Closed Tues. Cards: MC, V. Wine and
beer.

Szechwan: San Francisco
Chinese/Bamboo-trimmed dining room with quiet charm

According to history, Confucius divorced his wife because her cooking fell below his standards. When it comes to food, the Chinese get serious. That's why you'll find a lot of Chinese customers at the Szechwan. The Szechwan's chef, Uncle Wang, knows what they expect, and gives it to them.

Uncle Wang has been around a wok for a long time. For seven years he cooked at the famous O-Mei restaurant in Taiwan. Then, for the next ten years, he was the personal chef of Congressman Tze Lee of Taiwan. In 1974, when Congressman Lee's son, John, came to the United States to open the Szechwan restaurant, he brought Uncle Wang with him. At the Szechwan, Uncle Wang prepares many of the same dishes he fixed for John's father, including Chung King prawns and Cheng-Tu beef. Both these dishes have the kind of flavor that wakes up your mouth.

The Szechwan is a polished little restaurant. The dining room is decorated with bamboo, Oriental flower arrangements, and traditional Chinese paintings. And in this room you'll also find Helen Lee, the owner's wife. Dressed in Ching Dynasty silk, this gracious lady spends the evening giving every table personal attention. She's the perfect hostess. Helen Lee manages to be everywhere . . . like oxygen.

Menu Specialties: □ Chung King Prawns (big, moist prawns in a fresh Szechwan tomato sauce that's flavored with "homemade" rice wine. Yes, homemade. This restaurant's rice wine is made on the premises by Uncle Wang. As far as Uncle Wang is concerned, "store-bought" stuff just won't do.) □ Cheng-Tu Beef (strips of choice beef, cloud ear mushrooms, and fresh spinach in a garlic-scented Chinese brown sauce.) □ Ta-Chien Chicken (chunks of marinated chicken, mushrooms, and bamboo shoots in an interesting chestnut-colored sauce which owes some of its character to a special seasoning that Uncle Wang gets from Taiwan.)

□ Sliced Leg of Lamb Szechwan (slices of lamb stir-fried with green onions and Taiwanese baby corn in a mild pepper sauce with a ginger accent.) □ Pork Szechwan Style (moist pork slices with a just-cooked texture in a gently spicy sauce laced with black cloud ear mushrooms.) **Prices:** Medium. **Basics:** 2209 Polk St. (near Vallejo), San Francisco. Tel: 474-8282. Hours: Noon-2 pm, 5-10:30 pm Mon.-Sat.; 5:30-10:30 pm Sun. Cards: MC, V. Wine and beer.

Cafe du Nord: San Francisco
Basque/Big dinners, small prices, Old World building

People have different ways of getting their moneysworth. After seeing the prices on a restaurant's menu, Groucho Marx ordered one lima bean . . . and then sent it back to be peeled. Of course, there is a simpler way to get your moneysworth—go to Cafe du Nord. At this

Basque restaurant, your dollar gets extra mileage. A modest $6.25 is your ticket to travel through a 6-course dinner. Although the menu changes daily, a typical meal might include a tureen of split pea soup, kidney beans vinaigrette, a spicy lamb stew, roast beef, spinach, a bowl of salad, caramel custard, and coffee. (On Friday the main course is a thick steak with mushrooms, and the price understandably becomes $7.50.)

The Basques have to serve big meals. They have a reputation to maintain. The Basques are a hearty people who live in the Pyrenees mountains between France and Spain. And they're known all over the world for their huge appetites. The Basques even have clubs which exist for only one purpose—eating. In these clubs, sheepherders and doctors dine side by side. Each clubhouse is well stocked with food and wine, and each member has a key and the right to take as much as he wants.

Cafe du Nord is located in a sturdy old building erected by a group of Swedish Americans in 1907. At the Cafe du Nord, everything is mahogany paneling, fresh flowers, and warmth. It's a relaxing atmosphere that attracts all types of people, but hopefully the owners won't ever get a customer like Groucho Marx. After Groucho finished his dinner at the Warwick Hotel in Philadelphia, he threw all the plates out the window . . . so nobody would have to wash the dishes.

The Menu: Your 6-course meal begins with a "bottomless" tureen of soup (usually split pea or lentil) and a basket of "dunkable" sourdough bread. Next comes a chilled vegetable plate (maybe tomatoes, onions, and green peppers in a vinaigrette.) When you finish this course, you're ready for dish number three (Thurs.—oxtail stew in wine sauce; Fri.—fresh sand dabs; Sat.—lamb stew.) Some people think this is the main course. It isn't. The Basques consider this course just an "appetizer."

Now it's time for . . . that's right . . . the main course (Thurs.—Basque chicken with tomatoes and bacon; Fri.—a thick filet steak with mushrooms; Sat.—roast beef) served with a fresh vegetable. Then comes a bowl of salad, served along with the main course, Basque-style. Finally, there's caramel custard, and coffee flavored with chicory. **Prices:** Inexpensive to medium. **Basics:** 2170 Market St. (near 15th St.), San Francisco. Tel: 864-9420. Hours: 5:30-10 pm Wed.-Sun. Closed Mon., Tues. No cards. Full bar.

Le St. Tropez: San Francisco
French/Small, romantic bistro with Old World fireplace

Dinner with Mr. Brady

The Background: Millionaire Diamond Jim Brady was one of the most colorful men of his age. During the 1890s, Brady became famous for two things: spending and eating. Restaurants liked Diamond Jim. Once, Brady gave a dinner party for 50 people that cost him $1,000 a person just for the food and wine alone. Of course, Brady was used to running up big bills. He dined out regularly, and during the course of a typical meal, he'd consume 36 oysters, 6 orders of cracked crab, 2 bowls of turtle soup, 7 lobsters, half a dozen venison chops, 2 whole canvasback ducks, a sirloin steak, and for dessert, 14 or 15 French pastries. When Brady dined in restaurants, little crowds would form around his table and cheer him on.

The Scene: A table at Le St. Tropez, a small bistro that's been doing business on Clement Street since 1971. Seated on one side of the table—Russ Riera, restaurant reviewer. On the other side of the table—Diamond Jim Brady, the 1890s most famous eater. Note: Brady's dialogue below is based on biographical facts.

"Yeah, it's romantic alright," said Diamond Jim Brady, "but where are your lady friends?"

The two men didn't know it, but the girls weren't coming. That afternoon, Riera had said the wrong thing. Remembering the kind of entertainment Brady was accustomed to, Riera had asked the girls if they minded wearing French cancan outfits and dancing on Brady's table after dinner. When the girls heard that, they decided to stand Riera up. Too bad. Le St. Tropez is a romantic place for dinner. The dining room has a beam ceiling, handmade wooden chandeliers, pots of flowers in every corner, and a beautiful Old World-style fireplace.

"I d-don't think the girls are going to show up, Mr. Brady," Riera finally said.

"Oh, well," Diamond Jim Brady replied, "I've never had much luck with girls. I once offered Lillian Russell a million dollars to marry me. She refused. And that was after the gold bicycle. As you know, my Lillian was a stage performer. So to keep her in shape, I bought her a bicycle. And to get her to ride it, I made it special. It was plated with 24-carat gold, had mother-of-pearl handlebars, and I had the spokes of each wheel set with little chips of diamonds, rubies, and emeralds."

Forgetting about women, Brady and Riera started looking over the menu. It didn't take them long to discover that this small bistro had a lot to offer. There was rack of lamb coated with imported French herbs, shrimps and scallops in a white wine cream sauce, and duckling in a black cherry sauce. And a clipped-on menu card announced that the special tonight was the ever-popular filet of sole Marguery. When

Brady saw the card he laughed and said, "They ought to call it filet of sole Diamond Jim."

"Why?" Riera questioned.

"Well, it's like this," Brady answered, "Many years ago, the restaurant I frequented most was Charles Rector's in New York. In fact, the way I ate, Rector called me 'the best 25 customers' he had. Anyway, one night at Rector's, I heard about this fabulous seafood dish that was a secret recipe of the Cafe Marguery in Paris. So I told Rector, 'if you value my future business, I want that recipe.' The next day, Rector took his son George out of Cornell University, and sent him to Paris. The boy managed to get work at the Cafe Marguery as a dishwasher, and cautiously observed the chef whenever sole Marguery was being prepared. It took the boy two months, working 15 hours a day, before he learned the secret of the recipe. Of course, you must remember that young Rector's father had warned him not to come back to New York unless he knew how to make the dish."

Suddenly, Brady remembered he hadn't ordered yet. Spotting a waiter he waved him over.

"Ten sole Marguery," Brady said quickly.

"Pardon me, sir," the waiter questioned.

"Pay attention, young man. I said ten Marguery."

"What, sir?"

"Ten! Ten!" Brady roared, "I want ten orders of sole Marguery."

Two hours later, the men were finished eating. As Brady sat there rotating a cigar in his mouth, Riera asked him what he thought of Le St. Tropez's version of sole Marguery. "Tastes just like the dish Rector gave me the night his boy returned with the recipe," answered Diamond Jim Brady. "Like I said back then—if you poured Marguery sauce on it, I could enjoy eating a Turkish towel."

Menu Specialties: ☐ Rack of Lamb Provence (a six-rib rack coated with a mixture of eight imported French herbs, sourdough crumbs, and bits of fresh tomato, and then roasted.) ☐ Shrimp and Scallops St. Jacques (the seafood is braised in white wine with fresh mushrooms, and then put in a casserole and baked with a rich chablis-laced cream sauce.) ☐ Duckling Montmorency (a half duckling, slowly roasted for 40 minutes and then topped with a dark crimson-colored sauce laced with Cherry Heering liqueur and big black cherries from Willamette Valley, Oregon.) ☐ Steak Marchand de Vin (a choice New York steak in a burgundy wine sauce flavored with shallots and a whisper of garlic.)

Dinner includes . . . 3 courses: Soup (maybe cream of spinach or cream of fresh tomato), a large butter lettuce salad well-tossed in a fine house dressing, main course with three fresh vegetables, and coffee. **Prices:** Medium. **Basics:** 126 Clement St. (near 2nd Ave.), San Francisco. Tel: 387-0408. Hours: 5:30-10 pm Mon.-Sat. Closed Sun. Reservations suggested on weekends. Cards: MC, V. Full bar.

El Zarape: San Francisco
Mexican/Dishes rarely seen this side of the border

Francisco Venegas. We know how to increase your business 100%. Go to Hollywood and buy one of those wind machines used to blow around the fake snow in old adventure movies. Next, put the wind machine near your stove. Open the window. Then, turn the machine on while you're cooking. The exciting aromas of your dishes will drift over San Francisco, hypnotize people, and pull them into your restaurant.

When you arrive at El Zarape, you'll like the place even before you taste the food. You'll like the friendly atmosphere and the personal service. You'll like the modest prices. And you'll like Francisco's menu with its list of interesting specialty dishes that go beyond the standard tacos and enchiladas. At the El Zarape, you can enjoy specialties like Costillas Ternera—short ribs marinated for 24 hours and then charcoal broiled—and chicken Mole Poblano in a rich, velvet-smooth sauce flavored with 25 different ingredients. One taste of the Mole and you're in Mexico—where this dish was originally created over 300 years ago by a group of nuns to honor a Spanish Viceroy who was visiting their convent.

At the El Zarape, Francisco also offers five prawn dishes made with plump prawns from the gin-clear waters of the Gulf of Campeche, Mexico. Our favorite is Camarones Rellenos—moist prawns stuffed with crab and wrapped with bacon, and arranged around an egg-rich homemade tartar sauce. And framing the prawns is a fiesta of Valencia orange slices and bright bits of cherry. The dish looks so good, you don't know whether to eat it, or send it to Hollywood for a screen test.

Menu Specialties: □ Prawns Rellenos □ Chicken Mole Poblano (a moist half chicken blanketed in a dark, mahogany-colored sauce that's very rich and very good. It takes over five hours of blending and stirring to make the Mole sauce. El Zarape's chicken Mole is more than just a well-made dish. It's an experience.) □ Costillas Ternera (beef short ribs marinated for 24 hours in white wine, cumin, cloves, and just a rumor of ancho chile, and then charcoal broiled.) □ Prawns Alcaparrado (large, moist prawns in a fresh tomato sauce flavored with red wine and laced with capers, onions, and green olives.)

Dinner includes: Soup (beef broth packed with vegetables and little Mexican meatballs), and main course with refried beans, rice, and salad. **Prices:** Inexpensive. **Decor:** A small, cheerful-looking dining room with comfortable booths, tables inlaid with bright blue Mexican tile, wrought iron chandeliers, and colorful paper piñatas hanging from the ceiling. Another plus: good service by smiling waiters in red jackets and bow ties. **Basics:** 3349 23rd St. (betw. Mission and Valencia), San Francisco. Tel: 282-1168. Hours: 10 am-10 pm Tues.-Thurs., Sun.; 10 am-11 pm Fri., Sat. Closed Mon. Cards: MC, V. Wine and beer.

New Pisa: San Francisco
Italian/5 courses, bargain prices

Inflation has driven prices up 50% in the last ten years. Shhh. Don't tell Dante Benedetti. He's still selling 5-course Italian dinners for $5.50. It's one of San Francisco's best bargains.

The New Pisa is an old-time Italian restaurant—and looks it. Inside, there's mahogany trimmed booths, cafe curtains in the windows, and 57 years of mementos on the walls. Italian ladies wearing kitchen-print aprons serve the food, and in the North Beach tradition, long, sturdy tables dominate the middle of the room. At these tables? Everyone: families. Poets. Businessmen. Bus drivers. On these tables? Always huge bowls of minestrone, house-made ravioli, and platters of chicken cacciatora. What does all this mean? The people, prices, and portions make a happy combination.

Dante's father opened the New Pisa just after World War I, and Dante has been cooking in this kitchen all his life. When Dante was a boy, his first job was keeping an eye on the bubbling pots of spaghetti sauce on the ancient black stove. He's still behind that stove today—with no promotion in sight.

The Menu: The menu changes daily. Dishes to look for: Chicken cacciatora, veal osso bucco, stuffed zucchini, baseball-sized Italian meatballs, and veal saute. There are usually 10 different entrees offered each night, but only one price—$5.50.

Dinner includes . . . 5 courses: A thick minestrone soup, French bread (which, for some reason, always tastes better in North Beach), tossed salad with a spicy dressing, homemade ravioli, main course with hand-cut fries and fresh Swiss chard, spumoni ice cream, and coffee.
Basics: 550 Green St. (near Columbus), San Francisco. Tel: 362-4726. Hours:11:30 am-10:30 pm Mon., Thurs.-Sun.; 11:30 am-2:30 pm Tues. Closed Wed. No cards. Full bar. Public parking (60¢ per hour) available at the Vallejo Street Garage, 766 Vallejo St. (near Powell).

Jack's: San Francisco
Their trademark—San Francisco cooking
In the beginning, diners paid with gold dust

The building that houses Jack's is a sturdy, three-story relic of age-buffed brick. It gives you the impression that Jack's has been around for a long time. It has. This restaurant served its first meal 115 years ago. Jack's opened in 1864, back in the days when San Francisco was young, bawdy, and wild—the kind of town where anything could be bought, or at least rented for the evening.

But outward appearances can be misleading. What's inside? To find out, you part the heavy Nile-green curtain in the entrance-way and squeeze through. The twentieth century . . . *fades away*. It's as if you've slipped into a time warp. The room hasn't changed a bit since the days when customers paid their checks with a pinch of gold dust. It's a well-lit dining room with a high, scrollwork ceiling and parchment-colored walls decorated with gilt embossings of garlands and cornucopias. Everything from the milk-glass lamps to the straw-bottomed cane chairs tells you that this is no counterfeit but the real thing.

At the back of the dining room, you might spot a faint red glow coming from behind a partition. A fire? Right. And an important one. The soft glow comes from an ancient brick charcoal broiler in the surprisingly small kitchen. In an area no bigger than your living room, five men in starched whites are working. Very hard. You see, there's also a time warp in the kitchen. Everything is done by hand. They even make their own mayonnaise. In this kitchen, the only electrical convenience they have is the light bulbs.

The main product of all this work is a 115-year-old collection of dishes that has become known by a well-earned title—San Francisco cooking. On Jack's menu you'll find everything from elegant San Francisco dishes like chicken saute with fresh artichoke hearts to homespun dishes like braised spareribs and frankfurters.

Over the years Jack's food has attracted its share of "fans." If you could take a stroll through this restaurant's past, you'd spot President Hoover cutting into a juicy rack of spring lamb, and you'd see Edward G. Robinson biting into a golden brown piece of French-fried eggplant. Look! There's General Douglas MacArthur spooning bearnaise sauce over some fresh crab legs, and in the other corner, Ernest Hemingway is finishing off a bowl of rich sorrel soup. And Ernest is sitting in the same place where, years before, another author, Jack London, sat and ate his favorite dish—braised spareribs and frankfurters.

Yes, Jack's is a one-of-a-kind establishment. It's a restaurant that wins the *Holiday* award every year for its classic San Francisco cooking . . . yet still has frankfurters on the menu. This is a restaurant that's able to bend the rules—a privilege it's earned by being in business for 115 years. The proprietor of this restaurant is a man named Mr. Redinger. But Jack's real owner is Time.

Menu Specialties: □ Chicken Saute a Sec a la Jack's (each piece is coated with an intoxicating brown glaze, and comes buried under a fortune in fresh mushrooms and peak-of-the-season artichoke hearts. Serves two.) □ Filet of Sole Marguery (three beautifully fresh filets laid on a foundation of bay shrimp, mushrooms, and chopped shallots. Then baked with a halo of lemony cream sauce that shouts its richness. One of Jack's most famous dishes.) □ English Mutton Chop (aside from the old-fashioned name, what you get is a blue ribbon piece of lamb, *three inches thick*—cut from the choicest part of the lamb's loin. It's roasted for a full 30 minutes and comes out a masterpiece—its herb-perfumed ebony crust hiding a moist pink interior. This was Lucius Beebe's favorite dish.)

□ Crab Legs Saute (only the finest, fresh Dungeness crab legs are used. Served with an excellent bearnaise sauce.) □ Rack of Spring Lamb, Potatoes Boulangere (after being roasted for a full 25 minutes, this premium eight-chop rack comes out of the oven perfectly crisp outside, and perfectly tender inside.) □ Daily Specials: Braised Spareribs and Frankfurters; Smoked Briskets of Beef; Irish Stew, Dublin Style.

Starters: The Super Bowl (Jack's serves some of the best soups in town . . . probably because they're made from a stock that's been simmered for 21 hours. Whatever is offered—chicken gumbo, minestrone, or old-fashioned lentil—order it.) Cold Artichoke (served with a dipping sauce made with homemade mayonnaise.)

With your main course: Potatoes au Gratin (a dish big enough for two, rich enough for four); French-Fried Eggplant (one of Jack's most popular vegetable dishes.) **Prices:** Medium to a step above medium. **Basics:** 615 Sacramento St. (near Montgomery), San Francisco. Tel: 986-9854. Hours: 11:30 am-3:30 pm, 5:30-9:30 pm Mon.-Sat.; 4-9:30 pm Sun. Reservations necessary. Coat and tie requested. No cards. Full bar. Public parking (35¢ per hour) available at the Portsmouth Square Garage, Kearny St. (betw. Clay and Washington).

Mama's: San Francisco
Breakfast/Fluffy omelets and fresh fruit bowls

Zzzzzzz . . . Hey, wake up! It's morning. Time to crank yourself into a vertical position and have breakfast—the recognized method of stoking the body's fires. And at Mama's you'll find many forms of kindling: light, fluffy omelets bulging with Dungeness crab or smoked ham; Swedish cinnamon French toast; buttermilk pancakes rippled with blueberries; and without-a-doubt-fresh fruit bowls. Mama's breakfasts are simple but good, and often this kind of simple is hard to find.

Mama's also offers a breakfast bonus—its location. Mama's little vanilla-white building is located right across the street from Washington Square Park. What a combination: out the window there's a view of a beautiful green lawn and oak trees—and on your plate there's a view of a sun-yellow omelet and a rainbow of fresh fruit.

Menu Specialties: ☐ The San Francisco Experience (a fresh crab omelet cooked in a generous amount of pure butter), $4.25. ☐ Smoked Ham and Imported Swiss Cheese Omelet, $2.75. ☐ Mama's Children's Favorite (an omelet housing a combination of sauteed mushrooms, Monterey Jack cheese, chopped tomatoes, and green onions), $2.95. Omelets include baguette sourdough toast with apricot-pineapple jam.

☐ Swedish Cinnamon French Toast (this is French toast with a flavor that says "Good Morning."), $1.95. ☐ Mike Jr.'s Favorite (buttermilk pancakes laced with ripe blueberries), $1.50. ☐ Fresh Fruit Bowl (depending on the season, peaches, raspberries, honeydew melon . . . it's a California harvest in a bowl. Fact: In 1636, the central marketplace in the city of Antwerp, Belgium, offered so many varieties of exotic produce, the great still-life artist, de Heem moved there just so he could paint the fruit.), $1.25. **Basics:** 1701 Stockton St. (at Filbert), San Francisco. Tel: 362-6421. Hours: 8 am-8 pm daily. No cards. Public parking (60¢ per hour) available at the Vallejo St. Garage, 766 Vallejo St. (near Powell).

Scott's: San Francisco
Seafood/Charm-splashed Victorian building

In the past, people have sometimes made a special effort to get fresh seafood. Take Lucullus, the Roman general and gourmet. In order to have fresh seafood for his banquets, Lucullus wanted the pond next to his villa stocked with live fish from the ocean. But in order to keep these fish alive, the pond had to be connected to a seawater supply. Unfortunately, a mountain separated the general's villa from the sea. No problem. Lucullus had 5,000 men under his command dig a channel through the mountain. Flashback: 63 B.C. One of Lucullus' men: "Heck, this is nothing. Last year I was an oarsman on a galley ship when the captain decided he wanted to go water-skiing."

Today, there are still some people who make a special effort to get seafood. Like the head chef at Scott's Grill. He gets up at 6 a.m. every morning and tours San Francisco's wharfside suppliers, carefully selecting the fish that will appear on Scott's menu that day.

But he isn't the only one at Scott's making an effort. Back at the restaurant, the grill man, the saute man, and the woman who shucks the oysters and cracks the crab, all seem to be making a special effort. At least that's the way the food tastes. You can taste it in the freshness of Scott's fragrant seafood cioppino, in the delicate flavor of their buttergrilled filet of petrale, and in the deep richness of Scott's crab au gratin with cheddar cheese.

At Scott's, someone has also made a special effort with the decor.

Inside, there's a fine, oak-trimmed turn-of-the-century atmosphere; and at the entrance to the dining room, there's a classic fish market display case stocked with Scott's latest collection of Blue Point oysters, Maine lobster, and Dungeness crab. And the restaurant itself is housed in a rambling two-story Victorian building. The building's color? San Francisco Bay blue, of course.

Menu Specialties: □ Fried Seafood Platter (Gulf prawns, Blue Point oysters, Eastern scallops, and Pacific snapper encased in a crisp sourdough crumb crust. Served on a cloth napkin shaped like a starfish, and accompanied by a side dish of homemade tartar sauce.) □ Crab au Gratin (crab legs and body-meat baked with a rich veloute sauce and white wine, then topped with cheddar cheese and cooked until a golden brown crust forms. The flavors play a song you'll want to hear often.) □ Filet of Petrale (fresh, snow-white filets dipped in egg, dusted with seasoned flour, and gently grilled.) □ Scott's Cioppino (a giant earthenware tureen filled with scallops, prawns, bay shrimp, red snapper, and Dungeness crab in a spicy, herb-flavored tomato stock.) Dishes include fresh hand-cut fried potatoes.

Starters: Shrimp Bisque (a rich, coral-colored soup accented with brandy); Boston Clam Chowder (made with New England Little Neck clams that are trucked in 3 times a week.) **Prices:** Medium. **Basics:** 2400 Lombard St. (at Scott), San Francisco. Tel: 563-8988. Hours: 11 am-11 pm daily. Cards: AE, MC, V. Full bar.

Europa: San Francisco
Czechoslovakian/Dumpling-sized cafe, small prices

A 1965 edition of *Scientific American* stated that the Earth weighs 6,595,000,000,000,000,000,000 tons. A recent edition of the same magazine stated the weight as 6,595,000,000,000,000,000,000½ tons. The figures speak for themselves. The Earth has gained half a ton, and Anna Prill knows she's partly responsible. The rich, heavy, Central European dishes that this Czech woman has been preparing for the restaurant-going public over the years have apparently added a few pounds to the scale.

Anna Prill's beef goulash and dumpling dinners can be found at the Europa, a miniature Bavarian chalet that looks like it was built by a band of Black Forest elves. Anna runs this seven-table restaurant by herself. At the Europa, it's not unusual to see Anna trot out of the kitchen to offer her guests seconds on dumplings and gravy. This lady honestly wants her guests to be pleased. In fact, maybe that's why she keeps all her dinners in the $4.50 range.

Menu Specialties: □ Kassler Rippchen (pork chops smoked by a Czech butcher in Hayward. You get two broiled chops topped with onions.) ☐ Szegedi Goulash (beef nuggets in a thick, spicy sour cream sauce laced with sauerkraut.) Items above include salad, Bohemian dumplings, and red cabbage. And the food is served to the sound of polka music on the juke box.

Liquid Assets: 14 kinds of foreign beer available. How about a Dinkel Acker? Yes, that's a beer, not a dance. Note: this is simple, homestyle food. Don't expect anything more. **Prices:** Inexpensive. **Basics:** 2769 Lombard St. (near Lyon), San Francisco. Tel: 567-0361. Hours: 4-11:30 pm Mon.-Sat. Closed Sun. Cards: MC, V. Wine and beer.

Blanche's: San Francisco
Homemade Lunches/One-of-a-kind cafe, outdoor dining

Blanche's is one of those restaurants that could only happen in San Francisco. It's . . . too offbeat for Houston . . . too personal for New York . . . and too real for Las Vegas.

Blanche's can be found in the gray industrial outskirts of the City—a clapboard cafe resting on a pier overlooking the China Basin channel. A half-block away are the Southern Pacific railroad yards. Throughout the day, men in tugboats and Mack trucks parade by Blanche's, but it's safe to assume that none of these men have mistaken Blanche's for a stevedore's hang-out. The building is lipsticked in red; inside, the walls are decorated with bright watercolors; and behind the restaurant, pots of yellow daisies line a huge pier that's used as an outdoor luncheon area.

Once you enter this tiny cafe, the procedure is to walk up to the counter and order lunch. The choices are limited, but usually include

46

homemade meat loaf sandwiches on crusty French rolls, just-baked date-nut bread, and shrimp cocktails. There's a good reason why the selection isn't large—Blanche, a gentle, motherly woman in her fifties, runs this restaurant almost single-handedly. But even with all the work she has to do, Blanche always has a kind word, a bit of advice, and a cinemascopic smile for everyone. Sometimes, she even writes notes to her customers on a small blackboard by the door. The latest message read: "Dear friends, I have a surprise dish planned for today. Love, Blanche."

Menu Specialty: ☐ Blanche's Special Luncheon (a cup of homemade soup + a shrimp cocktail + a meat loaf and cheese sandwich on a French roll + oven-fresh date-nut bread for dessert + coffee), $3.95. **Basics:** 998 4th St. (near Channel, two blocks south of Townsend), San Francisco. Tel: 397-4191. Hours: 11 am-2:30 pm Mon.-Fri. Closed Sat., Sun. Cards: MC, V. Wine and beer. Easy parking.

Vasilis: San Francisco
Mediterranean/Romantic decor and a $45,000 light

Like a love potion made from powdered rhinoceros horn, Vasilis' charm should be saved for a special occasion. Just don't bring someone here who scares easily. Vasilis is hidden in an alley behind Gump's, and as you walk down this little street, you're suddenly confronted by a thirty-foot, dragon-like bird with bright yellow flames shooting out of its beak. This wrought-iron sculpture of the mythical Phoenix stretches across the entire front of the restaurant.

Inside Vasilis, the bird's wings form arches over the small dining room, and each iron feather is tipped with a gumdrop light. In this room you'll also find pastel tablecloths, bare red-brick walls, and a menu that features 3-course Mediterranean dinners.

At Vasilis, couples settle back in comfortable scallop-back booths, sip wine, drink up the atmosphere, and sometimes even remember to order dinner. After all, it's hard to concentrate on food while your dinner companion is gazing at you with a pair of eyes that have a romantic 200-watt glow.

Menu Specialties: ☐ Crab Diablo Mediterranean (underneath a thin parmesan cheese crust is Dungeness crab meat in a white wine sauce flavored with mushrooms.) ☐ Veal Rapallo (two medallions of veal sauteed in imported Spanish sherry with fresh mushrooms, capers, oregano, and marinated chives.) ☐ Chicken Zorba Paspara (a traditional wedding dish from the island of Crete. Butter-sauteed chicken in a light sauce kissed with Madeira wine. And the chicken is served with a moist rice pilaf dotted with currants and pine nuts.)

Dinner includes . . . 3 courses: Soup (maybe cream of asparagus or Athens-style tomato soup), a tossed romaine salad topped with bay shrimp, main course with rice pilaf or baked potato, and ratatouille (a spicy Mediterranean vegetable dish made with zucchini, eggplant, green peppers, and tomatoes.) **Prices:** Medium. **Basics:** 44 Campton Place (near Stockton, a half block from Union Square), San Francisco. Tel: 392-5373. Hours: 11:30 am-2:30 pm, 5-10 pm Tues.-Sat. Closed Sun., Mon. Cards: MC, V. Full bar. Public parking (65¢ per hour) available at the Union Square Garage, Geary St. (betw. Powell and Stockton).

La Croisette: San Francisco
French/Small candlelit bistro, gentle prices

Table conversation

We'll never forget our first dinner at La Croisette. We had just sat down, when we heard someone say, "You know something? I've got the feeling that you guys are restaurant reviewers. If you are, you're in luck. The food here is good. Believe me."

We looked around. The waitress wasn't visible. And we were the only customers in the room. Suddenly, the voice spoke again. "Quit looking around. I'm right here." We quickly glanced behind us again. No one was there. Then . . . slowly . . . we realized what was happening. The table was talking.

"Yeah, boys," the table continued, "the food's good here, and I've been around long enough to know. When I started, I worked topless. That's right, no tablecloth. Then I was discovered. I worked all the high class joints, including a continental place that featured flaming dishes. I hated that one. All those flames scared me. Listen, you'd be scared too if you were made out of wood. Anyway fellas, I've been close to food for a long time, so you can trust me when I say the food's good."

We could hardly believe what we'd just heard, but one thing was certain—the table sounded sincere.

"Listen fellas," the table continued, "I'll tell you what to order. The chef makes a fine veal dish with a sauce of cream, mushrooms, and Madeira wine. It's one of his specialties. Or try the lamb chops Printanier. You ought to hear the people rave. By the way, if you like seafood, don't miss the salmon with bearnaise sauce."

By the time we finished dinner, we'd learned something: the table knew what it was talking about. The food was good.

"Glad to see that you fellows agree with me. But remember, boys," the table added, "you've got to be careful who you listen to. I have a friend who doesn't know anything about food. What's he do? Oh, he's a picnic table at Shakey's."

Menu Specialties: ☐ Veal Croisette ☐ Lamb Chops Printanier (five small lamb chops marinated for one week in olive oil with thyme, bay leaves, and rosemary, and then sauteed in butter with garlic and a touch of Pernod liqueur.) □ Salmon Parisienne (salmon topped with a perfectly made golden bearnaise sauce.) □ Quenelles (air-light dumplings of scallops and shrimp in a rich crab sauce accented with cognac.)

Dinner includes . . . 3 courses: Soup (maybe cream of mushroom or country-style onion soup), tossed salad with a good house dressing, and main course with carrots sauteed in butter, broccoli puree, and crepes Parmentier—silver-dollar-sized French potato pancakes. **Prices:** Medium. **Decor:** A comfortable bistro with candlelight, fresh pink carnations, and crisp white linen. **Basics:** 745 Columbus Ave. (near Filbert), San Francisco. Tel: 981-1176. Hours: 5:30-10 pm Tues.-Sat. Closed Sun., Mon. Reservations suggested on weekends. Cards: MC, V. Wine and beer.

Hunan: San Francisco
Chinese/Hunan cooking: Mao was raised on it

World politics have a strong influence on people's eating habits. We're positive, for example, that tourists in Syria don't ask for kosher pickles with their sandwiches. And it was world politics that helped create the Hunan cafe. This tiny restaurant opened in 1972, soon after cold war relations between our government and mainland China began to defrost. Noticing the sudden interest in all things Chinese, the Hunan's owner, Henry Chung, felt that the time was ripe to introduce Hunan cooking to San Francisco. Hunan food is a hearty, farm-style cooking that was totally unknown in the United States before Henry and a few others came along.

Hunan is an inland province where the soil is rich, and the men have a reputation for being as tough as Kaiser steel. It was the Hunan army that stopped the Japanese invaders during World War II. Mao Tse-tung himself was from the Hunan area.

It's no surprise then, that the strong-willed people from Hunan like spicy food. In fact, their favorite seasoning is the small, fiery fagara pepper. These peppers are so powerful, in China they aren't picked— they're allowed to walk out of the field on their own. But don't worry, Henry keeps his spicing well under control.

Besides spicy country dishes, Henry offers another trademark of Hunan cooking—smoked ham. Henry built his own walk-in smoke box, modeling it after ones he remembers seeing in Hunan Province as a boy. In this box, the hams are smoked for five days over hickory wood and oolong tea leaves.

Although Hunan cooking is unique, this restaurant isn't, as Lincoln might say, for "all the people, all the time." The place is small and plain-looking, and the seating arrangement is an elbow-to-elbow situation. But we don't care. The Hunan could be located in a broom closet and we'd still go back.

Menu Specialties: □ Smoked Ham (thin slices of Henry's five-day smoked ham are stir-fried with Chinese vegetables and black bean sauce. The result? A unique, flavor-loaded dish. Don't miss it.) □ Hunan Spareribs (the spareribs spend 24 hours in a Chinese Five-Spice powder marinade. Then they're jacketed with rice crumbs seasoned with star anise, and cooked in a bamboo steamer. Finally, the spareribs are served in the bamboo steamer they were cooked in.) □ Harvest Pork (sliced pork wok-tossed with bamboo shoots, bok choy cabbage, marinated bean cake, and a mild, fragrant garlic sauce.)

□ Hot & Sour Beef (thin slices of beef, green onions, carrots, and strips of bell peppers in an unusual sauce with a mild, vinegary backtaste.) □ Hunan Crescent Dumplings (huge pillows of fresh Chinese dough bulging with a spicy meat filling.) **Prices:** Inexpensive to medium. **Basics:** 853 Kearny St. (near Washington), San Francisco. Tel: 788-2234. Hours: 11:30 am-3 pm, 4:30-9:30 pm Mon.-Fri. Closed Sat., Sun. No cards. Beer only. Public parking (35¢ per hour) available at the Portsmouth Square Garage, Kearny St. (betw. Clay and Washington).

Beethoven's: San Francisco
German/Moderate prices and owner-chef Baumann at the stove

When you were a baby and didn't get something to eat, you cried. Now, depending on what you get, you still may want to cry. In fact, just the thought of money wasted on bad restaurant meals tends to trigger the emotions. Well . . . stop sniveling . . . c'mon, dry your eyes. 'Cause with Alfred Baumann's cooking, there'll be no tears.

This man is going to treat you right — German style. Alfred started cooking when he was only slightly taller than a Bavarian beer stein, and by the time he was 14, he was an apprentice chef at a Black Forest resort. And that was 20 years ago. All this experience shows. Alfred's veal Geschnezeltes in Marsala sauce explodes with flavor; his potato pancakes are the best we've had in San Francisco; and his sauerbraten is so authentic, it tastes like it never left Germany. To make this dish, Alfred marinates a beef loin for 14 days in a red wine mixture that includes juniper berries he grows in his own backyard.

Alfred also uses an Old World recipe for his decor. The small dining room has wine-colored drapes, gilt-framed paintings, fresh flowers, and soft classical music to tenderize the atmosphere. It's all very European and soothing. Also very soothing is the check. Alfred has kept his prices very moderate. For example, on the 3-course dinner, Alfred's sauerbraten is $6.50. At Alfred's, John F. Kennedy's famous words won't ring in your ears. At a $200-a-plate gathering in his honor, President Kennedy confessed, "I could say I'm deeply touched, but not as deeply touched as you have been in coming to this luncheon."

Menu Specialties: ☐ Sauerbraten ☐ Veal Geschnezeltes (thin slices of veal sauteed with Marsala wine, fresh mushrooms, cream, and shallots.) ☐ Roast Pork Schweinebraten (a pork loin rubbed with garlic and caraway seeds, roasted, and then served with a hearty, flavor-packed pan gravy.) ☐ Beef Rindsrouladen (tender beef rolls with a bacon-flavored stuffing. Served with a rich burgundy wine sauce.)

Dinner includes . . . 3 courses: Soup (usually Alfred's German vegetable soup), a good house salad, main course with potato pancakes or spatzle dumplings and excellent red cabbage, and a *complimentary* glass of port wine. **Prices:** Inexpensive to medium. **Basics:** 1701 Powell St. (near Columbus, opposite Washington Square), San Francisco. Tel: 391-4488. Hours: 5:30-10:30 pm Tues.-Sat. Closed Sun., Mon. Cards: MC, V. Wine and beer. Public parking (60¢ per hour) available at the Vallejo St. Garage, 766 Vallejo St. (near Powell).

Are Steak Houses Rare?
Just the Good Ones.

This isn't just our opinion. Maurice Drecier thinks so, too. Drecier is a millionaire gourmet who has spent 25 years traveling to 80 countries looking for the perfect steak. So far, this search has cost him $600,000.

In a restaurant Drecier is easy to spot. He wears beautifully tailored Saville Row suits, keeps a monocle corked in one eye, and always carries a black surgeon's bag. What's in the bag? Plenty. There's a custom-made thermometer to measure the steak's saline level, a large magnifying glass to examine its texture, and an 18-carat gold steak knife. Drecier insists that a steak should be so tender, he can cut through it easily with his gold knife.

There's a good reason why this self-appointed Steak Detective has a hard time finding great beef—most ranchers aren't willing to invest the kind of money it takes to raise a blue-ribbon steer. To begin with, to produce a prime steer, a cow must be mated with a stud bull that's sometimes worth as much as a home in Tiburon. Then, when these steers are big enough to join the herd, *each one* needs a grazing area the size of ten football fields. Finally, the steer must be fattened on corn. For 3 months. At the end of this period, each steer has eaten enough corn to make 100 cases of bourbon.

It's possible to do even more. And some have. Hundreds of years ago, Chinese warlords had slaves who spent their whole day massaging cattle to keep the meat tender. Even today, in Kobe, Japan, the steers are bottle-fed beer, and here in California, at a feedlot near Salinas called Fat City, they really do something special—the steers' 250-acre pen has piped-in music. According to manager Ray Stanfield, the music keeps the cattle calm and prevents expensive stampedes. What kind of music works best? Country & Western, of course.

The result of all this effort is a good steak, and at this point, it really becomes clear why these steaks are expen$ive. A 1,000-pound steer only yields about 75 choice steaks. And this precious 75 has to satisfy a lot of demand. You want one; your neighbor wants one; and a while back, even Mark Twain wanted one. When Twain returned from Europe and was asked what he wanted most, he replied, "I want a county of beefsteak . . . a mighty steak an inch and a half thick, hot and sputtering from the griddle."

Yep, Mark, that's what we want, too. And we've found it at Grison's, Vanessi's, Original Joe's, and Scotty Campbell's. All these restaurants buy the kind of high-quality beef we've been talking about and have the good sense to employ a true broiler-master to tend their charcoals. Plus all of these places cut their steaks with a generous hand. Scotty Campbell's, for example, features something called the Highlander's steak. How big is it? Well, to put it simply . . . if this steak were any larger, they'd have to bring it to your table with a fork lift.

Grison's Steak House

The Grison salad, Kansas beef, homemade biscuits
All-American steak dinners since 1934

When Grison's opened in 1934, it had lots of competition. But times change. Today, Grison's represents a type of restaurant that, oddly enough, is getting hard to find: the classic, high quality, All-American steak house. Grison's reputation is based on some of the things that have made this country great—things like homemade biscuits with Florida honey, baked Idaho potatoes almost the size of footballs, and America's finest—Kansas corn-fed beef.

□ Grison's 22-ounce T-Bone Steak □ Grison's 18-ounce New York Steak □ Grison's 16-ounce Eastern Club Steak (all of Grison's beef is purchased from a company in Wichita, Kansas that operates its own cattle ranch. And when the beef arrives at Grison's, it's inspected and cut into thick steaks by the owner himself, Eddie Armendizo. Where steaks are concerned, he's a serious man. If a strip of beef doesn't meet his standards, as Eddie says, "It goes back." At this restaurant, second best just won't do. They even serve a steak like they're proud of it. The steaks are brought to the table on service carts. The arrival is a fine sight—especially if it's your steak that's arriving. You'll be looking at a thick, charcoal-crusted, juice-rich steak, sitting on a silver chafing dish that's kept warm by glowing charcoal briquettes.)

Dinner includes . . . 3 courses: The Grison salad (three kinds of lettuce tossed tableside in a special house dressing. It's a dressing that never varies. Why? The same assistant chef has been making it for the last 20 years.), hot biscuits with Florida honey, main course with a rich creamed spinach and a baked Idaho potato or Texas-style chile bean pot, coffee, and homemade cheesecake.

Side Order: Grison's dinners are big and filling, but maybe two or three of you might think about sharing an order of French fried onion rings. Grison's makes the best onion rings in San Francisco. And they're as proud of their onion rings as they are of their steaks. This is probably the only restaurant in America that serves onion rings in a sterling silver dish. **Prices:** A step above medium to expensive. **Decor:** Grison's still has the time-mellowed appearance of a Thirties steak house—revolving doors, potted palms, a maze of comfortable maroon-enameled booths, and oceans of white linen. Tuxedoed waiters provide excellent service. One of them even adds to the Thirties atmosphere: he sort of looks like Spencer Tracy and he sort of talks like Edward G. Robinson. **Basics:** 2100 Van Ness Ave. (at Pacific), San Francisco. Tel: 673-1888. Hours: 5-10:30 pm Mon.-Sat.; 3-10:30 pm Sun. All major cards. Full bar. Free parking at Grison's garage; the entrance is on Van Ness, just below Pacific.

Vanessi's

Steaks, house-made pasta, and exhibition cooking

☐ Vanessi's Top Sirloin Steak ☐ New York Steak (both these steaks come from corn-fed Idaho beef, and when they emerge from Vanessi's meat lockers, they've been aged for 4 weeks.) ☐ Vanessi's Special Culotte Steak (the culotte is taken from the best part of the sirloin and it's truly a premium cut. A steer yields only *two* culotte steaks. That's why you'll have to pay a little extra for this cut. But don't worry. Its noble flavor will pay you back.) ☐ Broiled Hamburger Sandwich (Vanessi's treats all beef with respect—even hamburger. You get a great, half-pound hunk of fresh-ground prime chuck cloaked with two mighty slabs of crusty French bread.)

Other Specialties: ☐ Breast of Chicken Bolognese (baked in white wine with a topping of two cheeses and a slice of home-cured prosciutto ham. This prosciutto is cured for 6 months by Vanessi's in a small downstairs room.) ☐ Tortellini Veneziana (a meat-stuffed, half-moon-shaped pasta, made exclusively for Vanessi's by a retired Italian chef who once worked in this restaurant's kitchen. The tortellini are topped with a cream-rich, tomato-flecked sauce.)

☐ Chicken Cannelloni Supreme (one of the best versions of cannelloni we've had. As far as we're concerned, the dish deserves 4 stars and a Halley's comet. You get two delicate crepes wrapped around a minced filling of chicken and fresh mushrooms, and topped with a silk-smooth supreme sauce and parmesan cheese.) **Prices:** Inexpensive to a step above medium. **Decor:** Vanessi's opened in 1936. And the atmosphere stopped changing in 1943. Inside, there are three small rooms done in Venetian trattoria style. And these rooms are always filled with a happy, lively crowd. Counterattack: Vanessi's has an open, exhibition-style Italian kitchen, so the best seats in the house are at the counter. **Basics:** 498 Broadway (at Kearny), San Francisco. Tel: 421-0890. Hours: 11:30 am-1:30 am Mon.-Sat.; 4:30 pm-midnight Sun. Reservations strongly suggested. All major cards. Full bar. Public parking (60¢ per hour) available at the Vallejo St. Garage, 766 Vallejo St. (near Powell).

Original Joe's

Sizzling steaks upstairs . . . Joe's own butcher downstairs

For the past 33 years, Original Joe's has relied on the best possible method for controlling the quality and freshness of their meat—they employ a full-time butcher on the premises. This man spends his whole day in Joe's specially-equipped basement shop, cutting and trimming 375-pound sides of beef. Then, after Joe's personal butcher is finished, the beef goes to the upstairs kitchen where it will soon appear on Joe's charcoal broiler.

□ The 18-ounce Top Sirloin Steak □ The 18-ounce New York Steak □ The Filet Mignon (ever been served a *full pound* of filet mignon? Well, they serve one here.) □ The Hamburger, Original Joe's Style (Joe's even grinds its own hamburger. When the chef gets your order, he takes a half-pound of fresh-ground meat, molds it into a patty, presses in some onions, broils it, tops it with a hunk of butter, and serves it between a quarter-loaf of French bread. What results? One of the best hamburgers in San Francisco.) Dishes include fresh hand-cut French fries, spaghetti, or sauteed vegetables.

Starters: Joe's Italian Salad Bowl (the lettuce is just the beginning, there's also salami, cauliflower, tuna, celery, hard-boiled eggs, peas, zucchini, black olives, and anchovies. The salad is easily big enough for two. As owner Louis Rocca puts it, "We feed heavy, we feed good." For dressing, ask for the can of Bertolli olive oil and the wine vinegar.); Garlic Bread (fresh garlic is used and what a difference it makes.) **Prices:** Inexpensive to medium. **Decor:** A friendly, well-lit room with big comfortable booths. At Joe's, there's an open, exhibition-style kitchen, so our favorite place to sit is at the counter— across that counter a performance by a cast of broiler-masters and skillet-showmen is always in progress. **Basics:** 144 Taylor St. (near Eddy), San Francisco. Tel: 775-4877. Hours: 10:30 am-1:45 am daily. No cards. Full bar.

Scotty Campbell's

Prime steaks, Highland decor, and "Maerd Eip" cheesecake

□ Prime Top Sirloin Steak □ Prime New York Cut Steak □ The Highlander (a huge 19-ounce hill of prime New York.) The adjective "Prime" isn't what Scotty's thinks of the steaks. And it isn't what we think of the steaks. It's what the U.S. government thinks. And they don't feel this way very often. Only 6% of all the beef that's inspected qualifies for the government's top grade of USDA Prime. In order to get their share, Scotty Campbell's has a contract with a large meat company that gives them first pick on any prime beef the company receives.

Dinner includes . . . 3 courses: A great Scotch onion soup, or a large tossed salad with a fresh herb dressing, hot cheese bread, main course with a stuffed baked potato flavored with seven different seasonings, coffee, and a large scoop of sherbet.

Dessert: Maerd Eip (an egg-enriched, chiffon-like cheesecake topped with brandied cherries. Don't miss it.) **Prices:** A step above medium. **Decor:** Walls covered with tartan cloth, big comfortable booths, a fireplace, waitresses in kilts, and in one corner, an authentic 15th century suit of armor. **Basics:** 2907 El Camino Real (near 5th Ave.), Redwood City. Tel: 369-3773. Hours: 4:30-10:30 pm Mon.-Thurs.; 4:30-11 pm Fri., Sat.; 4-10 pm Sun. Reservations suggested on weekends. All major cards. Full bar. Parking lot.

U.S. Restaurant: San Francisco
Italian/Homecooked meals at giveaway prices

This is the kind of restaurant everybody hopes to find. Even though nobody really believes it exists. To begin with, at the U.S. Restaurant the portions are dished out with a motherly generosity, and the sauce on the pasta has the kind of deep, rich flavor only pride can produce. Better still, the *adult dinners have children's prices*.

Then there's the seating arrangements. According to an unwritten rule at this restaurant, an empty chair at your table is an open invitation to the next stranger who drifts through the door. And when you discover that the dishwasher is the owner, you realize that the kind of place you didn't think existed . . . exists!

Luigi Borzoni is a modest man. His restaurant looks as humble as it did when his relatives opened it 50 years ago. His wife does the cooking, and the entire melting pot of people in North Beach pours through Luigi's doors to enjoy her recipes. Judging from the company we've had at our table, probably the only Italian who sees a greater variety of people is the Pope. We've shared a piece of sourdough and a slice of life with a Yugoslavian welder, a retired circus clown, and even a private detective known as The First Division because of the firepower he carries in his pocket.

Menu Specialties: □ Veal Parmigiana (veal with an Italian bread crumb crust, topped with Monterey Jack and a fresh tomato sauce.) □ Pot Roast (huge, tender, pink slices in a wine-flavored pan juice.) □ The Daily Specials (two to four specials are offered each day, including chicken with risotto on Tuesday, tagliarini with meatballs on Thursday, baked halibut Italian-style on Friday, and veal osso bucco on Sunday.) Dishes include "Vegetables U.S. Restaurant" (in other words, vegetables that are so fresh, they taste like they were grown in the kitchen.) □ Spaghetti or Rigatoni (in Mrs. Borzoni's fine, honest, homemade sauce.) □ Ravioli al Pesto (plump ravioli serve as a backdrop for a beautiful green pesto, a Genoan sauce made from fresh basil, garlic, olive oil, grated cheese, and chopped pine nuts. And this dish is $2.80, a price that deserves the spotlight.)

Starters: Minestrone Soup (a big bowl. And it's 30¢, a price that *really* deserves the spotlight.) A Final Word: Considering the size of the portions and the prices, the U.S. Restaurant is offering some of the best food values around. **Prices:** Inexpensive. **Decor:** The interior is plain, in the classic American beanery tradition—open kitchen and solid tables, circa 1940. All we need is Betty Grable to play the waitress. **Basics:** 431 Columbus Ave. (near Stockton), San Francisco. Tel: 362-6251. Hours: 6 am-8:30 pm Tues.-Sun. Closed Mon. No cards. Wine and beer. Public parking (60¢ per hour) available at the Vallejo St. Garage, 766 Vallejo St. (near Powell).

Basta Pasta: San Francisco
Italian/Homemade pasta and seafood from their own boat

This is a restaurant you can't help liking. The pasta is made on the premises, the seafood is Golden Gate fresh, the prices are reasonable, and the casual trattoria atmosphere tells you to relax, loosen up, laugh a little. And people do. On weekend nights, you get the feeling that at any minute everyone in the place is going to break into song, like a scene in an old Hollywood musical. Actually the mood is set as you walk in. At the entrance to this North Beach trattoria, the brass door handles are engraved with the words "Hold until quake stops."

But don't get the idea everything at Basta Pasta is relaxed and casual. At this trattoria, cooking your dinner is considered serious business. Owners Lorenzo Petroni and Bruno Orsi even have their own fishing boat. They went into partnership with three Sicilian fishermen and acquired a 60-foot commercial fishing boat, christened the North Beach Star. This boat supplies the trattoria with most of its seafood.

The menu's "Catch of the Day" is especially impressive. On a gold-colored metal platter that's shaped like a fish, you're served a *whole* broiled fish, usually rex sole or petrale, with a flavor that lets you know it's caught-at-5 a.m. fresh. The price? $4.50. That, paisanos, is a bargain.

As the name suggests, the other specialty here is pasta. At this trattoria, there is one man in the kitchen who does nothing but make homemade pasta. And we appreciate this gentleman's work. When we eat fettucine and clams at Basta Pasta, our cheeks tend to swell like a pair of Scottish bagpipes.

To go with the pasta, there's a special house Chianti. The wine is made for the restaurant at a small winery in Italy that's run by friends of owner Petroni's family.

We always enjoy Basta Pasta, and we should have gone there one night recently. Instead, we ended up trying this new restaurant across town. It was a mistake. The food was tasteless, overcooked . . . well, let's put it this way . . . if that meal had been served in a prison dining hall, it would've touched off a riot.

Menu Specialties: □ Catch of the Day □ Filet of Sole Mugnaia (snow-white filets in a light, golden crust. Served with a buttery, lemon-scented sauce.) □ Cioppino Livornese (you're presented with a huge tureen filled with fresh, sweet Dungeness crab, prawns, and clams in a hearty, garlic-flavored tomato sauce.) □ Gamberi (large, sauteed prawns in a sauce made with butter, lemon, and fresh Italian herbs.) □ Salmon or Halibut (both fresh from Basta Pasta's boat and broiled with stopwatch timing.)

□ Seafood Cannelloni (thin crepes stuffed with a mixture of crab, prawns, and sole, topped with a rich white sauce and romano cheese, and baked.) □ Fettucine Vongole (fresh pasta in a sauce made with clams, butter, white wine, and herbs.) □ Fettucine Pomodoro (the pasta is tossed in a long-simmered tomato sauce that's made with fresh tomatoes, and what a difference it makes.) □ Spaghettini "Basta Pasta" (the pasta is served with a distinctive sauce made with prosciutto ham, mushrooms, herbs, cream, and bits of fresh tomato.) □ Fettucine Pesto (the noodles are tossed in a classic sauce of fresh basil, olive oil, parmesan cheese, and pine nuts.)

Starters: Fisherman's Soup (an 8-hour-simmered broth well-stocked with fresh vegetables, pieces of halibut, and homemade garlic croutons.) **Prices:** Inexpensive to medium. **Decor:** A two-story restaurant with an open kitchen, solid, polished-wood tables, and an old-fashioned winepress on display. **Basics:** 1268 Grant Ave. (at Vallejo), San Francisco. Tel: 434-2248. Hours: 11:30 am-2 am daily. Cards: MC, V. Wine and beer. Public parking (60¢ per hour) available at the Vallejo St. Garage, 766 Vallejo St. (near Powell).

Golden Eagle: San Francisco
Creative Cooking/American Heritage decor

Restaurant ads are always filled with sparkling adjectives like "fine," "excellent," and "superb." But when you get to the place, you don't always get "fine" food. Or even average food. What's really needed to keep people from being mis-fed is "Truth in Dining Legislation." Then, if a place advertises that it serves "fine" food, it better have it.

The Golden Eagle is one place that wouldn't have any problem backing up its claims. The food is even better than the owner says it is. When owner John Hadley describes his food as "good," we can only assume he's being modest. John certainly has the right to use a more powerful adjective to describe his Mediterranean scallop chowder, or his sirloin beef strip rolled around a stuffing of ham and Monterey Jack cheese. And "good" is too modest a term for his Fisherman's prawns. These prawns come drenched in a thin, golden-yellow sauce that's a panorama of flavors: all at once you can taste a soft-spoken sweetness, a lemony tartness, and an oregano afterkick.

When it comes to desserts, John calls his selection "nice." More modesty. The Golden Eagle offers seven different homemade desserts each night, including a pecan pie laced with grated coconut, and homemade ice cream.

As you can see, the Golden Eagle wouldn't be affected by Truth in Dining Legislation. But there are other restaurants that would. Imagine the typical court case of the future . . . say, for example, The State of California vs. Joe's Fine Foods. Before the judge sits a paper carton of beef stew marked Exhibit "A." Pushing it aside, the judge solemnly announces, "Mr. Joe, it is the finding of this court that you have no right to call your food 'fine.' "

Menu Specialties: ☐ Fisherman's Prawns ☐ Broiled Beef Roll (thin slices of sirloin rolled around a filling of chopped ham, Monterey Jack cheese, and pine nuts. Then topped with a rich sauce of white wine, butter, shallots, and sour cream.) ☐ Casserole of Crab (a mound of delicate Dungeness crab meat is placed on a bed of fresh spinach, crowned with a light, flavorful cream sauce, and then baked.) ☐ Hunter's Stew (a triangle of flavors . . . chicken, beef, and veal in an unusual reddish-brown wine sauce with a mild sweet and sour character.)

Dinner includes . . . 4 courses: Soup (maybe green pea with asparagus or brandied crab bisque), Caesar salad, main course with two fresh vegetables, and any one of seven homemade desserts. **Prices:** A step above medium. **Decor:** An American Heritage decor—antique globe lights, salmon-colored walls, and classic gilt-framed oil paintings. **Basics:** 160 California St. (at Front), San Francisco. Tel: 982-8831. Hours: 11:30 am-2:30 pm Mon.-Fri.; 5:30-10 pm Mon.-Sat. Closed Sun. Cards: AE, MC, V. Full bar.

What kind of guy runs Sun Hung Heung? Is he...

Generous?

Right. This Robin Hood of Chinatown serves dishes that taste rich — at prices that won't make you poor.

Honest?

You bet. This Boy Scout of Chinatown never uses anything but fresh, high quality ingredients in his dishes.

Brave?

Yes. This Lone Ranger of Chinatown boldly features a menu that offers more than just the common variety of Chinese dishes.

Sun Hung Heung's Specialties: □ Mongolian Beef Steak Balls (before the meat is stir-fried with oyster sauce and green onions, it's given special privileges—for 24 hours it's allowed to lie in a pool of ginger-spiked soy marinade.) □ Fried, Stuffed Chicken Wings (this dish is the result of either amazing culinary skill or magic. Boned chicken wings are stuffed with a tasty shrimp, pork, and mushroom mixture until the wings reach *four times their normal size*. Then, they're deep fried. When a golden crust forms, the now-giant chicken wings are sliced into silver-dollar rounds and served with a Chinese brown sauce. A unique dish.)

□ Shelled Prawns with Virginia Ham (a Chinese dish receiving American aid. The prawns are toss-cooked with mushrooms, snow peas, and slivers of that famous ham from the town of Smithfield, Virginia. Why are they famous? The hams are from peanut-fed stock, smoked over corncobs, and cured for one whole year. Queen Victoria of England used to have a standing order for six hams a week from Smithfield.) □ Cantonese Chicken Salad (our favorite. A chicken is rubbed with wine and soy sauce, breaded, steamed, then deep fried until it's golden brown. Then, it's boned, sliced, and tossed with shredded lettuce, green onions, sesame oil, coriander, and crushed walnuts. Finally, this mosaic of flavors is topped with a snowcap of crisp rice noodles.)

□ Beef with Asparagus □ Prawns with Sweet Peas (both dishes are carefully stir-fried in a wok. And when cooked in a wok, meat seems juicier, prawns seem plumper, and vegetables seem crispier. Is there a reason? Sure. *The Wok:* About 1,000 years ago, someone in China invented an odd-shaped frying pan that looked like an iron salad bowl with handles. He probably figured he could cook with it or use it as a battle helmet. Anyway, it was a stroke of genius—the design has never been changed. The wok's round-bottom concentrates heat: food cooks fast. And when food is cooked quickly, it helps preserve the food's natural color, texture, and flavor.)

□ Pork Won Ton Soup (you're served a huge bowl packed with fresh, plump won ton dumplings in a flavorful broth laced with ribbons of barbecued pork. We think this is one of Chinatown's best won ton soups.) **Prices:** Inexpensive to medium. **Decor:** Sun Hung Heung has been in business at the same location since 1919. Outside, the building has a fine, time-mellowed look, complete with pagoda-style trim and a 1943 neon. Inside, there's a comfortable dining room decorated with traditional Chinese paintings. **Basics:** 744 Washington St. (near Grant), Chinatown, San Francisco. Tel: 982-2319. Hours: 11:30 am-midnight Mon., Wed.-Sun. Closed Tues. Cards: MC, V. Full bar. Public parking (35¢ per hour) available at the Portsmouth Square Garage, Kearny St. (betw. Clay and Washington).

Des Alpes: San Francisco
Basque/Big dinners, bargain prices

Jack Walsh calls himself "The World's Strongest Man." Jack has lifted a 700-pound motorcycle with one hand. He has carried a full-grown horse up a ladder on his back. And once, Jack kept a DC-3 airliner from taking off by holding it with a cable. But could Jack Walsh get up from the table after eating one of the Des Alpes' Basque dinners. We doubt it.

This old North Beach landmark begins their family-style dinners with a large tureen of Basque-style split pea soup and a basket piled high with fresh, crusty sourdough bread. The next dish to be put on the table is the Des Alpes' string bean salad laced with hard-boiled eggs and onions, and following the salad, comes a meat or seafood course—possibly steamed clams or a hearty, well-seasoned lamb stew. We can just see Jack Walsh now: as soon as he's finished the stew, he braces his powerful hands on the table, takes a few deep breaths and then . . . stands up. Jack thinks dinner is over. But while he's standing there flexing his muscles in triumph, a five-foot-tall Basque waitress walks up, gives him a stern look, and says, "Sit down, mister. You haven't had the main course yet."

The waitress then brings Jack Walsh a platter of roast beef, a generous helping of French fries, and in keeping with Basque custom, a tossed green salad, which is meant to be eaten with the roast beef as a side dish. And after this course, the waitress returns later with a pot of coffee and spumoni ice cream. That's when she notices—Jack Walsh is no longer trying to get up.

Big, family-style meals are a Des Alpes tradition. In fact, the only thing about a meal here that isn't big is the price. At Des Alpes, you can buy a 5-course dinner for $5.00. Now that's what we call a bargain.

The Menu: A 5-course Des Alpes dinner begins with a tureen of split pea soup and a basket of sourdough. Next comes a special string bean salad and after that, dish number three (Thurs.—oxtail stew in wine sauce; Fri.—steamed clams; Sat.—Basque-style lamb stew.) This is followed by the main course (Thurs.—roast lamb; Fri.—strips of filet mignon in a mushroom-wine sauce; Sat.—roast beef in a pan sauce) served with French fries and, in keeping with Basque custom, a tossed green salad. Finally, the waitress puts a pot of coffee on your table and a dish of spumoni ice cream.

Prices: Inexpensive. **Decor:** Inside you'll find red checkered tablecloths, pictures of Basque dancers, and over the entrance to the dining room, a hand-carved sign that says, "Ongi etorri"—Basque for "Welcome." **Basics:** 732 Broadway (near Stockton), San Francisco. Tel: 788-9900. Hours: 5:30-10 pm Tues.-Sat.; 5-9:30 pm Sun. Closed Mon. Cards: MC, V. Full bar. Public parking (60¢ per hour) available at the Vallejo St. Garage, 766 Vallejo St. (near Powell).

Angelo's: San Francisco
Italian/An authentic old country pasta house

The Declaration of Independence states that "all men are created equal." The Founding Fathers probably realized that this statement isn't totally accurate. Surely, they weren't referring to people who cook. Not everyone has the natural-born talent to duplicate some of the pasta dishes that Angelo Roselli sends out of his kitchen. When it comes to making fettucine, tortellini, and lasagna, Angelo has been created superior.

But talent alone doesn't make good pasta. It takes something else: hard work. At 8 a.m. each morning Angelo and an assistant arrive at his small pasta house in the Marina District. After a quick cup of strong black Italian coffee, the two men go to the rear of the restaurant and climb the steel ladder that leads to the upstairs loft where the pasta is made. Angelo and his assistant spend the next six hours in this room— sifting, mixing, kneading, and patting. But they're not alone. In the room there's also a beautiful, gleaming pasta machine from Milan. Of course, to Angelo it isn't just a machine. It's a partner.

Over the years there have been many people who have appreciated Angelo's talent. When he worked at the Riviera Hotel in Las Vegas, his cooking gained him a reputation among the headliners there, including Frank Sinatra and Dean Martin. One of the celebrities that especially enjoyed Angelo's cooking was Don Rickles. He asked Angelo a number of times to prepare dinner for him. And after each dinner Rickles would tip Angelo $30 and shout, "Hey, Angelo, buy yourself a villa in Italy."

Angelo's fettucine, tortellini, and lasagna. A visit to this restaurant makes you stop and think about the record. Italians: Discovered America. Invented pasta. These people have done a lot for us.

Menu Specialties: □ Lasagna Bolognese (wide, made-today fresh noodles layered with a thick Bolognese meat sauce and a trio of cheeses—mozzarella, fontina, and parmesan.) □ Green Fettucine, White Sauce (fresh spinach noodles tossed in a flavorful ivory-colored sauce made with three cheeses and whole cream.) □ Tortellini Papalina (tender rounds of pasta stuffed with a distinctively seasoned mixture of four meats, and served in a white sauce laced with paper-thin ribbons of prosciutto ham.) □ Fettucine Carbonara (slender, delicate noodles in a rich, silky sauce laced with lots of pancetta—Italian bacon.) **Prices:** Inexpensive. **Decor:** A small, friendly-looking trattoria with candles in red glass holders, and a semi-exposed kitchen displaying a huge brick oven. **Basics:** 2234 Chestnut St. (near Pierce), San Francisco. Tel: 567-6164. Hours: 5-11 pm Tues.-Sun. Closed Mon. No cards. Wine and beer.

Tadich Grill
Seafood

Schroeder's
German

In total, they've been open 216 years.
Big, casual, anytime places polished by time.

When it comes to cooking, Tadich and Schroeder's know what they're doing. They should. They've had a lot of practice. Schroeder's has been open since 1893, and Tadich has been around since 1849.

At Tadich, the specialty is fresh seafood. Repeat: *fresh* seafood—most of it either cooked on Tadich's antique charcoal broiler, or pan-fried in a combination of cooking oils that's a century-old house secret. When it comes to seafood, it's Tadich's, not the Wharf, where many San Franciscans head.

Schroeder's has been called "the oldest, most authentic German restaurant in the West." There is a number of reasons why Schroeder's has been called "authentic." For example . . . their German sauerbraten pot roasts are marinated for three days before they're cooked. They offer authentic German potato pancakes, homemade applesauce with their roast pork, and fresh huckleberry pastries with 2-inch-high whipped cream hats. Schroeder's even features made-just-for-them frankfurters almost the size of baseball bats.

Both restaurants have mahogany paneled interiors that look exactly like they did in the 19th century. At Schroeder's, there are deer heads, ancient murals of brauhaus scenes, and probably the largest collection of Bavarian beer steins outside of Munich. Schroeder's vast, wooden-pillored dining hall is also filled with seemingly mile-long rows of elbow-polished oak tables. At Tadich, the tables are covered with starchy white linen, and the veteran waiters wear old-fashioned white cotton jackets over almost floor-length white aprons. In fact, sometimes it's hard to tell the waiters from the tablecloths. At both restaurants, there is a casual, "drop-by-anytime" feeling. Tadich even has a long mahogany lunch counter. It's a friendly place to eat when you're by yourself.

The best test of a restaurant is the test of time, and few restaurants have passed that test as well as Tadich and Schroeder's. When Schroeder's opened in 1893, the automobile had just been invented. And Tadich opened in 1849—12 years before Abraham Lincoln was elected President.

Tadich Grill Specialties: The calendar tells Tadich what to do. When a fish is in season, it goes on Tadich's menu. Immediately. According to tradition, a new menu is printed each day to showcase what's fresh. The following seafoods are usually available: □ Charcoal Broiled Seafood—Halibut Steak; Sea Bass; Rex Sole (overcooking fish is a sin. But the anchorman at Tadich's broiler is no sinner. When a piece of fish reaches its finest moment, it's immediately swept from the charcoal broiler, drizzled with butter, and quickly sent in your direction.

□ Pan-Fried Seafood—Petrale Sole; Filet of Rock Cod; Sand Dabs (all have that tang-of-the-ocean freshness, all are pan-fried to a golden brown, and all are served with an unusual homemade tartar sauce.) □ Crab Meat & Prawns Monza (baked in a creamy, coral-colored sauce flavored with paprika and mushrooms.) □ Halibut Florentine (halibut placed on a bed of spinach, topped with a sherry-laced cheese sauce, and baked.)

Dishes come with large hand-cut French fries. Starters: Fresh Coney Island Clam Chowder; Tadich Special Dinner Salad (with fresh Dungeness crab and shrimp.) **Prices:** Medium. **Basics:** 240 California St. (near Battery), San Francisco. Tel: 391-2373. Hours: 11:30 am-8:15 pm Mon.-Sat. Closed Sun. No cards. Full bar. Public parking (70¢ per hour) available at the Golden Gateway Garage, Clay St. (near Front St., across from the Embarcadero Center).

Schroeder's Specialties: Schroeder's has a rotating menu featuring six German entrees each day. □ Tues./Fri.—Sauerbraten, Potato Pancakes (the beef is marinated for three days and then roasted. The result? The beef is fork-tender and the sauce shouts "sop-me-up!" Served with crisp, golden brown potato pancakes riddled with fresh apple bits.) □ Wed.—Roast Pork (tender slices resting on a mound of spicy bread crumb stuffing, and topped with a rich, mahogany-colored pan gravy. Served with homemade applesauce made from fresh green apples.) □ Thurs.—Holstein Schnitzel (thick, greaseless breaded veal cutlets topped with a fried egg, anchovies, dill pickels, and capers. Sounds crazy, but like a group of German folk dancers, the flavors work well together.) □ Daily—Authentic German-Style Frankfurters.

Items above include German potato salad, and two vegetables (maybe freshly-cooked red cabbage, and anise-flavored sauerkraut made by Germans in Oregon.)

Dessert: Huckleberry Squares (so rich, you could get fat just looking at one. These huckleberry pastries are a Schroeder's original and it's a recipe they protect. The squares are made just for Schroeder's by a local bakery. And a strict agreement between Schroeder's and the bakery prohibits the bakery from making huckleberry squares for anyone else.) **Prices:** Inexpensive. **Basics:** 240 Front St. (near California), San Francisco. Tel: 421-4778. Hours: 11 am-9 pm Mon.-Fri. Closed Sat., Sun. No cards. Full bar. Free one hour validated parking after 5 pm at the Golden Gateway Garage, Clay St. (near Front St., across from the Embarcadero Center).

Miniature: San Francisco
Russian/Bargain priced 4-course dinners

The Miniature's food is based on the simple fare of the Russian peasant, probably the only cuisine in the world to have a direct effect on history. In Czarist Russia, the aristocracy would pick the best meats and vegetables for themselves. The peasants had to take what was left. The Miniature's Selianka stew and borsch cabbage soup are the sort of dishes that the peasants made out of what they were given. Borsch is really tasty, but not when you're forced to have it three times a day. Then one night, 35,000,000 peasants decided they were tired of having borsch for breakfast. They asked the Czar for bacon and eggs. He said no. The next morning . . . the Russian Revolution.

The Miniature is a modest-looking place that is a combination bakery and restaurant. You dine in a simple, box-shaped room where the service is handled by a woman with a molasses-thick Russian accent. She brings you everything except the last course. For dessert, you're invited to step into the Miniature's bakery and pick whatever you want. You find yourself staring at a pastry case filled with walnut rum cakes, seven-layer cakes, and Russian cheesecake studded with candied fruit. It's a sight that will make your eyes reach the size of weather balloons. And you'll be just as pleased when you see your check. At the Miniature, $4.95 buys a 4-course dinner, including pastry.

Menu Specialties: ☐ Selianka (a hearty peasant stew . . . a flavorful union of Ukrainian pork sausage, fresh cabbage, green peppers, black olives, and mushrooms. One of the Miniature's most popular dishes.) ☐ Pelmeni (homemade pasta stuffed with meat—the Russian version of ravioli.) ☐ Zrazl (chubby hamburger dumplings flavored with Russian seasonings and topped with sour cream the owners make themselves.)

Dinner includes . . . . 4 courses: Soup (you can pick any one of the Miniature's four house soups, including barley, spinach, or a traditional borsch), salad with Russian dressing, main course, coffee, and for dessert, a trip to the Miniature's pastry case. **Prices:** Inexpensive. **Basics:** 433 Clement St. (near 6th Ave.), San Francisco. Tel: 752-4444. Hours: 11 am-8 pm Tues.-Sun. Closed Mon. No cards. Wine and beer.

Orsi's: San Francisco
Italian/Interesting specialties in a Florentine setting

Oreste Orsi is brave. Instead of serving the kind of family-style meals that made North Beach famous, he took the luxury approach to Italian cooking. Back in 1963, Orsi set out to build himself the Rolls Royce of Italian restaurants. And Orsi had the experience to do it. He'd been a chef for a long time. In fact, it's rumored that Orsi was picked to do the cooking on the night they invented fire.

The menu at Orsi's reads like an encyclopedia of Italian cooking. Among the one hundred dishes listed, you'll find house-made fettucine that shouts its freshness, chicken Etrusca baked in the ancient clay pot method, and veal saltimbocca topped with fontina cheese and a slice of prosciutto ham which Orsi cures himself. And for dessert, there's Orsi's famous cassata cake—a hollow spongecake filled with sweetened ricotta cheese, chocolate, and minced citron fruit, soaked in 5 liqueurs, and finally encrusted with toasted almonds.

To handle such a menu, this restaurant has two kitchens. In the basement, there's a prep room where loins of veal are scalloped, green lasagna noodles are made, and a trio of produce men chop away at vegetables with the swashbuckling motions of old buccaneers. The main kitchen is topside, between the bar and the dining room. No secrets here. A large window in the wall of the kitchen gives customers the chance to watch Orsi's chefs at work. But this isn't the only place where you can watch the food being prepared. Sometimes, the kitchen visits your table. As you sit in comfortable leather booths, tuxedoed waiters stand behind tableside carts, gently tossing fettucine and skillfully carving herb-perfumed meats—all against a background of crystal chandeliers and Roman columns.

The bill here may shake you up. When you sign the Visa slip, your hand may be registering 8 on the Richter scale. But then you settle down and reflect on the two-hour dinner you've just finished. Thinking about the food and the service you've received, you have to admit it: Orsi gave you a dinner that was worth the earthquake prices.

Menu Specialties: □ Breast of Capon alla Orsi (the breast of capon is boned, split, filled with a flavorful stuffing, pan-seared in sweet butter, and then finished with sauterne and cognac.) □ Orsi believes in freedom of choice. On Orsi's menu, eight different veal dishes are offered. Our favorite? Saltimbocca alla Florentina (tender veal scallops topped with a paper-thin slice of prosciutto ham and fontina cheese, and served in a light brown wine sauce flavored with fresh sage. It's a 1-2-3 dish. (1) white Eastern veal is used, (2) the fontina cheese is imported from Denmark, (3) Orsi cures the prosciutto himself . . . a process that takes eight months.)

□ Chicken Etrusca (the waiter rolls a serving cart to your table. On it, there's a large black clay pot. The top is lifted. A beautiful aroma fills the air. Inside, there's a whole chicken—encrusted with herbs and surrounded by fresh artichoke hearts, mushrooms, zucchini, and a chestnut-colored sauce with a rich, deep, intoxicating flavor. By using the clay pot cooking method, Orsi has created a dish that's "fit for a king." And Orsi has some practical experience in this area. Back in the late Forties, Orsi used to cook for King Humbert II of Italy. Note: the Chicken Etrusca takes 60 minutes to prepare. It's listed on Orsi's separate specialty menu. The dish serves two.)

Dishes include risotto rice and fresh spinach prepared Italian-style. Starters: ☐ Cannelloni Ripieni (homemade pasta filled with chicken, veal, and ricotta. Topped with fontina cheese and sauced with a creamy bechamel, and a red marinara made with fresh tomatoes. One of the best versions we've found in San Francisco.) ☐ Lasagna Verdi (fresh, thin sheets of spinach pasta layered with a rich combination of cheeses, sauces, and fresh herbs.) ☐ Fettucine Romana (ribbon-cut noodles, made-only-hours-before-fresh, in a sauce of butter, pure cream, parmesan cheese, and nutmeg.) Note: pastas can be split between two. ☐ Tossed Green Salad (a mixture of red leaf, chicory, Boston, and romaine lettuce. Tossed tableside with olive oil and vinegar. But not just any vinegar. Orsi's own homemade red wine vinegar. Before it reaches your table, Orsi ages the vinegar in oak casks *for 3 years*.) Dessert: Cassata Cake, of course. **Prices:** Expensive. **Basics:** 375 Bush St. (near Kearny), San Francisco. Tel: 981-6535. Hours: 11:30 am-11 pm Mon.-Fri.; 5-11:30 pm Sat. Closed Sun. Reservations suggested. Jackets requested. All major cards. Full bar.

Tia Margarita: San Francisco
Mexican/Candlelit dining room, Acapulco decor

Those of us who watch the thoroughbreds race at Bay Meadows are familiar with an educational little newspaper called the *Daily Racing Form*. The purpose of this publication is to help you predict a horse's performance. Do you know what's really needed? A similar newspaper for restaurants. We'd call it the *Daily Dining Form*.

Suppose you're looking for a place to eat. After reading the *Dining Form*, you immediately veto Joe's Grill. The paper reports that Joe's new chef is so inexperienced, he tried to fry ice cream; so the odds of getting a decent meal at Joe's are 800 to 1. Then, just as you're turning the page in search of a better bet, a suspicious-looking stranger appears.

"Psssst. Got a hot tip. Visit Tia Margarita. A sure winner."

But you don't take his word. You consult the *Daily Dining Form*. The statistics are all there ::::: Tia Margarita Recap ::::: Authentic Mexican cooking ** Besides the usual fillings, Tia Margarita stuffs their enchiladas with black olives or chorizo, a spicy Mexican sausage ** Uses choice Denver beef for the Carne Asada—a sirloin steak cooked with green peppers, onions, and imported Mexican spices **

Avoids the Tijuana gift shop look; decor is tasteful and romantic **
Track record: the restaurant has been a local favorite for the last 15
years ** The *Daily Dining Form's* summary: the odds of being satisfied
here are 1 to 1 . . . it's a sure bet.

Menu Specialties: □ Carne Asada □ Chorizo Enchiladas (rolled
tortillas bulging with a filling of tasty Mexican sausage. Topped with a
sauce of chopped tomatoes and mild imported chiles.) □ Tia Margarita
Special Enchiladas (filled with black olives, onions, and Monterey
Jack. Topped with parmesan cheese.) □ Chile Rellenos (long Ortega
peppers stuffed with Monterey Jack, dipped in egg batter, and deep
fried. Topped with a fresh, mild Mexican red sauce.)

Dishes include salad with a special house dressing, Spanish rice,
and refried beans. **Prices:** Inexpensive. **Basics:** 300 19th Ave. (at Clement), San Francisco. Tel: 752-9274. Hours: 4-11 pm Mon., Wed.,
Thurs.; 4-11:30 pm Fri., Sat.; 3-10 pm Sun. Closed Tues. Reservations
suggested. No cards. Full bar.

Pacific Cafe: San Francisco
Seafood/A place to go when fishing for modest prices

The Pacific Cafe is a fine neighborhood spot to enjoy seafood.
And the prices are very reasonable. This is one place that won't torpedo
your wallet.

Our favorite dish at the Pacific Cafe is the turbot, New Orleans
style. Besides being a good dish, at $6.65, it's an excellent value con-
sidering the preparation involved. The turbot is stuffed with crab and
shrimp, and covered with a sherried cream sauce. Then it's wrapped in a
parchment cooking bag which locks in every bit of moisture while the
fish bakes. When the turbot is done, it's brought to your table—bag and
all—and slit open with a jackknife. When a fragrant fist of steam hits
your face, you begin.

Menu Specialties: □ Halibut Steak □ Salmon □ Petrale Sole (all
three come directly from the ocean 16 blocks from your table. And
when they arrive here, all three are carefully broiled over charcoal.)
□ Pan-fried Pacific Oysters (fresh from Tomales Bay, 40 miles down
the road.) □ Turbot, New Orleans Style.

Dinner includes: A large tossed salad with an herb dressing, and
fresh hand-cut fries almost the size of 2 × 4's. **Prices:** Inexpensive to
medium. **Decor:** Inside there's booths of natural wood, and burnt
orange walls with 1890 nautical photos. **Basics:** 7000 Geary Blvd. (at
34th Ave.), San Francisco. Tel: 387-7091. Hours: 5-10:30 pm Mon.-
Thurs.; 5-11 pm Fri., Sat.; 5-10 pm Sun. No cards. Wine and beer.

Rue Lepic: San Francisco
French/Chef-owned bistro with a Nob Hill setting

Rue Lepic is a restaurant with genuine San Francisco charm. Located just down the hill from the Mark Hopkins Hotel, this friendly-looking bistro has a small, softly-lit dining room set with crisp linen and filled with fresh flowers. Even the kitchen has been made part of the atmosphere. Chef-owner Tyrone Aquino, dressed in a classic starched white uniform, cooks in full view of his diners. The only thing separating the dining room from the kitchen is a waist-high counter. At Rue Lepic, it almost feels like you have your own personal chef.

The food also gives you the impression that the chef is cooking just for you. Rue Lepic's duckling with peaches and veal in champagne sauce have the kind of flavor that can only be achieved when a dish is given personal attention. And it's not just the entrees that get this attention. The chef makes his vegetables taste like they were grown in butter.

The service at Rue Lepic is as personal as the restaurant itself. The hostess, Tyrone's wife Cecily, handles each party with a natural warmth, and the way Rue Lepic's waiter takes care of your needs, the man must have psychic powers. He is also helpful when it comes to describing Rue Lepic's dishes. On our first visit to Rue Lepic, we asked him what the chef's veal in champagne sauce was like. The waiter thought for a moment, gave us a sly smile, and said, "Well, gentlemen, if you taste the sauce and close your eyes, it's like dreaming of an affair with a beautiful woman." And you know something? He was right.

Menu Specialties: □ Veal in Champagne Sauce (Wisconsin milk-fed veal and fresh mushrooms in a buttery, silk-smooth cream sauce with a subtle champagne flavor.) □ Duckling with Peaches (a boned duckling, crisp and golden outside, and tender and moist to the bone inside. Served with peach quarters and a dark sauce that's fragrant with peach brandy.) □ Filet of Beef Rue Lepic (two medallions of filet mignon cloaked with a rich brown sauce made with brandy and green peppercorns from Madagascar.) □ Chicken Chambertin (boned chicken in a mushroom-laced red wine sauce with a deep, distinctive flavor.)

Dinner includes: Soup (maybe cream of cauliflower or crab bisque), or salad (butter lettuce, zucchini, tomatoes, cucumbers, and fresh mushrooms in a house dressing flavored with eight different herbs), and main course with rice pilaf and fresh vegetable (maybe purée of asparagus or purée of broccoli.)

Dessert: Chef Aquino makes his own pastries. Our favorite is his version of the strawberry tart—a flaky pastry shell filled with a rich custard laced with banana slices, and topped with fresh strawberries and a crown of whipped cream. **Prices:** Medium. **Basics:** 900 Pine St. (at Mason), San Francisco. Tel: 775-4535. Hours: 6-10 pm Tues.-Sat. Closed Sun., Mon. Reservations necessary. Cards: MC, V. Wine and beer.

Exploring San Francisco's
United Nation's Variety of Restaurants

As a U.N. ambassador, you must be prepared

Have you ever wondered what it would be like to be appointed the United States ambassador to the United Nations?

Monday morning. 9 a.m. You enter the Oval Office. You're greeted by the President of the United States. After a few minutes of pleasant conversation, the President gets down to business. "I want to make you aware," the President begins, "that your new position includes one important duty—dining at foreign embassies. It's a tough job. Your diet will vary from Russian pelmeni one night to Greek moussaka the next. Now, this kind of diet takes some getting used to, so I'm sending you to San Francisco to get some practice. Because . . . you must be prepared. Prepared to eat Russian pelmeni. Greek moussaka. Indonesian rijstaffel. As our ambassador, you must be able to eat all of these." The President pauses, and then adds, "Remember, the peace of the world may depend on it."

So there you have it. Your assignment. By Presidential order. Every night, a different cuisine. Just for the practice.

But if you were a U.N. ambassador, where would you go in San Francisco to get that practice? We have some suggestions.

For the food of Russia try

Cinderella

According to legend, Tolstoy was eating chicken Kiev when the idea to write *War and Peace* came to him. It's been called the world's greatest novel. Listen, why don't you try Cinderella's Kiev and see what happens?

Chicken Kiev (a boned, rolled chicken breast encased in a crisp bread crumb crust. And inside, there's a golden reservoir of sweet butter that squirts out when you plunge in the fork.), $3.10. Or try the Beef Stroganoff (in a tasty sour cream sauce with mushrooms. And to soak up the sauce, there's homemade Russian peasant bread.), $2.90. Another dish you might try is the Pelmeni (the Russian version of the ravioli), $2.40.

Decor: A modest-looking cafe with seven tables and an old country aroma of steaming borsch drifting through the air. **Basics:** 436 Balboa St. (near 5th Ave.), San Francisco. Tel: 751-9690. Hours: 9 am-6:30 pm Wed.-Sun. Closed Mon., Tues. No cards.

For the food of Indonesia try

Sari's

The owners of this small, friendly restaurant are Siti Atikah and Julda Asmara, two hard-working ladies from Indonesia. Just think . . . they traveled 7,640 miles to cook you dinner. And they'll be cooking you Indonesia's most famous kind of dinner—a rijstaffel.

Actually, a rijstaffel is a creation of the Dutch who colonized Indonesia in the 19th century. The Dutch liked two things—Indonesian food and variety. The result was a feast called a "rijstaffel." It was sort of an attempt by the Dutch to eat all their favorite Indonesian dishes at one sitting. During colonial days, a rijstaffel sometimes took three full days to prepare. And while Sari's isn't equipped to serve a feast of this size, their version of the rijstaffel is still a meal that lives up to its name.

Sari's rijstaffel includes 9 dishes: fried Krupuk shrimp chips, Lumpia (Indonesian egg roll), Gado-Gado (salad, Indonesian style), Ayam Goreng (lemon marinated, fried chicken), Udang Goreng (Indonesian fried shrimp with onions), Saté Daging (beef marinated in Javanese spices, skewered and charcoal broiled. Served with an Indonesian peanut sauce.), Sajur Lodeh (mixed vegetables cooked in coconut milk), Pergedel (Indonesian meatballs), rice, and for dessert, Spekkoek (spiced layer cake). The rijstaffel dinner, $7.25.

Decor: Inside, there's Javanese batik cloth on the walls, Balinese dance masks hanging from the ceiling, and a five-foot-high Indonesian ceremonial gong in one corner. **Basics:** 2459 Lombard St. (near Divisadero), San Francisco. Tel: 567-8715. Hours: 6-10 pm Tues.-Sun. Closed Mon. Cards: MC, V. Wine and beer.

For the food of Korea try

Korea House

The specialty here is marinated barbecued meats. Both the Bulkogi beef ($5) and Kalbi short ribs ($5) are marinated in a flavor-loaded Korean sauce for 24 hours and then broiled. And the result of this "down home" Korean barbecue is . . . mighty fine, neighbor. Dinner includes: Soup, vegetables tossed in a sesame dressing, rice, and green tea. Also included is a little dish of kimchee—cabbage pickled in red peppers for three days. In Korea, kimchee is eaten like we eat dill pickles here. But be careful. The stuff is so hot, one nibble and your tongue does a sit-up.

Decor: A bright, beige wood, Oriental decor and huge comfortable booths. **Basics:** 1640 Post St. (near Laguna, opposite the Japanese Cultural Center), San Francisco. Tel: 563-1388. Hours: 11:30 am-10 pm Mon.; 11:30 am-3 am Tues.-Sun. Cards: MC,V. Full bar.

For the food of Tunisia try

Carthage

Tunisia is a small Arab country bordering the Mediterranean. It's a nation with a proud heritage that dates back to when Tunisia was the center of the ancient Carthaginian empire. One of the characteristics of the Tunisian people is their genuine hospitality. And that's evident when you visit this small, eleven-table restaurant. Regularly during the evening, Mohsen Douihech, the restaurant's handsome owner-chef, leaves the kitchen and stops by all eleven tables in the dining room. At each table, he shakes the hand of everyone in the party and thanks them for coming. Now that's hospitality.

Chicken au Citron (a whole capon roasted with black olives, pearl onions, saffron, rosemary, marjoram, and pieces of lemon that are marinated Tunisian style for one full month. The pan sauce that results is rich, very gently tart, and excellent. Served with rice pilaf.), $7.25. Tunisian Brochettes (tender, well-trimmed pieces of lamb marinated for 48 hours with harissa and other Tunisian spices, then broiled and topped with roasted pine nuts. Served with rice pilaf and sauteed zucchini.), $7.95. Couscous (chef Moshen's couscous of imported semolina, lamb, and eight different vegetables is prepared with a special pot called a couscousier and comes out a caravan of flavors.), $7.25.

Dinner includes: Charba (a fragrant Tunisian lamb soup), or salad (butter lettuce topped with a mixture of marinated green peppers, tomatoes, and eggplant, and an Arabian dressing.)

Decor: A small dining room with handwoven Tunisian rugs, candlelight, and beige tablecloths. The walls are decorated with pictures of the ruins at Carthage and a photo of two camels—which belong to chef Moshen's father back in Tunisia. The room also benefits from the charm of Mohsen's dark-eyed wife Michelle, who acts as hostess. **Basics:** 2326 Judah St. (near 28th Ave.), San Francisco. Tel: 665-6400. Hours: 6-11 pm Mon.-Sat. Closed Sun. Cards: MC, V. Wine and beer.

For the food of the West Indies try

Connie's

At this Caribbean restaurant it's always easy to find owner Connie Williams. She's never very far away from her stove. Also, you may notice that many customers make a special point of saying hello to Connie. Some even hug her. Connie deserves this kind of attention—she radiates a kind of warmth you can almost feel. You might say that her restaurant has natural heating.

Caribbean Chicken (tender chicken seasoned with spices imported from Trinidad), $5.00. Connie's Favorite Gumbo (crab, shrimp, chicken, and rock cod in a fragrant long-simmered stock), $5.50. Curried Beef with Eggplant (chunks of beef cooked with vegetables and spices until the sauce is the rich red color of a Caribbean sunset. Served with a side dish of Connie-made chutney.), $5.00.

Dinner includes . . . 4 courses: Soup, tossed salad, homemade coconut bread, main course with a fresh vegetable, coffee, and West Indian pudding with rum sauce.

Decor: Colorful paintings cover the walls and soft island folk music plays in the background. **Basics:** 1907 Fillmore St. (near Bush), San Francisco. Tel: 563-8755. Hours: 5:30-10 pm Wed.-Sun. Closed Mon., Tues. No cards. Wine and beer.

For the food of Greece try

Xenios

This is as close to Greece as you're going to get without a passport. Owner Peter Stavros' father, Demetrios, has operated Greek restaurants continuously since 1935, and Stavros senior has taught his son all the right things to do. Peter also learned to be loyal to the homeland: in Xenios' kitchen the spice boxes bear Greek labels and the cooking wines come from Greek vineyards. And this loyalty is being appreciated. One of Xenios' customers is Mr. Velliadis, the Greek consul general stationed in San Francisco.

Moussaka (Greece's most famous dish. Layers of fresh eggplant and ground beef seasoned with Greek spices, topped with a rich white sauce, and baked in a special clay dish from Greece.), $5.75. Dolmades (lean ground beef, rice, and spices including fresh mint, wrapped in imported grape leaves and topped with a light lemon sauce), $5.50. Kotopoulo Krasato (sauteed chicken smothered with a mixture of minced tomatoes, white and green onions, and green peppers flavored with Castal Damielis, a Greek red wine), $6.00. Dishes include two fresh vegetables prepared Greek style and rice pilaf.

Decor: A small, romantic, brick-walled dining room with a Grecian-Roman fountain, a Mediterranean tile floor, and a beautiful antique brass chandelier that has over 750 hanging crystals. And you enter the restaurant through nine-foot-high, 300-year-old, hand-carved doors from Spain. **Basics:** 2237 Polk St. (near Green), San Francisco. Tel: 775-2800. Hours: 5:30-11 pm daily. Reservations suggested on weekends. All major cards. Wine and beer.

For the food of India try

Tandoori

This restaurant's moist, spicy chicken Tikka Tandoori ($5.75) and tender Boti lamb ($5.25) have a special flavor. Why? They're cooked in a very special oven. This restaurant has an imported Indian tandoor—a barrel-shaped oven made from Punjab riverbed clay. Inside this oven is a bed of charcoal that must be kept burning 24 hours a day. The tandoor cooking method dates back to the 11th century. Indian villagers found that meats cooked in round ovens made of Punjab clay were much more flavorful than meats cooked in regular ovens. And 900 years later, this Punjab clay magic still works.

Decor: Large, comfortable booths and waiters in Madras and turbans. **Basics:** 2550 Van Ness Ave. in the Vagabond Motel (near Filbert), San Francisco. Tel: 776-1455. Hours: 11 am-3 pm Mon.-Sat.; 5-10 pm Sun.-Thurs.; 5-11 pm Fri., Sat. Cards: AE, MC, V. Full bar. Free parking in the Vagabond Motel's garage.

For the food of El Salvador try

Coatepeque

Go ahead, think about it. How long has it been since you've had a first time? If it's been a while, you should have a Salvadorian dinner at the Coatepeque. They offer a kind of cuisine that's rarely found outside of Central America. But their food isn't just "different." It's also very good.

Bisteck de Puerco (thin pork scallops marinated for four days in homemade pineapple vinegar and spices, and then grilled), $3.15. Albondigas Meatballs (flavored with a whisper of fresh mint, and served in a tasty Salvadorian tomato sauce), $2.50. Salvadorian Stuffed Peppers (whole green peppers stuffed with a flavor-loaded combination of meat, diced potatoes, and spices. Topped with a fresh Salvadorian sauce.), $2.50. Cheese Pupusas (handmade Salvadorian tortillas filled with cheese imported from El Salvador), 75¢. Dessert: Torrejas (homemade pastry in a cinnamon-rum sauce), 45¢. And look at those prices. This is the home of the $4 adventure.

Decor: A bright, friendly-looking place with a simple but spotless decor. **Basics:** 2240 Mission St. (near 18th St.), San Francisco. Tel: 863-5237. Hours: Noon-8:30 pm Mon., Tues.; noon-9:30 pm Fri.-Sun. Closed Wed., Thurs. No cards. Beer only.

Harbin: San Francisco
Chinese/Inviting Oriental atmosphere

Eva Chang can prepare over 250 Chinese dishes, but considering her background, it's a miracle that she can boil water. As the daughter of a wealthy banker, Eva grew up on a 120-acre estate in China. Until she was thirty, Eva lived in a cushioned world of silk and jade splendor. Think about it: if you had an 84-room house, 23 servants, and 4 cooks, how much would you know about making egg foo yung?

Eva left China in 1951 due to Communist trouble, and when she arrived in the United States, she and the kitchen were still strangers. But once she entered the kitchen, she quickly learned to be a cook. And a good one. Although she lacked experience, Eva was born with the one characteristic you'll find in both great chefs and professional gamblers. As Eva admits, her culinary skill is the result of "lucky hands."

Eva's restaurant features dishes from Manchuria, a northern region of China which borders the Yellow Sea. The trick with the Manchurian style of cooking is to season each dish highly without going overboard and making a diner feel like someone's celebrating the Fourth of July in his mouth. And believe us, Eva knows the trick. To anyone who's tried her hot crispy shrimp, it's very obvious that this woman has "lucky hands." Imagine what hands like that could do in Las Vegas.

Menu Specialties: ☐ Hot Crispy Shrimp (Don't miss 'em. Shrimp with a golden brown crust, crowned with a spicy crimson red sauce that glows like Oriental jewels.) ☐ Mongolian Lamb (tender ribbons of lamb in a rich brown sauce laced with green onions. Served on a bed of crisp, snow white Chinese noodles.) ☐ Moo Sue Pork (you're served an egg-enriched pork mixture laced with cloud ear mushrooms and a stack of paper-thin Chinese pancakes. You spoon some pork onto a pancake and then roll the pancake around the mixture. It's sort of a do-it-yourself Chinese enchilada.)

☐ Crab a la Harbin (snow white crab meat stir-fried in sesame oil with ginger, eggs, and onions.) 22 Eggs Means Twin Boys: Onions and eggs are Chinese baby food. Instead of baby announcements, the Chinese send hard-boiled eggs—8 for a girl, 11 for a boy. Also, in some parts of China, they rub newborn babies with a freshly-cut onion. According to custom, this ensures that the child will be clever. It probably also ensures that no one will pick the baby up for a few days. **Prices:** Inexpensive to medium. **Decor:** In the dining room, there's Chinese art on straw paper walls, and linen tablecloths. And through an archway, there's a glassed-in dining patio with a reflecting pool and garden. **Basics:** 327 Balboa St. (near 4th Ave.), San Francisco. Tel: 387-0274. Hours: 11:30 am-11 pm daily. Cards: MC, V. Full bar.

Tired of this happening?

Then visit La Pantera,
where 5-course meals with wine are $6.25

Yep. After paying the bill at some restaurants you feel like your wallet has just been flattened with a rolling pin. Whenever we get this uncomfortable feeling, it means the time has come for another visit to La Pantera. This Italian restaurant tends to restore our confidence in the purchasing power of the dollar. La Pantera's 5-course dinners including wine are $6.25.

But it's not just the price that attracts us. The main attraction at La Pantera is the old-fashioned Italian homecooking that leaves the kitchen. The food tastes like someone cares. And someone does. Mrs. Nicolai, La Pantera's owner, is never more than a few feet away from her stove.

La Pantera has been around for a long time. In 1906, a small vaudeville house in North Beach went broke, and an Italian couple took over the building and turned it into a modest restaurant called La Pantera. And the policy they established in 1906 is still being followed by Mrs. Nicolai today. There is no menu. You just take a seat and the food starts coming.

You sit at large, round communal tables and are expected to share the steaming platters of food with your neighbors—whether you know them or not. In North Beach, the "everybody's welcome table" is a long standing tradition. At this type of family-style restaurant, you either make friends out of strangers or go for the dishes within reach. But with a platter of freshly-made ravioli sitting on the other side of the table, you tend to make friends fast.

The Menu: One main course is served nightly. Some examples: an authentic chicken cacciatora; a home-style veal parmigiana with a flavorful layer of cheese; cross ribs of beef roasted with Italian herbs; veal Bocconcino in a delicate tomato sauce.

Dinner includes . . . 5 courses: A tureen of fresh, hearty minestrone soup, a plate of wine-cured salami and pepperoncini, a pasta (maybe fettucine in basil sauce or homemade ravioli), or an appetizer course (maybe lemony sand dabs or stuffed zucchini), main course with fresh vegetable, a bowl of salad (traditionally served after the main course), and finally a plate of fruit and cheese for dessert. Also included—a small bottle of Parducci red wine.

Prices: Inexpensive. **Decor:** There are seven huge, elbow-polished mahogany tables, an old, stately, hand-carved bar, and a scrollwork ceiling. **Basics:** 1234 Grant Ave. (betw. Columbus and Vallejo), San Francisco. Tel: 392-0170. Hours: Noon-2 pm, 6-10 pm Tues.-Fri.; 6-10 pm Sat., Sun. Closed Mon. No cards. Full bar. Public parking (60¢ per hour) available at the Vallejo St. Garage, 766 Vallejo St. (near Powell).

Beginning: San Francisco
Soul Food/Basketball star scores with down home cooking

Several years ago a member of the Miami Dolphins football team opened a restaurant. Unfortunately, most of the people who tried his food were very unhappy—it tasted like AstroTurf. Five years ago, basketball superstar Nate Thurmond also decided to take some of his capital and open a restaurant. The difference is his food tastes good. The reason is very simple: 6'11" Nate has a talented 5'8" cook named Louis Love in charge of his kitchen.

The Beginning features soul food, a type of cooking that Louis has been preparing for 35 l-o-n-g years. You can taste this experience in the very first thing Louis puts on your table—homemade cornbread muffins. They're moist. Crispy. Golden brown. And just perfect for sponging up some of the rich herb stock in Louis' gumbo—a Creole dish of crab legs, chicken, rough-cut vegetables, shrimp, and smoked pork sausage.

After you've tried Louis' gumbo, we think you'll agree with us that the Beginning serves authentic soul food. How authentic? By the time you leave this place, you'll be doing the James Brown leap and the O'Jays kick.

Menu Specialties: ☐ Gumbo (the famous Creole dish midway between a soup and a stew. Louis authentically flavors it with New Orleans filé powder, a fragrant seasoning first used by the Choctaw Indians in Louisiana. Louis' gumbo of shellfish, fowl, sausage, and herb stock is tasty proof of his ability to balance and blend. Gumbo available Tues., Fri., and Sat.) □ Southern Fried Chicken (when a soul food cook makes fried chicken there are three commandments to obey: (1) the chicken must be greaseless, (2) the crust must be light and crisp, (3) the meat must be moist. And Louis obeys all the commandments.) □ Baked Ham (slices of flavorful ham and sweet yams in a sauce that's one of Louis' closely guarded secrets. And it will probably remain his secret. When Louis cooks, it's his policy never to let anyone watch him.)

Dinner includes: Soup (maybe Louis' beef chunk soup or his chicken Creole soup), or a crisp salad, homemade cornbread muffins, and main course with two Louisiana-style vegetables. Dessert: Homemade Sweet Potato Pie (great stuff. The pie has a rich, buttery, just-baked flavor.) **Prices:** Inexpensive. **Decor:** Dark wood walls hung with pitchforks and antique butter churns, lights made out of well buckets, a potbelly stove, patchwork-print wallpaper . . . it's the farmhouse theme done with style. **Basics:** 2020 Fillmore St. (near California), San Francisco. Tel: 563-9948. Hours: 4-11 pm Tues.-Sun. Closed Mon. No cards. Full bar.

Saigon: San Francisco
Vietnamese/A long list of authentic specialties

In 1968, the U.S. Army made it possible for author Riera to sample Vietnamese food on-location . . .

While in Vietnam, I gave my girlfriend, Phuong, 4,500 piasters a month. I realized that a GI in a war zone only has two choices: you either do without a steady girlfriend, or you lease some affection. At least I received a fringe benefit—Phuong gave me a thorough introduction to Vietnamese food.

To prepare for a night at Phuong's, I would first stuff the pockets of my jungle fatigues with candy. According to Army policy, Phuong's village was off-limits to GI's after dark, and the candy insured that I would be given plenty of warning before an MP raid. I found that the local Vietnamese kids who acted as lookouts adjusted their efficiency according to the number of Hershey bars they received. Around the barracks, my friends used to call me "the candy man."

Once I had recruited my palace guard, I made my way to Phuong's place—a pale yellow plaster shack with a roof made out of flattened soda pop cans. Dinner was usually waiting for me. Phuong would start the meal with Cha Gio, a Vietnamese-style egg roll, and then she'd serve me . . .

Hold it. Perhaps I should stop and let you know how this story relates to the Saigon.

It seems that Phuong and this Vietnamese restaurant think alike. To my surprise, the Saigon offers many of the dishes Phuong served me. And they serve them at very modest prices—most of their dishes are in the $3 range.

One of the Saigon's dishes especially brought back memories—the shrimp Tom Chua Ngot. Phuong served me this dish the night I passed up a Bob Hope show to visit her. Phuong said I wouldn't regret it. "Ooooooo," was she right.

Menu Specialties: □ Cha Gio □ Tom Chua Ngot (a rich, ruby-colored Vietnamese sweet & sour sauce serves as a backdrop for a star-shaped arrangement of shrimp encased in a delicate, golden-colored batter.) □ Ca Chua Nhoi Thit (you're served a platter of huge, flavorful pork and mushroom meatballs—each one set inside a whole tomato.) □ Ga Nhag (tender pieces of chicken toss-fried in a light sauce made with fresh ginger. The Vietnamese call this dish "singing chicken." It's a dish you'll want to "hear" again.)

□ Thit Heo Ram (ribbons of tender, well-trimmed pork stir-fried in a fascinating, mildly sweet sauce made with coconut milk.) □ Bo Xao Ca-Ry (a very good Vietnamese curry dish made with strips of beef and a garden of fresh, crisp vegetables. And it's not just the taste you'll remember. The curry is brought to your table on a sizzling metal platter that sends up such a cloud of steam, it looks like a monsoon just arrived.)

□ Ga Ngu Vi Huong (chicken marinated with a special Five-Spice powder for 24 hours and then roasted until a reddish-brown glaze forms. This Five-Spice powder has a magical quality—the ability to pull your taste buds in five different directions at once. With each bite, the flavor starts smoky, turns sweet, backtracks to sour, levels off spicy, and disappears nutty—all in a split second.)

□ Cua Rang Muoi Tieu (crab prepared southern Vietnamese style. You're served a whole, fresh, steaming-hot Dungeness crab in shell—with each piece coated with a thin, topaz-colored sauce with a buttery richness that dazzles. This isn't a dish you eat, it's a dish you experience. After you're finished, the waiter brings you a finger bowl filled with perfumed water.) Dessert: Chuoi Chien (excellent Vietnamese-style banana fritters made with a perfect air-light batter. Thankfully. We've been to some places where the banana fritters are so heavy, it takes two hands to lift the fork.)

Note: We suggest you have your dinner served Chinese style, with everyone helping themselves from central platters. Vietnamese food lends itself to this approach. Also, it tends to turn a Vietnamese meal into a Vietnamese feast. **Prices:** Inexpensive. **Decor:** A comfortable dining room with potted plants, candles in amber glass holders, and some Vietnamese dolls on display. Plus, owner-host Bill Sonsip provides helpful friendly service, while his wife handles the kitchen—teamwork at its best. **Basics:** 579 Geary St. (near Jones), San Francisco. Tel: 885-3332. Hours: 11 am-3 pm, 5-10 pm Mon.-Sat. Closed Sun. Cards: MC, V. Wine and beer.

San Francisco Pizzerias

Where to get the best pizzas in San Francisco

Ah, pizza. Everybody's favorite way of getting fat. The only problem is finding a place that knows how to make it properly. How disappointing to sit down expecting pizza . . . and get served a circle of cracker-thin dough topped with a watery tomato sauce, tasteless cheese, and enough oil to run a diesel from here to L.A.

Francis Ford Coppola has found a way to avoid those kind of disappointments. He's learned to make his own pizza. But can a man who's made a $10 million dollar movie about the Mafia make a good $6 pizza? Yep. Francis was lucky enough to find the right teacher—Tommaso's. In San Francisco, we've only discovered a handful of restaurants that make great pizza, and Tommaso's is one of them. Our other discoveries are Giorgio's and Gennaro's.

This trio has an important common denominator: fresh ingredients. They all make their own dough and make it daily, and never, no never, pound out a round lump of dough until they get your order. They also slice their own mozzarella from huge cheese rounds, and their toppings are the work of authentic Italian sausage makers. Best of all, their sauces are made in the mild Neapolitan tradition, which means that the spices that give the pizza its wonderful aroma won't turn your breath into a lethal weapon the next day.

So there you have it. We feel the best pizzerias in the City are Tommaso's, Giorgio's, and Gennaro's. But we'd like to stress that this is just our opinion. If there's one thing we've learned in talking to people about this popular food, it's that pizza is like sex—there are a lot of different opinions on "what's good."

Tommaso's Pizza: Salami, Italian sausage, mushroom, or pepperoni: small, $5.50; large, $6.50. *The shop's custom touches:* the crust of Tommaso's pizza is thick and takes on a special character from being baked in an old-fashioned pizza oven that burns oakwood logs. In fact, Tommaso's, which has been in business since 1936, has the only oakwood-fueled pizza oven in America. Dessert Your Family: for dessert try their homemade Cannoli (a crispy pastry shell stuffed with a sweet, creamy filling studded with candied fruit), $1.50. **Basics:** 1042 Kearny St. (near Broadway), San Francisco. Tel: 398-9696. Hours: 5-11 pm Wed.-Sat.; 4-10 pm Sun. Closed Mon., Tues. Cards: MC, V. Wine and beer. Public parking (60¢ per hour) available at the Vallejo St. Garage, 766 Vallejo St. (near Powell).

The Coppola Pizza
Francis Ford Coppola, director of The Godfather, *making a pizza at Tommaso's in San Francisco. What more can we say?*

Giorgio's Pizza: Salami, sausage, mushroom, or pepperoni: small, $3.60; medium, $4.70; large, $5.75. Or don't play favorites . . . invite 'em all aboard—Giorgio's Special Pizza: small, $5.00; large, $7.00. *The shop's custom touches:* they offer the rare Calzone, a pizza turnover stuffed with salami, pepperoni, mozzarella, and ricotta cheese: small, $4.20; large, $5.90. And they have Italian health food, a Vegetarian Pizza (mushrooms, bell peppers, onions, and black olives), small, $5.00; large, $7.70. **Basics:** 151 Clement St. (at 3rd Ave.), San Francisco. Tel: 668-1266. Hours: 11:30 am-11:30 pm Mon.-Thurs.; 11:30 am-12:30 am Fri., Sat.; 11:30 am-11 pm Sun. No cards. Wine and beer.

Gennaro's Pizza: Pepperoni, fennel sausage, salami, or mushroom: small, $3.25; medium, $4.25; large, $5.50. Or try Gennaro's Godfather Pizza—sort of four pizzas in one. The pizza is divided into four sections: ¼ sausage, ¼ mushroom, ¼ bell peppers, and ¼ anchovy: small, $3.50; medium, $4.50; large, $5.75. *The shop's custom touches:* Gennaro's pizzas are baked in a hand-crafted, brick-lined oven that was built especially for Gennaro's father in 1949. According to Gennaro, this oven gives his pizza crust its special character. In fact, the oven is so unique, it was once featured on the TV show, "You Asked For It." **Basics:** 2113 Polk St. (near Broadway), San Francisco. Tel: 771-7220. Hours: 4-midnight daily. No cards. Wine and beer.

Swiss Louis: San Francisco
Italian/On Pier 39, huge dinners in the Louis tradition

For forty-three years, Swiss Louis was located in North Beach. Then, in 1978, they moved to the Pier 39 complex. Swiss Louis now has a new decor and a beautiful view of the bay.

What else changed? Nothing.

This establishment still believes in an old Italian custom: The Big Meal. At Swiss Louis, dinner begins with a round, 13-item appetizer tray that's almost the size of a roulette wheel at Harrah's. There's two kinds of salami, coppa ham, marinated artichoke hearts, mortadella . . . well, anyhow, the tray is stocked better than some Italian delicatessens. Along with the appetizer tray comes a large tossed salad topped with bay shrimp and an Italian herb dressing that begs to be sopped up with a piece of crusty sourdough.

Next, you're served a cup of chef Salvatore Chiavino's minestrone. Then, it's time for the main course. You like veal? Try his saltimbocca Romana—veal rolls stuffed with prosciutto ham and cheese, and topped with a rich mushroom sauce. You like chicken? Chef Chiavino takes a half spring chicken, sprinkles it with fresh herbs, including rosemary he grows himself, and broils it in an iron Schiacciato-style device—which keeps the chicken moist and tender, yet gives it a beautiful crisp crust. Or maybe you'd like a steak. Chef Chiavino offers a thick New York steak that's so tender, it's as if the cow had spent most of its time laying on a couch.

Finally, the last course is served—a cocktail glass of fresh sugared strawberries in red wine. But that's not all. Also placed on your table is a huge wooden bowl of fresh, ripe fruit and nuts that looks like it was arranged by a still-life artist. You don't know whether to paint it or eat it. Go ahead, eat.

Menu Specialties: ☐ Broiled Chicken ☐ Veal Saltimbocca Romana (veal rolls stuffed with prosciutto ham and Monterey Jack cheese, and seasoned with oregano, sage, and thyme. Topped with a mushroom sauce that traces back to a good rich stock. Served with wild rice sauteed in butter with green onions and bits of Italian ham.) ☐ New York Steak (a well-aged steak that's been cut with a generous hand. But maybe you're wondering—is this an authentic Italian dish? Yes. Just before serving it, chef Chiavino leans down, waves his hand over the steak, and whispers, "You're Italian.") Note: All Swiss Louis' dishes are available a la carte.

Dinner includes . . . 5 courses: A 13-item appetizer tray, salad, soup, main course with fresh Italian green beans and potatoes au gratin, coffee, and dessert. **Prices:** Medium to a step above medium. **Basics:** Pier 39, San Francisco. Tel: 421-2913. Hours: 11:30 am-10:30 pm daily. All major cards. Full bar.

Adriatic: San Francisco
French/A bistro with elegant dishes at everyday prices

During the period the French were in Vietnam, many Vietnamese people gained a knowledge of French cooking; in Vietnam's big cities, Vietnamese-run restaurants with French menus were relatively common. So it's not really too surprising to find that the owner of this small French restaurant is a Vietnamese lady named Madame Sinh. For her, running a little bistro is a comparatively easy task. In Saigon, Madame Sinh owned and managed two hotels, two restaurants, a nightclub and a coffee factory, which is said to have produced "the best coffee in southeast Asia."

In the kitchen of the Adriatic is a chef Madame Sinh knew in Saigon—a Vietnamese gentleman named "Pierre" Hoa. Mr. Hoa learned to cook from the French. And he learned well. Chef "Pierre" Hoa's cooking is his unemployment insurance. The Adriatic's menu is filled with elegant French dishes.

But this is one French restaurant where you don't need a wad of money the size of a beach ball. The prices are almost unbelievably reasonable: filet of sole Cardinal with lobster sauce is $6.50, breast of chicken Marechale with Perigourdine sauce is $5.75, and noisettes of lamb with sauce Choron is $6.25.

Of course, this kind of rich cooking can quickly expand your waistline. We saw an example of this on a recent visit to the Adriatic. An overweight gentleman seated next to us had apparently been coming here too often. In fact, if that gentleman gets much bigger, he's not going to be allowed on the streets unless he's wearing a set of license plates.

Menu Specialties: □ Filet of Sole Cardinal (three rolls of poached petrale sole—one roll is topped with a lobster medallion, one with a fluted mushroom, and one with a pinch of black truffles. Served with a silk-smooth lobster sauce.) □ Chicken Marechale (a butter-sauteed breast of chicken topped with a classic, dark brown Perigourdine sauce.) □ Noisettes of Lamb Ambassade (three filets of lamb served with an artichoke bottom, and a golden, tarragon-flavored sauce Choron that's accented with fresh, diced tomatoes.) □ Prawns Miramar (prawns sauteed in butter with herbs, garlic, and a squeeze of fresh lemon, and then flambéed in brandy with a touch of white wine and Pernod liqueur.)

Dishes include three fresh vegetables. **Prices:** Inexpensive to medium. **Decor:** A corner bistro with soft lighting and tables set with dark blue linen and red carnations. **Basics:** 1755 Polk St. (at Washington), San Francisco. Tel: 771-4035. Hours: Noon-3 pm, 5-10 pm Tues.-Sat.; 5:30-10 pm Sun. Closed Mon. Reservations strongly suggested on weekends. Cards: MC, V. Wine and beer.

What can three couples do?
HAVE A CHINESE BANQUET

Okay, you've rounded up two other couples. Now what? First, you'll need a restaurant with a list of interesting specialties. Our suggestion? **The North China Restaurant.** Next, you'll need a phone: you should always call the North China Restaurant in advance and plan out the evening's meal with David Lee, the owner's son. David will customize a banquet to suit your tastes. And to give you some ideas for your banquet, let's take a look at what over 4,000 years of Chinese dinner parties have produced—or how the Chinese conduct a banquet.

When the Chinese gather for a *Chiu-Hsi,* or "banquet," they like to take things slow. Although a banquet will consist of many dishes, each dish will be served separately. The sequence of courses a host will order for a Chiu-Hsi usually looks something like this: one *Ping Pan* or "appetizer platter"—→ three *Chow* or "stir-fried" dishes —→one *Teem* or "sweet dish"—→three *Daah Tsai* or "big affair" dishes.

At a Chinese banquet, the host starts by being an actor. No matter how dazzling a meal the host has planned for his company, ancient Chinese custom says the host must face his guests, clutch his heart (optional), sniffle (even more optional), and apologize for the "insignificant display of food about to be placed before such honorable company." Of course, this is just a custom. And that's obvious as soon as the North China's *Ping Pan* or "appetizer platter" arrives. On it will be honey-glazed spareribs, home-smoked whitefish, sliced beef seasoned with star anise, and Chinese chicken salad flavored with ginger and tossed in sesame oil.

In picking the *Chow* dishes, the host will follow Chinese custom and try to achieve a contrast of flavors, textures, and colors in the dishes. At the North China, three Chow dishes to try might be: Twice-Cooked Pork, Chung King Style, which are stir-fried with a black bean sauce and cloud ear mushrooms; the North China's Assorted Vegetables; and Kung Pao Shrimp robed with a rich, crimson sauce flavored with wine, ginger, and Chinese spices.

Intermission. Some Chinese hosts, depending on their background, may punctuate the middle of a Chiu Hsi with a *Teem* or "sweet" dessert-like dish to give the palate a flavor contrast. But we recommend you skip this course. Save your sweet tooth for the North China's Glazed Bananas at the end of the meal. The Glazed Bananas are too sweet for the middle of a Chiu Hsi, but too good to miss.

Now, it's time for the *Daah Tsai* or "big affair" dishes. Two of the North China's most popular "big affair" dishes are Sweet & Sour Fish and Smoked Tea Duck. The duck is a house specialty. To make this dish, a duck is left for twelve hours in a marinade that contains Jasmine tea leaves, and then smoked for two more hours over oak in a special oven designed by the North China's owner.

The third Daah Tsai dish served is soup. While not in the "big affair" class of the other two Daah Tsai dishes, tradition says that a soup is the last course of a Chinese banquet. Why? There are so many special dishes in a Chiu Hsi, the Chinese don't want to start the meal with something as filling as soup. So, a simple preparation like Egg Flower Soup is served last, as the Chinese say, just to "fill in the corners of the mouth."

At the end of the banquet, the host is presented with the check. If you're the host, there's an ancient saying of unknown origin that fits this moment perfectly. You should stand, face the rest of your party, smile, and then say," 還 頭﹐誰 也 呢 我 老 這 樣 來 ," which means: "A check is like a Chinese banquet—it is meant to be shared."

Note: The North China is also a good place to go when there's just two of you. All the dishes mentioned in this article are on the regular menu and can be ordered as part of a dinner for two.

The North China's Specialties

Ping Pan: □ The North China's Appetizer Platter. *Chow* or "Stir-Fried" Dishes: □ Twice-Cooked Pork, Chung King Style □ Kung Pao Shrimp □ Assorted Vegetables (six different Oriental vege- tables all stir-fried separately and then quickly cooked together. This technique preserves each vegetables's snap. The Chinese like to "hear" their vegetables . . . in other words, the faint sound of crunchy fresh- ness that's produced as they bite into them. The Chinese call it "Shung," or "the voice from the dish.") □ Ming's Beef (slices of beef stir-fried with mushrooms and broccoli.) □ Chow San Shen (a flavorful union of chicken, shrimp, and abalone in a light sauce. A Chinese chef's idea of peaceful coexistence.)

Daah Tsai or "Big Affair" Dishes: □ Smoked Tea Duck □ Sweet & Sour Fish (a whole rock cod that spent its afternoon swimming in an aerated tank in a Chinatown fish market. The cod is deep fried until golden brown and then topped with a classic, well-balanced sweet & sour sauce.)

Teem or "Sweet" Dish: □ Glazed Bananas (Step one: banana slices are battered and fried. Step two: the fruit is transferred to a pan of melted sugar and glazed. Step three: the bananas are rushed to the table and dunked in a bowl of ice water. Result—the coating crystallizes, leaving the bananas with a glass-like candy crust and a molten-hot interior. Step four: open your mouth.) **Prices:** Inexpensive to medium. **Decor:** One of the most attractive Chinese restaurants in the City . . . turquoise-blue chairs, hand-carved pinewood screens, a beautiful twenty-foot mural by artist Shih Kuiang, and a live tropical tree grow- ing in the middle of the dining room. **Basics:** 2315 Van Ness Ave. (near Vallejo), San Francisco. Tel: 673-8201. Hours: 11:30 am-2 pm, 4-10 pm Mon.-Sat. Closed Sun. Reservations suggested on weekends. Cards: MC, V. Wine and beer.

"What makes you think the food here is hot?"

Unlike some places, Mrs. English's excellent barbecue sauce won't start a fire in your mouth

In 1978, Carl English decided to open the Station No. 1 Barbecue. And Carl knew what it would take to make the place a success—his mother's barbecue sauce. So he asked her if she'd make the sauce for the restaurant. Mom said yes. Carl was in business.

Mrs. English's grandfather operated a legendary barbecue stand in Leavenworth, Kansas in the 1890s, and while she has apparently inherited this gentleman's skill, she didn't need his recipe for barbecue sauce. She came up with a better one. And it's a closely-guarded recipe. It takes Mrs. English four hours to prepare the sauce and she won't let anyone come around her while it's being made. That's not all. Mrs. English won't even tell *her own son Carl* how to make the sauce. We didn't believe it either, until we asked Carl about this bit of information. He said just one word, "True."

The actual cooking of the beef ribs and spareribs is Carl's department. Each batch of ribs spends three hours in a huge, wood-burning brick oven that Carl had custom-designed for the restaurant. And the flavor of the ribs tells you that they benefit from every minute in Carl's oven.

The food at Carl's reminds us of this very good barbecue we discovered in an old section of Los Angeles. But we've never recommended it to anyone. The place has a serious flaw. They attract the meanest, toughest clientele we've ever seen in a restaurant. In fact, when you arrive the doorman frisks you to see if you have a gun. If you don't—he gives you one.

Menu Specialties: ☐ Barbecued Spareribs ☐ Barbecued Beef Ribs. **Prices:** Inexpensive. **Decor:** A small, friendly-looking place with red cloth napkins on the tables and 1890 photos of firemen on the walls. **Basics:** 501 Clement St. (at 6th Ave.), San Francisco. Tel: 386-5882. Hours: 11 am-10 pm Mon.-Thurs.; 11 am-midnight Fri., Sat.; 2-9 pm Sun. No cards. Wine and beer.

Gold Spike: San Francisco
Crab Cioppino Feeds/5 courses, bargain prices

Wear something stainable. Roll up those sleeves. If you must, find a baby and steal his bib. On Friday nights during crab season, the Gold Spike throws cioppino feeds. Primitive instincts surface. Crab cioppino must be eaten with the hands. You get a large plate of fresh crab legs and body meat in shell, drenched in a spicy sauce of tomatoes, white wine, onions, and Italian herbs. Everyone reacts the same. With hands hovering over the plate, you mumble an oath to finish everything, and . . . dig in.

The Gold Spike has been throwing cioppino feeds since 1920. Originally, the owners called the restaurant the "Columbus Candy Store." Candy? Remember, it was Prohibition. In the front, the store offered jawbreakers and licorice sticks—in the back, crab cioppino and bathtub gin. And even back then, the Gold Spike was known for the same thing it's known for today—the size of its meals. For $6.75, you get a 5-course cioppino dinner that includes a tureen of minestrone, a large, tomato-topped salad, a side dish of marinated red beans and salami, a platter of homemade ravioli and rigatoni, fresh Swiss chard, spumoni ice cream, Italian cookies, and coffee. Whew! Meals of this size are hard to come by, unless, of course, you have an Italian grandmother stashed away somewhere.

Menu Specialty: ☐ Crab Cioppino (made with fresh Pacific Dungeness crab. Served during the crab season: Nov. 15—May 15. Friday nights only.) The cioppino dinner includes the 5 courses described above. **Prices:** Inexpensive. **Decor:** A small trattoria with a time-mellowed look and walls that seem to be a vertical curio shop. Every inch of wall space is covered with a maze of items—including duck decoys, bamboo ski poles, and life preservers. **Basics:** 527 Columbus Ave. (near Green), San Francisco. Tel: 986-9747. Hours: 5-9:45 pm Mon., Tues., Thurs.-Sun. Closed Wed. No cards. Full bar. Public parking (60¢ per hour) available at the Vallejo St. Garage, 766 Vallejo St. (near Powell).

Tuba Garden: San Francisco
Continental/A fine old house with outdoor dining in back

This is a small, personal restaurant with good food, moderate prices, a charming setting, and friendly service. Like they said back in the days of vaudeville, that's a tough act to beat.

The restaurant is located in a two-story house of 1929 vintage. Inside, you'll find a small, nine-table dining room with brass Parisian chandeliers and hardwood floors covered with antique throw rugs from Afghanistan. There's even a view. The room looks out on a plant-filled patio that's used for dining on warm nights. And watching over these dining areas is owner-host Anthony La Cavera. The way he looks after customers, you can tell that this is a man who honestly enjoys what he's doing. Mr. La Cavera has such a bright smile, he could give you a sunburn.

The kitchen is also in good hands. Co-owner Gerd Wenske used to cook for the Duke of Liechtenstein. In fact, you may have seen Wenske's former employer—the Duke's picture is on a postage stamp.

At the Tuba Garden, chef Wenske features a rotating menu that offers four different main courses each week. Filet of sole stuffed with shrimp, a classic butter-stuffed chicken Kiev, and beef bourguignon have all been on the menu. Dinner includes an appetizer, maybe ham roulade or marinated mushrooms, and a salad or soup, maybe chef Wenske's consomme Siciliano dotted with bits of tomato and little meatballs.

But it's not just the food that's pleasing. Most of the restaurant's 3-course dinners are in the moderate $6.50 to $7.50 range. And, in our opinion, dinner is usually more relaxing in a moderately priced restaurant. At an expensive restaurant, it always makes us feel uncomfortable when someone looks at the check and then falls down and starts pounding the floor like it was a Congo drum.

The Menu: Chef Wenske changes his menu each week. There are always at least four main courses to choose from—with a good balance between land and sea. Dishes frequently featured: Fresh sea bass with Mornay sauce; stuffed chicken breast with a brandy-laced cherry sauce; Hungarian beef goulash with homemade spatzle dumplings; shrimp, scallops, and crab in a lobster bisque sauce; chicken saute Chasseur in a sauce of mushrooms, tomatoes, white wine, and herbs; and baked lasagna a la Cassa made with five Italian cheeses.

Dinner includes . . . 3 courses: Appetizer (maybe curried shrimp or cherry tomatoes stuffed with crab), soup or salad, and main course with three fresh vegetables. **Prices:** Medium. **Basics:** 3634 Sacramento St. (near Locust), San Francisco. Tel: 921-8822. Hours: 11 am-3 pm Mon.-Sat. and 5-9 pm Thurs.-Sat.; Sun. brunch 11 am-3 pm. Closed Sun.-Wed. evening. Reservations suggested; necessary for brunch. Cards: MC, V. Wine and beer.

Sun Wah Kue: San Francisco
Prime Rib/Price? It's like stealing legally

Scientists might be interested to know that this small Chinese restaurant performs a feat even more amazing than acupuncture: somehow, for $3.60, Sun Wah Kue manages to serve you a 4-course dinner including—drum roll, please—*a thick, juicy slice of prime rib*.

Although Sun Wah Kue is located in the middle of Chinatown, the menu is strictly American. This may seem peculiar unless you remember your history. After gold was discovered in California, thousands of San Franciscans marched out of town behind the Pied Piper of Greed, thinking there was no longer a stop sign at the entrance to Easy Street. Caucasian restaurant proprietors, along with everyone else, joined in the mad dash for gold. When they left, their Chinese employees took over the abandoned cafes and, to keep customers happy, continued cooking American dishes.

Sun Wah Kue dates back to this period. And the place looks it. White-haired Chinese bachelors sit around old wooden tables in a room where the walls have turned alfalfa-yellow with time; the cashier stands behind the kind of iron cage you used to see in old banks; and the dining room is ringed with veiled dining compartments. Your imagination plays tricks. You almost feel that behind one of those curtains there's a black-clad Chinese slave trader slowly smoking an opium pipe—while his eyes spin like the cherry wheels on a slot machine.

Menu Specialty: ☐ Prime Rib of Beef, $3.60. And the prime rib dinner includes 4 courses: Pearl barley soup, salad, main course with real mashed potatoes, buttered green beans, house-baked rolls, coffee, and a piece of flaky, homemade apple pie with a fresh, all-American flavor. Now, that's a deal. Note: Sun Wah Kue tends to run out of prime rib early—so try to get there before 5:30 pm; or go for lunch. **Basics:** 848 Washington St. (near Grant), Chinatown, San Francisco. Tel: 982-3519. Hours: 7 am-8 pm Mon., Wed.-Sun. Closed Tues. No cards. Public parking (35¢ per hour) available at the Portsmouth Square Garage, Kearny St. (betw. Clay and Washington).

Salmagundi
What This Country Needs
San Francisco Soup Shops/Take water, add creativity

Most restaurants have been plagued by skyrocketing costs, but that's one problem the creators of Salmagundi and What This Country Needs probably won't have to worry about. The owners of these two restaurants decided to specialize in soup. This was a wise business decision. The major ingredient in soup is water, an item, even in these hard times, that tends to remain reasonably priced.

Once these restaurants fill a pot with a couple of gallons of water, they don't leave the H_2O alone until it has assumed a new personality. At Salmagundi this could mean San Joaquin Valley vegetable soup, shepherd's Scotch broth, or U.S. Senate ham hock and bean; at What This Country Needs, the H_2O might be changed into anything from Creole gumbo to Zoo Tosphy—a spicy South African lamb soup.

These places may be soup kitchens, but they certainly don't look like 1935 Depression cafeterias. At What This Country Needs, there's an interesting Art-Camp decor with female-mannequin legs used as table legs; at Salmagundi, the decor is a sophisticated blend of red lamps, bright blue chairs, and white tables—just the right setting to enjoy a steaming hot bowl of homemade soup. And we do enjoy. Once, we made so much noise as we sipped away on our soup, six couples got up and started to dance.

Salmagundi: □ Three different soups are featured each day from a list of 40 soups—a list that includes Barbary Coast seafood bouillabaisse, Barcelona black bean, Italian sausage soup, Grant Ave. Chinese chicken soup, Ukrainian beef borsch, and Proper Bostonian clam chowder. You get a large bowl—sort of a tureen for one. And you can have *seconds of another soup* if you want. Soup + egg twist or sour-dough rolls, $1.95. □ Large, fresh tossed salad, 65¢ extra. □ Homemade fruit spice cake, 85¢.

Basics: 442 Geary St. (near Mason, across from the Curran Theatre), San Francisco. Tel: 441-0894. Hours: 11 am-midnight daily. No cards. Wine and beer. Public parking (65¢ per hour) available at the Union Square Garage, Geary St. (betw. Powell and Stockton).

What This Country Needs: □ Three different soups are offered each day from a list of 35—including a vegetable-packed Marco Polo chicken soup, Russian soldier's soup, a rich cream of mushroom, a hearty peasant Bigos soup laced with Polish sausage, and Royal St. soup (a spicy New Orleans blend of ham, bacon, clams, okra, lima beans, and green peppers in a tomato stock.) The soups are served in big earthenware bowls. Soup + a hunk of crusty baguette French bread, $1.55. □ Large, fresh tossed salad, 70¢ extra. □ Soup + "half" a sandwich (salami, roasted peppers, and provolone; or ham, cheddar cheese, and guacamole), $2.40. □ Homemade, 24-carat-rich fudge pie, 95¢.

Basics: Located in the Hyatt Hotel on Union Square (betw. Post and Sutter), San Francisco. Tel: 397-9129. Hours: 7 am-8:30 pm Mon.-Sat. Closed Sun. No cards. Wine and beer. Public parking (65¢ per hour) available at the Union Square Garage, Geary St. (betw. Powell and Stockton).

Caravansary: San Francisco
Middle Eastern/Interesting setting, moderate prices

Like a bank, the Caravansary can boast of having a lot of "assets." To begin with, the restaurant is in an interesting setting: the dining room is located in the back of a food specialty shop. After a little stroll through a land of imported cheeses, exotic coffees, and gourmet cookware, you come to a small oasis of a dining room—an area with a Mediterranean decor, candlelit tables, and a quiet charm. Another of the restaurant's assets is the fact that you can pick up a bottle of wine in the specialty shop and have it with your dinner . . . at liquor store prices plus a nominal $1.50 corkage fee.

The Caravansary also respects your wallet in another way. Their 3-course dinners, which include a fine four-item Meza appetizer course, are all moderately priced. This is one place where you won't have to worry about getting a check with a total that looks like your Social Security number.

Is that it? No. The restaurant's best asset is its food. The Caravansary's chef, Setrak Injaian, is following in his father's footsteps, and his father was once chef to King Abdullah of Jordan. And the talent genes have passed from father to son. At least it tastes that way when we have the Caravansary's mushroom-stuffed lamb Mantar in a light, herb-seasoned pomegranate sauce, or chef Setrak's chicken Geras—a boneless breast stuffed with wild rice and pine nuts and baked in a dark, rum-laced cherry sauce that glows like liquid jewels.

Chef Setrak's orange-scented cheesecake with an almond-paved bottom crust is also very good. Setrak somehow achieves that perfect balance of sweetness, lightness, and rich cheese flavor. Of course, the people of the Middle East have always had a "special talent" with desserts. For example, one of the world's most unique desserts is a Middle Eastern creation. According to the book, *Aphrodisiac Cookery*, in the 1700s Arabian sheiks had the nude bodies of harem girls painted with honey. The girls were then told to run through fields of pollen-laden hashish plants. When they returned, the sheiks would lick the hashish-speckled honey-glaze off the girl's nude bodies for dessert. Well, there's no doubt about one thing. It sure beats a Hershey bar.

Menu Specialties: □ Chicken Geras (chef Setrak rotates the Geras nightly with two other dishes—chicken Tabaka and Chicken Tsi-Tsi Belli. But whatever dish is available, it will have the special Setrak touch.) □ Lamb Mantar (a tender, two-inch-thick cut of lamb is marinated for 24 hours so it becomes even more tender. Then, it's stuffed with fresh mushrooms and slowly broiled for 20 minutes until a fine charred crust forms. Topped with a light pomegranate sauce, and garnished with giant whole mushrooms.) □ Shish Kebab (huge, perfectly trimmed chunks of lamb carefully broiled over lava rocks. But before the lamb reaches the fire, it's marinated for 12 hours. With this dish, you're buying time, and the resulting flavor of the lamb tells you that your money's well spent.)

Dinner includes . . . 3 courses: Meza (a very generous array of four Middle Eastern appetizers. We can describe them all in one word—good.), Armenian lavash cracker bread, a large romaine salad tossed in a tasty, dill-flavored dressing and topped with crumbled feta cheese, and main course with an authentic rice pilaf. Dessert: Cheesecake, chef Setrak-style. **Prices:** Medium. **Basics:** 2263 Chestnut St. (near Pierce), San Francisco. Tel: 921-3466. Hours: 11 am-3 pm, 5-10 pm Mon.-Sat.; 11 am-3 pm Sun. for brunch. Closed Sun. evening. Reservations suggested on weekends. Cards: AE, MC, V. Wine and beer.

Guido's: San Francisco
Italian/Small, romantic North Beach trattoria

North Beach used to be the site of one of the largest Italian colonies in the country. And author Riera is very familiar with the area—his father, Rosario Riera, was born and raised there. Any Saturday night in 1937, you could find Rosario hanging around some Columbus Avenue street corner, dressed in a chalk-striped, petroleum-blue zoot suit, with so much garlic on his breath, he could drive away vampires.

Over the years, the fact that San Francisco has an Italian colony has created a belief that it's easy to find good Italian food in the City. At one time, that may have been true, but this is no longer the case. Today, good Italian food is getting hard to find. Maybe that's why Guido's was an instant success. Unlike the old days, there's not a lot of competition around.

Guido's radiates the feeling of a romantic New York trattoria. The dining room is filled with candlelight, baskets of fresh fruit, white carnations, and pink linen tablecloths. And the room holds only twelve tables. Guido Piccinini has purposely limited his seating capacity, and also purposely limited his menu to eight carefully-made specialties—for one reason: so he can exercise total control. Guido wants to be a "ping-pong" owner. Ping! He's in the kitchen guiding the preparation of your dinner. Pong! He's at your table pouring wine.

Menu Specialties: ☐ Veal Scallopine (Guido personally selects his own veal daily, cuts it into scallops, and then has his chef saute it in butter with mushrooms, shallots, and slices of fresh eggplant.) ☐ Cannelloni della Casa (homemade pasta generously stuffed with minced veal, spinach, and three cheeses—ricotta, Monterey Jack, and parmesan. Topped with a fresh, gently-herbed Neapolitan tomato sauce.) ☐ Chicken Toscana (flavored with garlic and fresh rosemary, and roasted in butter with shallots, mushrooms, and marinated artichoke hearts.) □ Gamberi Dijonnaise (sauteed prawns topped with a cream-rich, white wine mustard sauce.)

Dinner includes . . . 4 courses: A butter lettuce salad sprinkled with sliced mushrooms, hot French bread with a baked-in parmesan cheese crust, a basket of golden brown French fried zucchini dusted with hand-grated cheese, main course with fresh vegetable and broiled tomato, coffee, and for dessert, a basket of fresh fruit and nuts that looks like it was arranged by a still-life artist.

Starters: Fettucine al Pesto (the pasta is made especially for Guido. Topped with a fresh green basil sauce.) **Prices:** Medium to a step above medium. **Basics:** 347 Columbus Ave. (near Broadway), San Francisco. Tel: 982-2157. Hours: 5:30-10:30 pm Tues.-Sat. Closed Sun., Mon. Reservations necessary. Cards: MC, V. Wine and beer. Public parking (60¢ per hour) available at the Vallejo St. Garage, 766 Vallejo St. (near Powell).

After Dinner: Have a drink at the Tosca Cafe—two blocks from Guido's. The Tosca is a San Francisco institution. It's an old, well preserved bar that has somehow made time stand still. Inside the Tosca, it's always 1935. There's a juke box stocked with opera records, mahogany walls dark with age, two huge gleaming expresso machines, and a long bar worn smooth by Italian elbows. The Tosca is famous for their version of cappuccino. To make the drink, the bartender puts a spoonful of custom-blended cocoa in a glass, adds some cream, then steams the mixture on the expresso machine, and finally tops it with a shot of brandy . . . Bosco revisited ($1.25). Also within reach on the Tosca's bar—baskets of cialde, thin rolled Italian cookies flavored with anise liqueur. Tosca Cafe: 242 Columbus Ave. (near Broadway), San Francisco. Tel: 986-9651. Hours: 9:30 pm-2 am Mon.-Sat. Closed Sun.

Sears: San Francisco
Breakfasts so good, you'll look forward to waking up

Breakfast. Many restaurants make it. But few make it well. And none make it better than Sears. In our opinion, Sears serves the best breakfast in San Francisco. Now, let us show you why.

The Fruit: Begin your breakfast with Sears seven-item Fresh Fruit Bowl, $1.10. Sears fruits are exceptionally choice. And not by accident. Owner Al Boyajian personally goes to the produce market at 4 a.m. daily and squeezes, fondles, and thumps until he's found the thoroughbreds of the harvest. The fruit bowl contains seven types of fruit marinated in freshly-squeezed orange juice: bananas, Florida grapefruit, freestone peaches, watermelon, honeydew melon, and more—depending on the season, but not just our seasons. Al buys strawberries from New Zealand, cantaloupes from Puerto Rico, and papayas from the Philippines.

A Matter of Batter: Swedish Pancakes (only air is lighter than these 18 little pancakes. The secret is a batter made with three flours. The mix is so popular, Sears sells packages of it at the restaurant and by mail order. President Eisenhower used to send orders in regularly.), $1.45. Pecan Waffle (golden brown, crisp, and totally greaseless, with finely chopped pecans mixed into the batter), $1.95. Sourdough French Toast (sourdough bread dipped in a blend of fresh eggs and cream and then carefully grilled. Served with Sears homemade strawberry preserves.), $1.85.

The Eggs: Beautiful, farm fresh, AAA specimens—each one almost the size of the Goodyear blimp. And they're cooked in the purest, sweetest, 93-score butter. Served with your choice of Hickory Smoked Ham, $2.95; Canadian Bacon, $3.15; or Smoked Country Sausage made especially for Sears, $2.95. Or have a 3-egg omelet . . . our favorite is the Spanish Omelet (the Spanish sauce is made with fresh tomatoes), $2.95. Plates include real hash browns and toast.

The Light Breakfast: Baked Apple (loaded with flavor . . . the balance between sweetness and tartness is perfect. Only large, premium Rome apples are used.), $1.10. Swedish Coffee Cake, or Banana Nut Bread (both have a light texture and a buttery just-baked flavor), 85¢.

Temptation at 10 A.M.: Besides great breakfasts Sears also makes the best pies in San Francisco. And if we're at Sears around 10 when the pies start leaving the oven . . . temptation starts whispering, "Order pie. Order pie." So we whisper back, "Okay, okay," and have pie for breakfast. House specialties: Fresh strawberry cream pie; a pecan pie that gives new meaning to the word "rich"; a three-inch-thick banana cream pie; old-fashioned deep dish blueberry or apricot pie; a lemon meringue pie that looks like it just won the first prize at the Iowa State Fair; and sometimes, there's even papaya and pineapple cream pie. All pies are 85¢ to 95¢ a slice.

Decor: A large, sunny dining room with table and counter seating. It's a restaurant that almost smiles "good morning" . . . maybe it's the yellow lace tablecloths or the exceptionally friendly waitresses. Or maybe it's the little things. Like Sears Cadillac waiting room. On chilly Sundays when the waiting line sometimes gets long, the owners park their Cadillacs in front, with heaters and radios on, and let customers wait in them. **Basics:** 439 Powell St. (near Post, half a block from Union Square), San Francisco. Tel: 986-1160. Hours: 7 am-3 pm daily. No cards. Public parking (65¢ per hour) available at the Union Square Garage, Geary St. (betw. Powell and Stockton).

Bangkok Cafe
Siamese House
Two San Francisco places offering the food of a colorful land

The U.S. Army gave author Riera the opportunity to try the cooking of Thailand. And meet Can-Do Samm . . .

In 1968, the U.S. Army decided to give me a firsthand look at Vietnamese food, and later that same year, they also supplied me with the chance to have a few dinners in Thailand. Once a GI had completed about six months of his tour of duty in Vietnam, he was entitled to five days of R & R—rest and recuperation—in any one of ten countries. I chose Bangkok, Thailand.

The first person I met in Bangkok was a driver—a man who made his living by carting around GI's while they were on R & R. I was standing in the lobby of the Olympic Hotel when up walked this driver. First he said, "Hello, GI." Then he grabbed my hand, and began shaking it like he was a U.S. Senator up for reelection. "I'm Can-Do Samm," he continued, "for you, I get good time, good food, good girls." Sold.

The first place we visited was a Siamese bathhouse. It was sort of the Baskin-Robbins of sex: 31 choices. And like Mr. Can-Do, all the girls talked in terms of "a good time." Also, under Mr. Can-Do's direction, I rode an elephant, saw a Buddhist statue that was 5½ tons of solid gold, and ate a lot of "good food." Which brings me to San Francisco's Bangkok Cafe and Siamese House. Their dinners are just like the ones I was served in Thailand. Except they're only half as big. In Bangkok, Can-Do Samm ordered for me in Thai. And he always ordered twice as much as I could eat. Then, halfway through the meal, he'd say, "You no can finish, I can do."

Bangkok Cafe Specialties: □Chicken Kai Pad Phed (sliced boneless chicken spiced with sweet basil leaves that the owner's mother sends from Thailand.) □ Beef Saté (eight bamboo skewers of thinly sliced beef are broiled over charcoal, and then topped with a fresh peanut sauce that's rich, spicy, and excellent.) □ Chicken Ka-Ree Kai (chicken in a flavorful curry sauce based on imported Thai curry powder and coconut milk.)

Dinner includes: Chicken ginger soup, rice, and fresh broccoli, sauteed Thai-style. Dessert: Mango ice cream. Also try their O-Leang, sweet iced coffee made with imported Thai coffee. **Prices:** Inexpensive. **Decor:** A small, modest-looking cafe where the owner's daughter serves you, and the walls are decorated with Air Siam posters. **Basics:** 208 Clement St. (near 3rd Ave.), San Francisco. Tel: 386-9669. Hours: 11 am-9:30 pm Mon.-Sat. Closed Sun. No cards. Wine and beer.

Siamese House Specialties: □ Chicken Kai Tod (on the outside there's a tasty dark brown crust, and inside there's moist chicken spiced with imported Thai herbs.) □ Beef Nor Tod (thin sauteed sirloin strips flavored with garlic and mystery.) □ Prawns Kung Yang (the prawns spend the day marinating in a lagoon of Thai sauce. Then, they're rubbed with butter, broiled, and topped with sauteed mushrooms and green peppers.)

Dinner includes: Soup, fresh vegetable, rice, tea, and a "very scenic" main course: your plate will be garnished with at least eight kinds of fresh fruit—banana, melon, pineapple, pomegranate—well, you're surrounded by so much fruit, you feel like a plantation owner. **Prices:** Inexpensive. **Decor:** Walk through the door and into Thailand. There's a low bamboo ceiling, floor-style seating at handmade Thai tables, and brass art objects imported from Bangkok. **Basics:** 2448 Clement St. (near 26th Ave.), San Francisco. Tel: 752-4090. Hours: 5:30-9:30 pm Tues.-Sun. Closed Mon. Reservations suggested on weekends. No cards. Wine and beer.

Kichihei: San Francisco
Japanese/Traditional 4-course dinners, modest prices

There are very few culinary daredevils among San Francisco's Japanese chefs. Rather than take any chances, they've kept their menus safely centered around the standard Big Three—tempura, teriyaki, and sukiyaki. And we can't say that Kichihei is any different. But . . . one thing separates Mr. Kichihei Ohara from his competitors: Care. At Kichihei, the deep-fried tempura prawns are as greaseless as they should be, the teriyaki sauce has all the rich flavor it's supposed to have, and the vegetables in the sukiyaki are as fresh as nature meant them to be. And the prices are as enjoyable as the food. Kichihei's 4-course dinners are all around $6.25.

Kichihei Ohara is a chef with nothing to hide. At his restaurant, he has an open kitchen with a custom-made viewing counter. It's located down a hallway from the dining room. After you've finished your meal in the small, artistically-decorated dining room, you can retire to ringside, sip a glass of plum wine, and watch Kichihei at work. As you sit there on stools made from bamboo soy sauce barrels, you may notice a lot of salmon on Kichihei's teppan grill. It's Kichihei's specialty, and it's very popular—especially with his Japanese customers. Which is understandable. According to statistics, the Japanese are the world's biggest fish eaters. And we can verify that. We have a Japanese friend who is living proof of that fact. Our friend eats so much seafood, his lips move in and out with the tide.

Menu Specialties: □ Tempura (butterflied prawns, whole mushrooms and vegetables dipped in a special batter and deep-fried. The oil's temperature and the chef's timing must be perfect to achieve the desired result—tempura with a light, thin crust. And at Kichihei, each piece comes out with a crust as light and thin as a bride's nightgown.) □ Sukiyaki (you're served a small black iron pan covered with a hand-carved wooden top. The top's removed . . . and enough steam puffs out to fog eyeglasses four tables away. When the mist clears, you find a carefully arranged selection of thin beef strips, fresh mushrooms, green cellophane noodles, bean cake, green onions, and napa cabbage in a tasty soy broth.) □ Chicken Teriyaki (a boneless chicken breast coated with an ebony glaze that could serve as a classroom example of what teriyaki sauce should be.) □ Salmon Shioyaki (salmon broiled in a special salt coat that keeps the fish moist yet gives it a beautiful crust.)

Dinner includes . . . 4 courses: First, you're given hot *shibori* hand towels. "Most" people think this is a nice custom; "some" think it's a practical idea; and a "few" think it's something to eat. Then, you're served an ice-cold bean sprout and shrimp salad topped with a rice vinegar dressing, a beautiful sunomono soup, main course with fresh, soy-flavored spinach sprinkled with sesame seeds, rice, green tea, and for dessert, Mandarin oranges. **Prices:** Inexpensive. **Basics:** 2084 Chestnut St. (at Steiner), San Francisco. Tel: 929-1670. Hours: 5-10 pm Mon., Tues., Thurs.-Sat.; 4:30-9:30 pm Sun. Closed Wed. Reservations suggested on weekends. All major cards. Wine and beer.

A Final Note on the Kichihei Restaurant: The fugu fish is a very popular Japanese delicacy, but because of certain laws it can't be served in the United States. Too bad. Chef Kichihei Ohara has an official fugu license. Why the license? Certain small, hard-to-identify glands of the fugu carry toxins that can cause unconsciousness. To make the fugu edible these glands must be removed. And only specially trained, government-licensed chefs are allowed to do this. It's an important job. Fugu toxin is powerful stuff. In *From Russia with Love,* someone slipped James Bond some fugu toxin, and according to the book, "Bond pivoted slowly . . . and crashed headlong to the floor." Yes, if a fugu chef in Japan isn't extremely careful, he may find his customers getting dizzy and passing out. Of course, in America, some restaurants can achieve the same effect just by showing you the bill.

Sam Wo: San Francisco
Chinese/The main attraction, a waiter named Edsel Ford Fong

A first-timer at Sam Wo might wonder why this ancient three-story brick building is constantly jammed with people waiting to eat. The dining areas on the second and third floors are just two small, plain rooms with banana-colored wallpaper and police-station lighting. You sit on 1930-era wooden stools and if there's an empty place at your table within minutes you'll have a new dinner companion. And to reach these upstairs rooms, you must pass through a tiny street-level kitchen which is always overflowing with five Chinese cooks hard at work with their cleavers.

The mysterious appeal of Sam Wo is on the second floor—the lair of Edsel Ford Fong, a Chinese warlord turned waiter. His theme is rudeness and the people love it. Being yelled at by this one-man spectacle is considered an honor in some circles.

Here's what we mean. While we were sitting there one night, a raven-haired beauty bathed in perfume passed by Edsel. As she floated by, Edsel roared, "You smell up place!" She tried to answer, but he cut her off with, "I no can talk now—too busy." Then Edsel spotted a man in a three-piece suit standing by the doorway. "Hey you, take teapot upstairs. Refill cups. Do now! Customers like plenty hot tea." With the proud look of one who has been singled out, the man did as he was told.

Along with the floor show, Edsel manages to serve food, shout orders down a dumbwaiter in machine-gun Chinese, and carry on conversations with five different tables at once. Edsel has been called "The Greatest Show on Earth"—and he doesn't even charge for the performance.

Menu Specialties: Sam Wo is sort of a Chinese version of an Italian pasta house. And the noodles that are used in Sam Wo's dishes are all made on the premises—or as Edsel boasts, "Tonight, you lucky. You got numbah one waiter who got numbah one noodles." □ Chow Fun Fried Rice Noodles with Shrimp (wide, flat noodles toss-cooked with shrimp, fresh bean sprouts, and Chinese seasonings.) □ Tomato Beef Chow Mein (thin noodles stir-fried with beef strips, fresh onions, tomatoes, and sweet and sour sauce.) □ Roast Pork Rice Noodle Roll (a steamed roll with a pork stuffing.) **Prices:** Inexpensive. **Basics:** 813

Washington St. (near Grant), Chinatown, San Francisco. Tel: 982-0596. Hours: 11 am-3 am Mon.-Sat. Closed Sun. No cards. Public parking (35¢ per hour) available at the Portsmouth Square Garage, Kearny St. (betw. Clay and Washington).

Iron Pot: San Francisco
Italian/5-course meals, 1934 decor, yesterday's prices

The Iron Pot caters to people who like 5-course dinners. And that includes us. In fact, we're such big eaters, the government is thinking about putting our picture on Food Stamps.

But it's not just the size of the Iron Pot's dinners that attracts us. We also like this restaurant's prices. At the Iron Pot, $5.50 buys you a big tureen of minestrone soup, tossed green salad with a plate of salami and mortadella, house-stuffed ravioli, choice of a lemony veal Dore, or a wine and mushroom-flavored chicken saute Luciano, roasted potatoes with onions, mixed vegetables, coffee, and dessert. There's only one thing to call a dinner like this—a good deal. And for $6.25, you have your choice of an eight ounce "Baby" steak, or veal saltimbocca layered with ham and Monterey Jack cheese.

The Iron Pot has been around since 1934. And looks it. The place has the kind of atmosphere only age can produce. There's chianti bottles hanging from the ceiling, ancient wooden booths, dim lights, and a huge collection of paintings in every conceivable style, size, and shape. Why so many paintings? Tradition. In the Thirties, the Iron Pot was a Bohemian hangout. If an artist was broke and hungry, the management would accept one of his paintings as payment for a meal. Before long, the restaurant turned into an informal art gallery, and although the painting payment plan is no longer in effect, the management still follows the tradition of keeping its walls open to local artists.

There's no telling who you'll see at the Iron Pot. We've sat across from bankers and longshoremen. Everybody likes a good deal. Once, we even sat across from *Chronicle* columnist Herb Caen. And on our last visit, a stout, gray-haired gentleman across from us was having dinner with the kind of woman you just can't help but notice. She had big blue eyes, long, platinum blonde hair, a Las Vegas body, and a voice that sounded like Rice Krispies if they could talk.

Menu Specialties: ☐ Veal Dore (thin slices of veal dipped in an egg batter and sauteed in butter with white wine and a squeeze of fresh lemon juice.) ☐ Chicken Saute Luciano (a half chicken sauteed with fresh mushrooms, chablis, and Italian herbs.) ☐ Baby Steak Iron Pot (an eight ounce New York strip steak, owner-aged and then carefully grilled.) ☐ Veal Saltimbocca (veal slices layered with ham and Monterey Jack cheese, battered, and then sauteed in wine.)
Dinner includes . . . 5 courses: A tureen of minestrone soup, a

102

salad partnered with side dishes of salami and mortadella, house-stuffed ravioli, main course with mixed Italian vegetables and potatoes roasted with onions, coffee, and ice cream. **Prices:** Inexpensive. **Basics:** 639 Montgomery St. (near Washington), San Francisco. Tel: 392-2100. Hours: 11 am-2 pm, 4:30-10 pm Mon.-Fri.; 5-10 pm Sat. Closed Sun. Cards: V. Full bar. Public parking (35¢ per hour) available at the Portsmouth Square Garage, Kearny St. (betw. Clay and Washington).

Yenching: San Francisco
Chinese/Behind the kitchen door, co-stars Cho and Lu

In the past, it wasn't just the food that attracted people to San Francisco's Chinese restaurants. As late as 1927, customers were allowed to smoke opium in the dining rooms of Chinatown restaurants. Back then, it was easy to spot people who had gone to Chinatown for dinner. They were the ones driving their cars around San Francisco backwards.

But today, people go to Chinese restaurants for only one reason—the food. And that's what attracts them to the Yenching.

Although the Yenching has been doing business in Chinatown for many years, in 1978, a couple of changes were made. First, they remodeled. The decor is now bright and modern. And what's more important they hired Mr. Cho and Mr. Lu to head their kitchen staff.

These men make a great team. Chef Cho prepares the Szechwan dishes and chef Lu specializes in Peking-style cooking, and together they can do just about anything. There are 3,000 taste buds on the surface of the tongue and between Cho and Lu, they know how to entertain all of them. In fact, this duo usually has the audience yelling for more.

The Yenching certainly shines in comparison with some places. One Chinese restaurant in particular comes to mind. They were bad. But honorable. When we opened our fortune cookies there was a couple of Alka-Seltzer tablets inside.

Menu Specialties: □ Mongolian Beef (strips of tender beef and green onions coated with a deeply flavored, mahogany-colored sauce.) □ Mo Shu Pork (you're served a steaming-hot mixture of minced pork, eggs, and Chinese vegetables, a side dish of paper-thin Chinese pancakes, and plum sauce. You take a pancake, dab it with some plum sauce, then spoon on some of the mixture, roll, and eat. There you have it. A Chinese burrito.) □ Ta-Chien Chicken (tender pieces of chicken toss-cooked with green peppers and Chinese spices.)

□ Princess Prawns (golden-battered prawns framed against a unique sweet & sour-style sauce.) □ Sliced Scallops with Garlic Sauce (ivory-colored coins of scallop in a reddish-brown sauce.) □ Hunan Smoked Pork (home-smoked pork stir-fried with bok choy cabbage, scallions, and ginger.) **Prices:** Inexpensive to medium. **Basics:** 939 Kearny St (at Columbus), Chinatown, San Francisco. Tel: 397-3543. Hours: 11:30 am-10 pm Mon.-Sat. Closed Sun. Cards: MC, V. Full bar. Public parking (35¢ per hour) available at the Portsmouth Square Garage, Kearny St. (betw. Clay and Washington).

Atlantis: San Francisco
Seafood/High "net" worth at easy-to-take prices

In the Fifties, my (author Riera's) father owned a small seafood restaurant on San Francisco's Fisherman's Wharf. It was there that I learned how seafood should be cooked. I was helping around the kitchen one Saturday when I spotted a pan of fresh crabs, clams, and oysters sitting on the counter. I asked my father how he was going to cook them. In a voice that was loud enough to be heard by his cousin Vito in Sicily, he replied, "The right way."

I never forgot that. And it's the reason why I like Atlantis—they, too, believe in cooking seafood "The right way." At Atlantis, the petrale sole is pan-fried with stopwatch timing; the prawns and oysters are encased in a bronze-colored breading that's crisp and totally grease-less; and the five kinds of seafood in their fish stew are served in a buttery fish-stock broth that's been simmered for a full 8 hours. Another specialty is their baked seafood cannelloni—thin, delicate crepes stuffed with crab, shrimp, scallops, and ricotta cheese, then topped with Monterey Jack cheese, a little fresh tomato sauce, and a silky Mornay sauce. One taste and it's obvious that the man in the kitchen knows how to make seafood cannelloni "The right way."

Atlantis has a light, airy dining room with white tablecloths, ocean-blue place mats, and a rainbow of fresh flowers on each table. It's a friendly-looking, likeable restaurant. With likeable prices. Most seafood dinners, which include shrimp bisque soup and thick, hand-cut French fries, are in the $5 to $7 range. At Atlantis, the thought of getting the check won't make your pulse start throbbing like an Apache war drum.

We have a suggestion: after a seafood dinner at Atlantis, have a drink by the sea. Since Atlantis is located just a short drive from the beach, we suggest that you take a ride along the Pacific's edge and stop by the Cliff House for a drink. This legendary establishment was re-modeled a few years ago and now features a comfortable, antique-filled bar with a fine old fireplace. The setting is still one of the best San Francisco has to offer. Why visit the beach? Scientists tell us that the evolution of man began in the oceans. Occasionally, it's nice to go back and see the old neighborhood.

Menu Specialties: ☐ Seafood Cannelloni ☐ Petrale Sole (a fresh, boned filet coated with a light egg batter and pan-fried. Topped with a golden yellow sauce made with butter and white wine.) ☐ Combination Seafood Platter (deep-fried oysters, prawns, scallops, and whitefish jacketed with a fresh bread crumb crust. Served with a homemade tartar sauce and a tasty red cocktail sauce.) ☐ The Atlantis Fish Stew (a steaming cast iron pot is set on your table. And inside that pot, it sort of looks like they've included the entire catch of a thirty-boat fishing fleet. The pot arrives packed with crab legs, baby clams, red snapper, scallops, and prawns, all in a fragrant, buttery broth. What happens now? You feast.) ☐ Salmon Steak Supreme (a fresh filet of salmon poached in a fine court bouillon, then crowned with a coral-colored, cream-rich shrimp sauce.)

Dinner includes: A tasty shrimp bisque, or an equally good Boston clam chowder, or salad, and main course with hand-cut fries, or almond rice. **Prices:** Inexpensive to medium. **Basics:** 361 West Portal Ave. (near Sloat Blvd.), San Francisco. Tel: 665-7920. Hours: 11 am-11 pm daily. Cards: MC, V. Wine and beer.

South Pacific Grotto: San Francisco
Polynesian Seafood/Tropical setting and soothing prices

Polynesian cooking . . . ruby-colored sweet and sour sauces, golden seafood curries nestled in scooped-out papayas. Dishes garnished with pineapple, coconut, and miniature Japanese umbrellas. Plum-sauced kebabs served on Ti leaves. This is food that's gone Hollywood. In Technicolor. With special effects. And at the South Pacific Grotto, their dinners finish with a happy ending—a very modest check. On a dinner with salad and dessert, sea bass Polynesian-style is $5.95, sea-food curry is $6.95, and Hawaiian seafood kebabs are $6.25.

It's not just the food that's in show biz. The decor is Hollywood tropical. There's tiki masks on the walls, an outrigger canoe hanging from the ceiling, and bamboo everywhere. You almost expect Mitzi Gaynor to show up on the shoulders of a 300-pound Samoan and sing *Bali H'ai*. Of course, who needs Mitzi? After three or four rum drinks, you may decide to stand up and do a few songs yourself.

Menu Specialties: ☐ Hawaiian Seafood Kebabs ☐ Sea Bass Polynesian-Style (broiled sea bass in a light sweet & sour sauce.) ☐ Seafood Curry (prawns, scallops, crab, petrale sole, and calamari in a rich curry sauce. Served in a fresh papaya.)

Dinner includes . . . 3 courses: Salad with sesame seed dressing, main course with Polynesian vegetables and rice, and coconut ice cream. **Prices:** Inexpensive to medium. **Basics:** 2500 Noriega St. (at 32nd Ave.), San Francisco. Tel: 564-3363. Hours: 5-10 pm Tues.-Thurs.; 5-11 pm Fri., Sat.; 4-9 pm Sun. Closed Mon. Cards: MC, V. Full bar.

Short Takes

Noble Frankfurter
The best hot dogs in San Francisco

This place has its hot dogs shipped in from New York. They're all-beef kosher-style dogs that explode with flavor (90¢). The hot dogs are partnered with a French sesame seed roll. And to decorate your dog, there's a selection of 12 different condiments, including three kinds of mustard and sauerkraut. Even the decor is a plus—natural wood tables, stained glass, indoor plants, and carpets. Note: Last year, Americans ate 15 billion hot dogs. If placed end to end, that's enough hot dogs to reach the moon and back. Hot dog lovers— do your part and next year we'll reach Mars.

Basics: 1900 Polk St. (at Jackson), San Francisco. Tel: 441-5307. Hours: 11 am-1 am Sun.-Thurs.; 11 am-3 am Fri., Sat. Wine and beer.

La Taqueria
The Best tacos and burritos in California

In our opinion, La Taqueria's tacos and burritos are the best in the state. And we're not the only ones who think so. One night at La Taqueria we were sitting next to a man who commented he was from Los Angeles. Just to make conversation, we asked the man what brought him to San Francisco. He stopped eating, gave us a look like we had asked something obvious, and said, "Tacos."

We don't know if he was serious or not, but we do know of people who come here from all over the Bay Area for a taco. Yes . . . a taco. At La Taqueria, the tacos and burritos are special. But we won't try to describe what makes them special. On paper, they wouldn't sound that unique; basically La Taqueria uses the same ingredients as everybody else. It's what the kitchen *does* with the ingredients. And magic is hard to describe.

Our favorites at La Taqueria? The chorizo sausage burrito ($1.35) and the taco filled with broiled, marinated beef strips ($1.10). Decor: A good-looking place with the cheerful feeling of a sidewalk cafe in Guadalajara—lots of white stucco, wrought iron, and Mexican tile work.

Basics: 2889 Mission St. (near 25th St.), San Francisco. Tel 285-7117. Hours: 11 am-9 pm Mon.-Sat.; 11 am-8 pm Sun.

Heshie's
The best hot pastrami sandwiches in the City

See that friendly Jewish man behind the slicing machine? That's Mr. Heshie—professional pastrami slicer. At Heshie's, you listen for a *wrrr* and pick up your sandwich. The pastrami is sliced per order from large briskets. Heshie says pastrami is at its best right after it's sliced. And after one taste of a Heshie sandwich, it's obvious the man knows what he's talking about. The Pastrami Sandwich (a thick stack of pastrami on Jewish egg bread; served with kosher pickles Heshie imports from Chicago), $2.50.

Basics: 636 Clay St. (near Montgomery, one block from the Transamerica pyramid), San Francisco. Tel: 397-9331. Hours: 11:30 am-3 pm Mon.-Fri. Closed Sat., Sun. Wine and beer.

Pasquale's
Authentic, hand-spun Neapolitan pizza

Hey, paisano, you looking for the real thing? Then look no more. 'Cause that's just what the owner of this pizzeria makes. Pasquale Ussorio is from Naples, the city where pizza originated, and this Neapolitan gentleman still does things the old country way. At Pasquale's, the pizza sauce is prepared fresh daily, the Italian sausage is made on the premises, and the dough is hand-spun to order. And when you see a Pasquale pizza spinning through the air, you can be sure you'll have a Close Encounter of the Best Kind. Salami, pepperoni, or Pasquale's homemade sausage pizza: small, $2.95; medium, $3.75; large, $4.80.

Basics: 700 Irving St. (at 8th Ave., one block from Golden Gate Park), San Francisco. Tel: 661-2140. Hours: 5 pm-12:30 am Mon., Tues.; noon-12:30 am Wed., Thurs., Sun.; 1 pm-2 am Fri., Sat. Wine and beer.

Balboa Cafe
Half-pound hamburgers on sourdough baguettes

At the Balboa, the hamburger has been remodeled. You're served a half-pound of carefully broiled choice ground beef that's been hand-molded to fit a long, slender sourdough baguette loaf. The resulting sandwich is about the size of a small telephone poll. And to give the sandwich even more personality, the hamburger is topped with sauteed onions, melted Monterey Jack cheese, and fresh tomato slices. Plus served along with the burger is a wedge of ripe watermelon or cantaloupe. The Balboa Hamburger, $2.95.

But it's not just the hamburgers that have been remodeled. The Balboa has been operating primarily as a bar since 1914, and when Jack Slick purchased the place in 1977, he restored the Balboa to its original luster. Mr. Slick is now the owner of a very handsome saloon. There are also some old-time bar policies to go along with the atmosphere, like making screwdrivers with freshly-squeezed orange juice.

Basics: 3199 Fillmore St. (at Greenwich, one block off Lombard), San Francisco. Tel: 921-3944. Hours: 11 am-11 pm daily; bar open until 2 am daily.

Just Desserts
The best cheesecake in San Francisco

This friendly, attractive-looking cafe specializes in authentic New York-style cheesecake by the slice. The cheesecake is so good, people eat it s-l-o-w-l-y, while going "mmmmmm" like well-oiled sewing machines. 90¢ a slice. And its rank among cheesecakes is now a matter of public record. In a cheesecake tasting contest sponsored by *New West* magazine, it was judged the number one cheesecake in the Bay Area.

Basics: 1469 Pacific Ave. (near Larkin, 2½ blocks off Van Ness), San Francisco. Tel: 673-7144. Hours: Noon-11 pm Tues.-Thurs.; 11 am-midnight Fri.-Sun. Closed Mon.

Seal Rock Inn
Breakfast just up the hill from the ocean

This restaurant has what it takes to make a beautiful morning—good omelets and a great setting. The place is located near the entrance to Sutro Heights Park, just above the legendary Cliff House. After breakfast you can take a walk along the beach or drop by the Cliff House and watch the crashing surf while wrapping yourself around a Ramos Fizz. The Seal Rock Inn itself is a comfortable little restaurant with an outdoor dining area for sunny days, and a menu that offers nineteen different omelets to choose from. Specialties: The Sutro Omelet (filled with ham, bacon, and cheese), $3.00; The Spanish Omelet (served with a sauce of tomatoes, onions, and green peppers), $2.75; The Greek Omelet (filled with feta cheese, black olives, and fresh tomatoes), $2.95. Omelets include hash-browns, toast, and a fresh fruit garnish—usually a whole tangerine.

Basics: 545 Point Lobos Ave. (at 48th Ave.), San Francisco. Tel: 752-8000. Hours: 7:30 am-3:30 pm Mon.-Fri.; 7:30 am-6 pm Sat., Sun.

Swan Oyster Depot
Seafood salads and Boston clam chowder since 1911

At Swan's, you'll find an antique marble counter and eighteen old-fashioned stools—which are usually occupied by eighteen seafood lovers. Swan's has a loyal following. And there's a good reason. Over the years, Swan's has continually proven it has real "net worth."

Specialties: A big, meal-in-itself combination shrimp, prawn, and crab salad topped with a fine San Francisco Louie dressing laced with hard-boiled eggs, $4.90. Rich, creamy Boston clam chowder loaded with fresh clams, 80¢ a cup. Huge Olympia oyster cocktail, $1.95. Shell Game: A man arrives at Swan's at 7:30 a.m. each morning and works until 11 a.m. doing nothing but shelling oysters.

Basics: 1517 Polk St. (near California), San Francisco. Tel: 673-1101. Hours: 8 am-5:30 pm Mon.-Fri.; 8 am-5 pm Sat. Closed Sun. Wine and beer.

New York City Deli
High-rise sandwiches, Jewish deli-style

Former New Yorker Mel Lefer tries hard to run a good deli. Mr. Lefer slices all his sandwich meats to order, uses an excellent, crusty corn-rye bread, and gets his cheesecake from a bakery in Albuquerque, New Mexico because he feels it's better than anything available locally. But that's not all. His pastrami and corned beef come from a firm in L.A. that supplies exclusive Beverly Hills delis, and his pickles come from a Stockton source because "they taste really kosher." True. If those pickles were any more kosher, they'd be able to speak Hebrew.

New York City's two-inch-thick, "need-two-hands-to-hold'em" sandwiches: Hot corned beef, $2.15; hot pastrami, $2.20; kosher salami, $2.10. Cheesecake, 85¢.

Legal Notice: Going to a Jewish deli is not only enjoyable, it's a constitutional right. In 1974, Federal Judge Jack B. Weinstein, citing a previous decision that Jewish prisoners have a constitutional right to eat kosher food, ruled that jailed Rabbi Meir Kahane be allowed to leave prison during mealtime so he could eat in kosher restaurants.

Basics: 2295 Market St. (at 16th St.), San Francisco. Tel: 431-8390. Hours: 9 am-2:30 am Sun.-Thurs.; 9 am-3 am Fri., Sat. Wine and beer.

Tung Fong
The best dim sum house in San Francisco

Question: what do you call it when two people can have a meal that includes *ten* different dishes for *only* $3.75 a person? Answer: a Chinese dim sum luncheon. What are dim sum? They're steamed dumplings and other luncheon delicacies that the Chinese call "little jewels." This is the way it works. An endless parade of waitresses pass by your table, and each one is carrying a tray loaded with small plates of dim sum. Using your finger like a baton, you point at whatever looks good to you. At the end of lunch, the waitress counts the stack of empty plates on your table and figures up the bill (75¢ a plate). A few of Tung Fong's dim sum specialties: Bonnet-shaped shrimp dumplings. Plum sauce spareribs. Char Sil Bow barbecue pork buns. Stuffed meat turnovers. Silver-wrapped chicken. And for dessert, don't miss Tung Fong's Chinese custard tarts.

Basics: 808 Pacific Ave. (near Stockton), Chinatown, San Francisco. Tel: 362-7115. Hours: 10 am-3 pm Mon., Tues., Thurs.-Sun. Closed Wed. Public parking (35¢ per hour) available at the Portsmouth Square Garage, Kearny St. (betw. Clay and Washington).

La Quiche
A friendly-looking crepe and quiche bistro

This small bistro has a cheerful, Parisian atmosphere and a convenient downtown location. But best of all, it has a man in the kitchen with a talent for making flaky-crusted quiches and air-light crepes. Quiche Lorraine (a freshly-baked, individual-sized pie with a rich filling that contains imported Gruyere cheese and bits of ham and bacon. Served with salad.), $3.25.

The Crepes: This bistro cooks its dinner-plate-sized crepes on a special crepe grill that the owner brought back from Brittany, France. But even with this piece of equipment, cooking these thin, delicate crepes on a hot grill takes a chef with quick hands. And in this area, La Quiche's chef is certainly qualified. Probably the only guy who works faster is a pickpocket. A crepe filled with imported Swiss cheese and Parisian ham, $3.30; a crepe filled with bacon and ratatouille—a spicy vegetable mixture, $4.15; a crepe filled with creamed spinach and Parisian ham, $4.05.

Basics: 550 Taylor St. (near Geary, two blocks from Union Square), San Francisco. Tel: 441-2711. Hours: 11:30 am-2:30 pm Mon.-Sat.; 5:30-10:30 pm daily. Cards: MC, V. Wine and beer. Public parking (65¢ per hour) available at the Union Square Garage, Geary St. (betw. Powell and Stockton).

Stella Pastry
The home of Sacripantina cake, pleasure by the slice

The Mona Lisa has been appraised at $100,000,000. Can't afford it? Well, how about an Italian masterpiece for 80¢? That's what a slice of Sacripantina cake costs. A Sacripantina cake is a four-inch-high, pale-gold tower that's one part sweet Genoan spongecake and three parts rich . . . rich . . . rich zabaglione cream flavored with Marsala wine, rum, and maraschino liqueur. This is one of our favorite desserts. Walk-away slice, 80¢. A cake that serves 4-6 people, $4.00; 6-8 people, $6.00. Take-out only.

Basics: 446 Columbus Ave. (near Vallejo), San Francisco. Tel: 986-2914. Hours: 8 am-6 pm Tues.-Sat.; 8 am-2 pm Sun. Closed Mon.

La Cumbre
Burritos and tacos with three-star flavor

La Cumbre's burritos and tacos better be good. That's all they sell here. At La Cumbre, you'll find a friendly Mexican family that works with the precision of a drill team as they carefully put together your order . . . mama chops, papa fills, son rolls, and daughter serves. What results? Big, fat burritos and tacos packed with lots of meat and loads of flavor. Barbecued pork burrito, $1.25; chicken taco, $1.00. Thirsty? Try a mango soda, 45¢. The decor here is a bonus: a cheerful Acapulco-style setting of stucco and Mexican tile.

Basics: 515 Valencia St. (near 16th St.), San Francisco. Tel: 863-8205. Hours: 11 am-9 pm Mon.-Sat.; noon-8 pm Sun. Dos Equis and Carta Blanca beer available.

Tip Toe Inn Deli
The only place in town serving Russian pizza

Russian Pizza—a dictionary definition: Rus · sian piz · za (rŭsh'ən pēt'sə) *n.* 1. A flaky, pie-like crust completely enclosing a filling made up of four different kinds of European sausages, sliced onions, and a fresh Russian tomato sauce. 2. A dish that can only be found at the Tip Toe Inn Deli. 3. A snack that costs $1.30 for a good-sized portion. 4. Since there is no table seating at the Tip Toe Inn, Russian pizza is served "to go" only, but because of its tempting aroma, most purchasers never seem "to go" very far before eating it.

Basics: 5423 Geary Blvd. (near 18th Ave.), San Francisco. Tel: 221-6422. Hours: 9 am-7 pm Mon.-Sat. Closed Sun. Wine and beer.

Lucca Deli
One of San Francisco's best Italian delicatessens

Walk by Lucca's window and you lose control. Your hand automatically points at the hanging salami, your feet start pulling you toward Lucca's door, and a soft voice inside your head begins to whisper, "Ravioli, ravioli, minestrone, an Italian sandwich . . ." You can't help yourself. You go into the shop. And as soon as you do, the voice whispers, "It's me again. I forgot to mention the Italian vegetable salad. It'll go well with the sandwich."

Lucca's ravioli (fresh, homemade pasta squares bulging with a flavor-loaded filling and topped with a meat sauce that's made with imported Italian mushrooms), pint, $2.00. Minestrone (a richly flavored bean and vegetable-thick soup that's based on a prosciutto hambone stock. It's a soup that takes chef Stefano Magnani 20 hours to make.), pint, $1.00. Look at it this way: you're paying 5¢ an hour.

The Lucca Sandwich (Lucca's features custom-built sandwiches. At Lucca's, when you tell the counterman what combination of meats and cheeses you want, that's what you get. And you can choose from four kinds of crusty rolls, five kinds of cheese, and a parade of quality Italian meats, including Genoa salami, galantina, coppa, Toscana salami, and Veneziana.), a generously stacked sandwich is about $1.80. Italian Vegetable Salad (a harvest of 13 vegetables, including cauliflower, asparagus, and zucchini in an Italian dressing that's made with homemade wine vinegar), half pint, $1.00.

Basics: 2120 Chestnut St. (near Steiner), San Francisco. Tel: 921-7873. Hours: 9 am-6:30 pm Mon.-Fri.; 8 am-6 pm Sat., Sun. Wine and beer.

Scandinavian Deli
Danish ham, Swedish meatballs, and 10 different salads

After working for seven years as a cook in the Danish merchant marines, Ernst Meyer came to San Francisco in 1960 and opened this homey, neighborhood establishment. It's a popular self-service eating place and it's easy to see why. Ernst has spent the last 19 years ignoring inflation. At Ernst's deli-cafe, a plate of moist, tasty Swedish meatballs is $2.90, baked Danish-style ham is $3.75, and a hearty Danish stew prepared with roast beef and Scandinavian knekpolse sausage is $2.25. Plus these dishes come with three vegetables and any one of 10 different Scandinavian salads, including Swedish "folk" salad with apples, grapes, and pears, and Danish potato salad.

Basics: 2251 Market St. (near 15th St.), San Francisco. Tel: 861-9913. Hours: 9 am-8:30 pm Mon.-Fri. Closed Sat., Sun. Wine and beer.

THE EAST BAY

Included in This Section

Norman's: Berkeley
Continental/Inviting neighborhood dinner house

What kind of restaurant do you like best?
1. A place with moderate prices?
2. A place with a variety of well-made dishes?
3. A place with a good decor?

Can't decide? Then just go to Norman's—they feature all three. Norman's offers dinners with moderate prices. And they also offer variety. Beef. Chicken. Seafood. Whichever door of choice you open, there will be a dish to greet you. Among the dishes you can choose are a richly-sauced beef stroganoff, chicken breast Rosemary stuffed with fresh mushrooms and covered with a sherry-laced cream sauce, and a cross-country match of Eastern scallops and baby Western shrimp in a white wine sauce. With each of these dinners you'll also get an individual loaf of crusty homemade bulgur wheat bread, and either soup, or a chilled Salinas valley artichoke ready to be dipped in a side dish of bordelaise butter.

Ah, then there's Norman's decor. The soft lights, the antiques, the beam ceiling, and the polished maple tables all combine to give the dining room the warmth of a sip of good brandy.

Menu Specialties: ☐ Chicken Rosemary ☐ Beef Stroganoff (a classic, done right. Butter-sauteed strips of beef in a smooth, mushroom-dotted sauce.) ☐ Scallops and Shrimp Vin Blanc (the shellfish are first sauteed and then topped with a richly seasoned white wine sauce.) ☐ Roast Beef Blintzes (an original—thin crepes encircling a sherry-flavored filling of diced roast beef, onions, mushrooms, and herbs. Then grilled in butter and topped with sour cream. Kosher, it isn't. Good it is.)

Dinner includes: A fresh chilled artichoke, or soup (maybe cream of asparagus), an individual loaf of crusty bulgur wheat bread baked on the premises daily, and main course with two vegetables. **Prices:** Medium. **Basics:** 3204 College Ave. (at Alcatraz), Berkeley. Tel: 655-5291. Hours: 11:30 am-2 pm Mon.-Fri.; 5:30-10 pm Mon.-Thurs.; 5:30-10:30 pm Fri., Sat.; 5-9:30 pm Sun. Reservations necessary on weekends. All major cards. Full bar.

Casa de Eva: Berkeley
Mexican/Interesting specialties, hacienda decor

The food at many Mexican restaurants is so hot, they ought to attach seat belts to the chairs to keep customers from going through the ceiling. But not at Casa de Eva. They believe in showing your mouth some respect.

Besides featuring dishes that won't blister your tongue, Casa de Eva has other ways of showing you they care about your mouth: Casa de Eva's owner goes to the produce market at 4 a.m. to hand-pick the green peppers for the chile relleno; hand-shredded flank steak instead of hamburger is used in the flauta; and even the chorizo sausage for the chalupas is homemade.

The chalupas are a Casa de Eva specialty. To make this dish, Mexican-style cornmeal is hand-shaped into a little boat and then loaded with some tasty cargo: smoky refried beans, chorizo sausage, shredded lettuce, sour cream, and guacamole.

Casa de Eva shows you they care about your eyes, too. In their hacienda-style dining room, you'll find red brick floors, handmade wooden tables, comfortable highback chairs, and a tiled archway giving you a view of Casa de Eva's open kitchen. What a contrast to the atmosphere found in some Mexican restaurants, where the decor looks like the interior of a Tijuana taxicab.

Menu Specialties: □ Chalupas □ Flautas (crispy rolled tortillas shaped like a Federale's nightstick and about half as long. The tortillas are filled with hand-shredded flank steak and seasoned with tomatillo imported from Mexico.) □ Quesadillas (large tortillas folded into a half moon shape and stuffed with avocado, Monterey Jack cheese, and slivers of smoked ham. The plate comes with a small bowl of fresh fruit marinated in its own natural juices.) □ Tamales (very homemade, very tasty, and very popular. Available weekends only. This tamale should interest Pacific Telephone—it's a Long Distance Tamale. What's a Long Distance Tamale? At 6:01 a.m., Casa de Eva finishes making the tamales in Berkeley, and at 6:02 a.m., someone in L.A. comments how good they smell.)

Dishes include refried beans and rice. **Prices:** Inexpensive. **Basics:** 2826 Telegraph Ave. (two blocks from Ashby), Berkeley. Tel: 845-9091. Hours: 11 am-10 pm Tues.-Fri.; 3:30-10 pm Sat., Sun. Closed Mon. No cards. Wine and beer.

Warszawa: Berkeley
Polish/Traditional homecooking and Old World hospitality

The two ladies who own the Warszawa feature traditional home-cooked Polish dinners. They are dedicated women and it shows—their food is excellent.

But since this is the first Polish restaurant in the Bay Area, it's our guess that the main requirement for such a venture is a sense of humor. At this restaurant, some diners are bound to get an irrepressible urge to tell a few Polish jokes. At least once a night, someone is likely to suggest that inside the kitchen there's a Polish chef holding a spoon while four assistants rotate him around the pot. Or that a lifeguard must be posted at the sink to keep the dishwasher from drowning.

When the Polish-joke-telling session ends, it's usually time for more serious matters—the food. You'll find that Polish cooking is a tapestry of influences. Over the years, Polish chefs have taken recipes from neighboring Russia, Germany, and Hungary and woven them into their cuisine. The Warszawa's bacon-filled, rolled Zrazy beef is German rouladen in principle; their homemade pierogi pasta shells stuffed with cheese and chives are a Polish version of Russian pelmeni; and their stuffed cabbage is Hungarian with a spice change.

The Warszawa's owners go to great lengths to make their food authentic. They even have relatives in Poland send them wild Polish mushrooms. They insist that other mushrooms are not effective stand-ins for the Polish variety. And this extra concern seems to be paying off. With the first bite of the Warszawa's food, you'll immediately discover that Polish food is no joke.

Menu Specialties: ☐ Duckling Kaczka (this is a dish that looks like it's getting ready to pose for the cover of *Gourmet* magazine. Spanning a huge plate is a duckling that's been roasted until the skin is a beautiful shade of golden brown. And surrounding this plump duckling is a fence of cooked apple slices and prunes and a rich pan sauce.) ☐ Zrazy Beef (thinly sliced sirloin steak rolled around a stuffing of onions, bacon, and wild Polish mushrooms. Topped with a chestnut-colored sour cream sauce.) ☐ Bigos (one of Poland's most famous dishes—a spicy stew of beef, pork, sausage, and sauerkraut in a hearty, deeply-flavored red sauce.) □ Pierogi (large homemade pasta shells with three different fillings—some have a pork filling; others are stuffed with wild Polish mushrooms; and still others hide a cream cheese filling.)

Dishes include fresh vegetable or homemade dumplings, and a basket of warm brown bread. Starters: Barszcz Soup (peasant borsch. This is no watery counterfeit. The Warszawa's red borsch is a rib-sticking, long-simmered product, filled with chunks of Polish kielbasa sausage.) Dessert: Torte Orzechowy (a homemade rum-walnut torte filled with whipped cream.) **Prices:** Medium. **Decor:** In a European-style white brick building, and inside there's Polish folk art decorating the walls and waiters in old-fashioned Polish jackets. **Basics:** 1730 Shattuck Ave. (near Virginia), Berkeley. Tel: 841-5539. Hours: 5:30-10 pm Mon., Wed.-Sun. Closed Tues. No cards. Wine and beer.

Driftwood: Alameda
Italian/4-course dinners, bargain prices

Four years ago, the Driftwood's owner decided to feature Italian food at his restaurant. This was a wise decision. Italian food is like sex . . . it's something people like to have often. And at the Driftwood, you can afford to have it often. Their 4-course dinners all have bargain prices: the Driftwood's prawn cioppino is $4.75, the chicken cacciatora is $4.00, and their veal parmigiana is $4.25. And dinner includes a tureen of soup, hot sesame bread, a family-style bowl of salad, spaghetti, vegetables, and spumoni ice cream.

The Driftwood's large dining room is filled with soft lights, big booths, and friendly waitresses. And a former occupant, a Polynesian restaurant, left behind its seashells and fishnets. But there are red checkered tablecloths—a quiet announcement that the kitchen is now under the influence of Italy rather than Pango Pango. Overall, the decor will sort of remind you of 1953 . . . and thankfully, so will the prices.

Menu Specialties: □ Prawn Cioppino (sherry-sauteed prawns are served in a bowl that's filled to high tide with a fresh, spicy marinara sauce. This is our favorite dish here.) □ Chicken Cacciatora (topped with an oregano-spiced red sauce laced with green peppers and onions.) □ Veal Parmigiana (breaded and topped with grated parmigiana cheese.) □ Prime Rib (even the prime rib is priced right. For $6.25, you get a tender, juicy 14 oz. cut.)

Dinner includes . . . 4 courses: An all-you-can tureen of mine-strone soup, hot sesame bread, a big bowl of salad, main course with spaghetti or baked potato, vegetables, and spumoni ice cream. **Prices:** Inexpensive. **Basics:** 1313 Park St. (near Encinal), Alameda. Tel: 522-5141. Hours: 5-9:30 pm Mon.-Thurs.; 5-10:30 pm Fri., Sat.; 2-9:30 pm Sun. Cards: MC, V. Full bar.

Bay Wolf Cafe: Oakland
Creative Cooking/In a time-polished blue and white house

Here's how to collect that $5 your friend has owed you for the past three years. Results 100% guaranteed.

The next time you're talking with your friend, casually bring up the subject of restaurants. As you're talking, try, more or less, to follow this script:

"By the way, I've made a discovery. I've found a restaurant that has creative 3-course dinners at moderate prices. Every night they have a new menu. A couple of weeks ago they served me roast sirloin of beef in a special sauce. The following week, I had loin of pork braised in champagne and served on a bed of minced mushrooms. Yesterday, I had fresh trout. The waiter told me that it comes from a trout farm in Big

Sur. He said the trout are put on a Greyhound bus at two and are in the chef's pan by six.''

"What's the name of this restaurant?" your friend asks.

Don't give it to him. Keep following our script. Raising your voice just slightly, say, "Wait a minute. Let me tell you a little more about this place. For dessert, they serve a fruit bowl packed with some of the biggest, sweetest fruit I've ever had. Why, the cherries are almost the size of doorknobs. And when this place says the vegetables are fresh, they mean it. The waiter told me that they have a vegetable garden out back where they grow their own vegetables and even the herbs used in their salad dressing. Part of the dishwasher's duties include tending the garden.''

"Interesting. But what's the name of this restaurant?" your friend asks.

You ignore his question and continue talking: "You'd like the atmosphere there. The decor is an artistic blend of modern and Victorian touches. The staff is friendly and helpful, they have an outdoor deck . . .''

"The name! The name! Tell me the name of this restaurant!" your friend shouts.

"Calm down," you say. "I'll tell you. But first, remember that $5 . . .''

The Menu: The menu changes daily with two different entrees offered each night. Frequently featured: Veal Madeira. Baked ham with homemade chutney. Filet of sole seasoned with fresh herbs and baked New Orleans style in a parchment cooking bag. Chicken breasts Bocconcini layered with prosciutto ham and Gruyere cheese and served with a light cream sauce flavored with Italian mushrooms.

Dinner includes . . . 3 courses: Soup (maybe cream of asparagus, fresh salmon chowder or Mendocino corn soup), salad with an olive oil and sherry wine vinegar dressing, and main course with risotto rice and sauteed vegetable (maybe homegrown green beans with almonds or homegrown snow peas with carrots.)

Dessert: A bowl of premium fruit (possibly homegrown plums or figs, freestone peaches, grapes, kiwi, and pineapple.) **Prices:** Medium. **Basics:** 3853 Piedmont Ave. (near MacArthur), Oakland. Tel: 655-6004. Hours: 11:30 am-2 pm, 6-9 pm Wed.-Sun.; 11:30 am-2 pm Mon. Closed Tues. Reservations necessary on weekends. No cards. Wine and beer.

Beau Rivage: Alameda
French/Candlelit dining room overlooking a yacht harbor

The movies have a rating system. How about a similar system for restaurants? The ratings could be painted in bold letters on the restaurant's window. For example, an "X" rating would stand for "excellent." Let's take the case of Beau Rivage.

You drive by and see . . .

Beau Rivage ┌─────────────────────┐
                │ **X** EXCELLENT FOOD │
                └─────────────────────┘

You slam on the brakes.

Now, let's say next week you want to try another French restaurant.

Remember the rating . . .

┌────┬──┐
│ **PG** │ PARENTAL GUIDANCE SUGGESTED   │
├────┴──┤
│ SOME MATERIAL MAY NOT BE SUITABLE FOR CHILDREN   │
└───┘

As you drive by you see . . .

Le Chaumont ┌────┬──────────────────────────────────────┐
                │ **PG** │ PALATE GUIDANCE SUGGESTED   │
                ├────┴──────────────────────────────────────┤
                │ SOME MEALS MAY NOT BE SUITABLE FOR ANYONE │
                └───┘

You step on the gas. Hard. And head back to Beau Rivage.

Chef Lucien Vigney deserves an "excellent" rating. This man has real talent. And we're not the only ones who think so. Lucien spent one and a half years cooking for Georges Pompidou—the former President of France.

At Lucien's candlelit restaurant in Alameda there are a number of dishes that spotlight chef Lucien's talent, including his beef Wellington with Perigourdine sauce, his veal in champagne sauce, and his French vanilla-chocolate mousse spiked with Kahlua liqueur. All of these dishes are very good. And, as we've all experienced, good food has an effect on people. You'll discover that, like a romantic scene in an X-rated movie, Lucien's food can get you . . . excited.

Menu Specialties: ☐ Veal au Champagne (tender veal scallops in a cream-rich, pale gold champagne sauce rippled with fresh mushrooms.) ☐ Filet of Beef Wellington (a two-inch-thick filet steak jacketed in a flaky pastry crust. Served with a Perigourdine sauce, a classic brown sauce based on a stock that chef Lucien simmers for a full 24 hours.) ☐ Filet of Sole Monte Carlo (three boned filets of petrale sole rolled around a salmon stuffing, and topped with a rich shrimp-laced cream sauce.) ☐ Chicken Chasseur (a boned, butter-cooked half chicken in a distinctive sauce that's made with white wine, bacon, and a fortune in fresh mushrooms.)

Dinner includes: Soup (maybe cream of asparagus or cream of

broccoli), or salade Roquefort (butter lettuce tossed in a tarragon-spiced dressing and then topped with a huge cloud of grated Roquefort cheese), and main course with fresh sauteed green beans and potatoes noisette. Dessert: Chocolate mousse, Lucien style. **Prices:** Medium to a step above medium. **Decor:** The restaurant overlooks the Ballena Bay yacht harbor. It's a beautiful setting. From the dining room there's a view of gleaming white sailboats and dark blue water, and inside the wood-paneled room, there's candlelight, gold linen, baby roses on every table, and a fireplace hung with copper pots. Plus, a friendly staff of tuxedoed waiters provide excellent service. Note: not all of the tables face the yacht harbor, so we suggest that you reserve one when you call for a reservation. **Basics:** 1042 Ballena Blvd. (about half a mile off Central, in the Ballena Bay Yacht Club), Alameda. Tel: 523-1660. Hours: 11:30 am-2 pm, 5:30-10:30 pm Tues.-Fri.; 5:30-11 pm Sat.; 5-9 pm Sun. Closed Mon. Reservations necessary on weekends. Cards: MC, V. Full bar. Parking lot.

Phoenician: Berkeley
Middle Eastern/Outdoor dining and modest prices

The Phoenician is a tribute to hard work and good cooking. Two Lebanese brothers, Adnan and Ghassan Jarrouge, opened a plain, tiny lunch room on this site three years ago. And the success of their venture gave the brothers the capital they needed to remodel. They expanded the lunch room into "the Jarrouge Dream"—a small, polished Middle Eastern dinner house that celebrates the cooking of the Arab world. The place now has imported brass lamps and a colorful hand-painted Lebanese mural inside and a plant-filled patio outside.

The cooking at the Phoenician is handled by Ghassan. But he doesn't have to work alone. Most of the time "oum" is in the kitchen with him—"oum" being the Lebanese word for mother. Mrs. Jarrouge can usually be found in the kitchen helping Ghassan fix the pilaf and stir the soup. She even makes homemade Lebanese pastry for the restaurant.

Mrs. Jarrouge also helps her son prepare the marinades for the lamb and chicken kebabs. And what marinades they are. It's as if the best spice stalls of Baghdad and Cairo are located just outside their kitchen door. Not that any of this has affected the Phoenician's prices—most of their dinners are in the $4.75 to $6.50 range.

The food at the Phoenician has attracted many members of the Bay Area's Middle Eastern community. And some out-of-town visitors. One night we were seated across from this Middle Eastern gentleman who we later learned was "in the oil business." But that was fairly obvious. When he left, we saw him get into a black limousine that was so big, it probably had its own zip code.

Menu Specialties: ☐ Lamb Mishwi (tender, perfectly trimmed chunks of choice, skewered lamb flavored with a seven-spice marinade that includes an aromatic spice called "sumac." Ghassan considers this seasoning such an important ingredient in the marinade, on a recent visit to the Middle East he purchased a large quantity of sumac and brought it back with him.) ☐ Prawns bi Salsa (large, moist sauteed prawns in a Mediterranean-style sauce of tomatoes, fresh mushrooms, and herbs.) ☐ Chicken Mishwi (pieces of chicken first spend 24 hours in a multi-spiced marinade that includes imported Lebanese thyme. Then they're skewered and carefully broiled.) ☐ Sheikh-El-Mehsi (each order consists of three whole garden-fresh baby eggplants that are fried, then stuffed with a flavorful mixture of lamb, onions, and pine nuts, and served in a very light, fragrant tomato sauce.)

Dinner includes: Soup (a Middle Eastern lentil soup with a lemon accent), hot Arab pitta bread, and main course with an authentic rice pilaf. Dessert: Homemade Baklawa (the Lebanese version of Greek baklava. You're served a pale gold square of air-light layers of fresh, flaky filo pastry spread with chopped walnuts and honey.) **Prices:** Inexpensive. **Basics:** 2441 Dwight Way (near Telegraph), Berkeley. Tel: 843-5788. Hours: 11:30 am-2:30 pm, 5-10 pm Tues.-Sat.; 5-9 pm Sun. Closed Mon. Cards: MC, V. Wine and beer. Parking lot in back.

Cornucopian: Oakland
Continental/Country inn atmosphere

In the last few years, big corporations have built a number of impressive-looking restaurants in the area. While some of these operations have succeeded in siphoning off business from the smaller restaurants, Cornucopian has remained unaffected. The only place where you stand a better chance of constantly seeing the same faces is the dining hall at San Quentin.

Cornucopian's customers have done some comparison shopping. When they visited the corporation restaurants, all they received was a plainly broiled steak. But at the Cornucopian, they never have to face a piece of meat that's plain and lonely. The Cornucopian's chef is a skilled matchmaker, and his menu is filled with happy marriages: the beautifully marinated rack of lamb is partnered with a classic, deeply-flavored bordelaise sauce; the filet of beef is wedded to a mushroom-rich red wine sauce; and the Cornucopian's crisp, golden brown duckling is escorted by a unique, mahogany-colored sauce that's based on a good stock, crushed walnuts, and the juice of pomegranates.

But it's not just the main course that gets the chef's attention. The Cornucopian's 3-course dinners include a cream of mushroom soup that lives up to its name, and a fresh romaine salad topped with either an herb-laced Italian dressing or a blue cheese dressing that's thick with cheese. Another point in the kitchen's favor is the flavorful vegetable saute that comes with the main course. The Cornucopian's chef doesn't try to fool Mother Nature. He uses only fresh vegetables and cooks them "per order."

The Cornucopian also hasn't forgotten the decor. The dining room has an inviting French country inn look with its white, wood-trimmed walls, cocoa brown tablecloths and powder blue napkins. And to top it all off, the service is good. In fact, it may even get better. The rumor is that next year, the Cornucopian is doing away with doggie bags. They're going to have a bus boy carry it home for you.

Menu Specialties: □ Duckling Cornucopian □ Filet of Beef Cornucopian □ Rack of Lamb (a choice eight rib rack marinated for 24 hours in wine, lemon juice, and fresh sweet basil and then roasted. Served with a classic bordelaise sauce.) □ Crab Amandine (fresh Dungeness crab legs and body meat in a light, buttery cream sauce laced with fresh mushrooms and slivers of toasted almonds.) □ Chicken Cornucopian (four tender pieces of chicken are first sauteed with cherry tomatoes, scallions, pearl onions, mushrooms, and herbs, and then flambéed in white wine.)

Dinner includes . . . 3 courses: Cream of mushroom soup, romaine salad (we suggest you try the Italian or blue cheese dressing), main course with fresh vegetables and rice pilaf, and coffee (a rich custom-blend that's as strong as love and black as night.)

Dessert: Each night a special homemade dessert is offered—maybe Genoise cake layered with mocha buttercream, German chocolate cake, or almond cake topped with fresh raspberry sauce. **Prices:** Medium to a step above medium. **Basics:** 5912 College Ave. (one block from Claremont), Oakland. Tel: 658-9700. Hours: 11:30 am-2:30 pm, 5-10 pm Tues.-Fri.; 5-11 pm Sat.; 11 am-2:30 pm (brunch), 5-9 pm Sun. Closed Mon. Reservations necessary on weekends. Cards: AE, MC, V. Wine and beer. Parking lot.

split pea soup
tossed salad
homemade rolls
PRIME RIB
fresh broccoli
baked potato
coffee
lemon chiffon pie

$5.75

BARGAIN GOOD DEAL

T. Cervenak

This is one of Walker's dinners.
It's their idea of a balanced meal.

Walker's is a small restaurant in Albany that serves homecooked meals in a friendly neighborhood setting. You might say it's a classic American-style restaurant. But more important, Walker's is a restaurant that understands what America needs: a 4-course prime rib dinner for $5.75. Or for $5.50, you can order Walker's Southern-fried chicken, or baked ham. And these prices include everything — a hearty soup, a crisp green salad, homemade popover rolls, fresh vegetable, a steaming hot baked potato, coffee, and dessert. Plus, when it comes to dessert, Walker's also understands that Americans want freedom of choice. So they offer nine kinds of homemade pie daily, including berry, pecan, apricot, and chocolate cream pie.

Dinner at Walker's — it's like celebrating the Bicentennial all over again.

Menu Specialties: ☐ Prime Rib ☐ Southern-fried Chicken ☐ Baked Ham. Dinner includes . . . 4 courses (see above). **Prices:** Inexpensive. **Basics:** 1491 Solano Ave. (near Curtis), Albany. Tel: 525-4647. Hours: 8 am-3 pm, 5-8 pm Tues.-Sat. Closed Sun., Mon. No cards. Wine and beer.

Lorenzo's: Oakland
Italian/Romantic multi-course meals, very appealing prices

The Italian's intense concern over food is a deeply-rooted characteristic that traces all the way back to ancient Rome. In fact, during the days of the Roman empire it was common practice to put cooks who had prepared an unsuccessful meal on special platforms and spank them in public. We can see it now: "Okay, chef Claudius, bend over . . . (whack!) . . . that's for the tasteless chicken . . . (whack!) . . . that's for the overcooked vegetables . . ."

Lorenzo Picchi wouldn't have had anything to worry about. The way he prepares his chicken cacciatora and veal Lucchese would have certainly kept him off the spanking platform. The sauce for the veal dish is one of our favorites at this restaurant. Although the "Lucchese" sauce is a simple, tomato-based preparation, the cooking method, a two-hour process, gives the sauce a subtle, unique flavor.

Another plus at Lorenzo's is the atmosphere. There are two small, romantic dining rooms with soft lighting, and a single pink carnation on each linen-covered table. The restaurant itself is located in a rustic-looking bungalow that's part of Jack London Village—a charm-filled collection of shops and restaurants overlooking the Oakland Estuary.

We saved Lorenzo's best feature for last—the prices. Lorenzo's dinners give a new meaning to the word "bargain." His dinners start with an asparagus appetizer, then shrimp Etruscan, and after that tortellini pasta in cream sauce. This is followed by the main course, say veal valdostana, and finally dessert, maybe fresh strawberries in a sour cream-Grand Marnier sauce. The price . . . $5.50. That's not a misprint. The price of Lorenzo's 5-course veal valdostana dinner is $5.50. Lorenzo's is what we call a "Christmas restaurant"—considering their prices, the food is almost a gift.

Menu Specialties: □ Veal Valdostana (Eastern veal rubbed with Lorenzo's six-herb butter and layered with fontina cheese and prosciutto ham. Then it's rolled and sauteed with white wine and shallots.) □ Chicken Cacciatora (chicken in a fresh wine-accented tomato sauce laced with mushrooms, green peppers, imported olives, and artichoke hearts.) □ Veal Braciole Lucchese (veal in a golden bread crumb crust. Served with Lorenzo's distinctive tomato sauce.) □ Filet of Sole Mugnaia (ocean-fresh filet of sole gently sauteed and topped with a lemon-scented, butter-rich sauce.)

Dinner includes . . . 5 courses: Asparagus della Casa, shrimp Etruscan, pasta Lorenzo, main course with fresh zucchini, and dessert. **Prices:** Inexpensive. **Basics:** 55 Alice St. (three blocks east of Broadway in Jack London Village, *next* to Jack London Square), Oakland. Tel: 465-4876. Hours: 11:30 am-9 pm Tues.-Sun. Closed Mon. Reservations suggested on weekends. Cards: MC, V. Wine and beer.

125

Narsai's: Berkeley
French/The 5-course Narsai dinner, a two-hour affair

When it comes to cooking, Narsai David is the Wizard of Ah's. Narsai features 5-course dinners, with each course a showcase of careful preparation and skill. At Narsai's, dinner is a relaxed, gently-paced, two-hour affair.

Even choosing an entree takes time. The decision isn't an easy one. There's medallions of milk-fed Wisconsin veal sauteed with fresh artichoke hearts and imported Bulgarian mushrooms; rack of lamb marinated for two days in pomegranate juice and red wine, then roasted and served with a classic sauce bordelaise; and fresh filet of salmon poached in white wine with shrimp and served in a flaky golden pastry boat topped with an ivory-colored cream sauce.

But eventually, decisions are made and your tuxedoed waiter will quietly begin to serve you a 5-course dinner . . . Narsai-style. It's a dinner that may include a quiche Lorraine appetizer, a rich mushroom soup, heart of romaine salad, and summer squash stuffed with spinach. After the entree, your waiter will bring you an ornate silver pot of fresh, custom-blended coffee and dessert—maybe Narsai's "Chocolate Decadence" cake topped with raspberry sauce. And the service matches the elegance of the food. Narsai's waiters seem to know what you want before you want it.

When concert promoter Bill Graham gave a dinner for musicians in New York, he flew Narsai there in his private Learjet to cater it. The reason is obvious. When it comes to the pleasures of the table, Narsai does things right. And that's the way he does things at his restaurant. Narsai has developed blue ribbon sources for all his meats, and equally good suppliers for his seafood. And for produce, he has a man on his payroll who arrives at the Oakland produce terminal at 3 a.m. each morning to hand-pick fruits and vegetables for the restaurant.

Finally, to make sure all these ingredients are given the attention they deserve, Narsai staffs his kitchen with five chefs, including one chef who does nothing but make pastries. Yet, although the demands of the kitchen take up a lot of Narsai's time, he sometimes finds it necessary to go underground . . . to take inventory. His wine cellar is stocked with 50,000 bottles; it's considered one of the best in the state.

Narsai's. The owner's talent, care, and concern for quality has created something special. At this restaurant you'll find the six-month dinner: six months after you have dinner at Narsai's, you still remember how good it was.

Menu Specialties: ☐ Medallions of Veal Robert ☐ Rack of Lamb Assyrian ☐ Filet of Salmon en Vol-au-Vent (when fresh salmon isn't available, Narsai uses fresh filet of petrale sole.) ☐ Supremes of Chicken Alexis Bespaloff (five faultlessly trimmed filets of chicken breast sauteed in butter with fresh cream and flambéed with sauterne to create a velvet-smooth, golden yellow sauce.) ☐ Lamb en Croute (the lamb is topped with a mushroom duxelle, then wrapped in a light pastry crust and roasted. Served with a deeply-flavored sauce bordelaise.) ☐ Prawns a l'Armoricaine (large, moist sauteed prawns in a distinctive sauce of butter, shallots, fresh diced tomatoes, and brandy.)

Dinner includes . . . 5 courses: Appetizer (choice of two each night—possibly Blue Point oysters Florentine, crepes Maxim stuffed with ham and Gruyere cheese, or duck paté with port wine aspic), soup (maybe tomato-shrimp bisque or cream of asparagus), heart of romaine salad, main course with two fresh vegetables (possibly an artichoke heart stuffed with carrots, and sauteed snow peas), coffee, and dessert (choice of three each night—maybe Swiss almond torte with mocha buttercream, strawberry layer cake topped with Italian meringue, or Amaretto liqueur soufflé pie.) **Prices:** Expensive. **Decor:** It's a dining room of simple elegance, with a quiet yet dramatic effect. You enter through 15-foot-high doors of polished virgin redwood into a room with white walls, thick burgundy carpets, highback chairs, and tables set with snow-white linen, gleaming silverware, and custom-made candle lamps. **Basics:** 385 Colusa Ave. (one mile from the corner of Solano Ave. and Colusa), Berkeley. Tel: 527-7900. Hours: 5-10 pm Sun.-Thurs.; 5-midnight Fri., Sat. Reservations suggested. All major cards. Full bar. Parking lot.

Au Coquelet: Berkeley
French/Huge dinners with wine at a bargain price

Over the years Berkeley has been the birthplace of many causes and campaigns. And this tradition has apparently had an effect on Berkeley restaurateur Jean-Marie Labourgue, the owner-chef of Au Coquelet. Jean-Marie is a man that has taken a stand on an important issue: he believes in ecology for your wallet's greenery. Chef Labourgue serves 5-course family-style French dinners *including wine* for $7.00.

Dinner begins with a basket of sourdough and a steaming hot tureen of soup that's almost the size of a swimming pool in Hillsborough. Next, you're served an appetizer course, maybe a classic quiche Lorraine, or homemade paté. Now it's time for the main course, which changes nightly. On Saturday, for example, the entree is tender slices of pork in a rich orange sauce and on Sunday roast beef with Madeira sauce is featured.

Along with the entree comes a fresh vegetable, and then, in the European manner, they bring you a bowl of salad tossed in the house dressing. This is a large salad—in fact at first glance, it looks like they're serving you Salinas' entire lettuce crop for the current season. Finally you're given coffee and dessert, maybe chocolate mousse or a raspberry custard tart.

You'll enjoy the food at Au Coquelet. But it may be a while before you return to Jean-Marie's restaurant. After one of Au Coquelet's huge family-style dinners, most people don't get hungry again for about six or seven weeks.

The Menu: One set 5-course meal is served nightly. Dinner includes a carafe of wine, soup, appetizer, main course (Tues.—veal Jeanette; Wed.—leg of lamb with a classic brown sauce; Thurs.—beef bourguignon), fresh vegetable, salad, coffee, and dessert. **Prices:** Medium. **Decor:** Inside, there's fine, old bare brick walls, colorful modern oil paintings, and long, custom-made blond wood tables. **Basics:** 2000 University Ave. (at Milvia), Berkeley. Tel: 845-0433. Hours: 6 am-2 am daily (dinner served from 5-10 pm). Cards: MC, V. Wine and beer.

Love's Pagan Den: Oakland
Filipino/The Love brothers bring Manila to you

What will $7 buy you today? Well, Van Imports of New Jersey stocks a personalized coffee mug with a built-in whistle—which helps you get quicker refills at lunch counters. And the Mars Boutique in Hollywood will sell you a $7 pair of strap-on headlights for your shoes—so people won't step on your feet in dark nightclubs. Or $7 will buy you a two-hour vacation in Manila. With dinner included.

At the Love brothers restaurant, it feels like you're in the Philippines. The small dining room is filled with bamboo, carved Filipino teakwood, and Tagalog fishing spears which serve as curtain rods.

Outside, wind chimes tinkle in the breeze. And through the window, you can see tropical plants, a pond, and a little covered bridge with a roof woven out of Nipa palm leaves.

Owner Art Love also adds to the charm of this restaurant. In his polite South Seas manner, Art will greet you and make sure you're comfortable, and then he'll go on to tell you a little about his country's food. Art will explain that Filipino cuisine developed as a committee effort. The fierce Tagalog natives, the Indonesians, the Chinese, the Spanish, and the Americans have all played a part in Filipino history, and they all left their mark on the food. Art points out that these varied influences have produced some unique dishes. And Art also shyly notes how well his brother cooks them.

Art has a right to be proud. His brother Ben's cooking is good. In the restaurant's tiny kitchen, Ben prepares such dishes as Rellenong Manok, a boned game hen that's marinated for 24 hours, then stuffed with chorizo sausage and baked. Another dish Art can be proud of is his brother's Sugpo—large Tiger prawns sauteed with fresh crushed ginger, mushrooms, and banana blossoms, a Filipino delicacy similar to our artichoke heart.

Is there any problem getting such exotic ingredients? "Sometimes," Ben sighs. He points out that just last week, for example, the banana blossoms didn't arrive on time. His brother Art was stuck in Rapu-Rapu for three days while they put a new sail on his outrigger.

Menu Specialties: ☐ Sugpo Prawns ☐ Rellenong Manok (must be ordered two days in advance.) ☐ Fried Pancit Molo (a huge turnover . . . almost the size of a small Philippine island . . . stuffed with wine-sauteed chicken, water chestnuts, shrimp, bamboo shoots, pork, and mushrooms. Then it's fried in coconut oil until the exterior becomes crisp and turns a beautiful shade of tropical gold.) ☐ Stuffed Top Sirloin (a thick, grilled steak stuffed with crab legs, shrimp, and mushrooms, and topped with a Filipino wine sauce. The flavors work on you separately and together—good partners.) ☐ Chicken Adobo (three tender pieces of chicken in an excellent reddish-brown sauce. This is one of the Philippine's most popular dishes.)

Dinner includes: Salad with a Caesar-like dressing (fresh romaine tossed with olive oil, lemon juice, parmesan cheese, and special seasonings until the leaves wear the dressing like a custom-made suit), main course with vegetable, rice, and a fresh pineapple wedge garnish.

Dessert: Leche Flan (one of the best custards we've had. It has a rich, nutty, caramel-like flavor.) Macapuno Sundae (mango ice cream topped with a Filipino coconut sauce.) **Prices:** Inexpensive to medium. **Basics:** 760 East 8th St. (three blocks east of Laney College; from downtown Oakland drive east on 7th St., which becomes East 8th St. once past Laney College), Oakland. Tel: 832-3383. Hours: 5-10 pm Tues.-Sun. Closed Mon. Cards: V. Full bar. Parking lot.

Giovanni's: Berkeley
Italian/Author Riera: "After 186 meals, I'm sure."

The food at Giovanni's is good. I'm positive. Absolutely sure. Do you know why I'm so confident? I've eaten 186 meals there. Do I always test a restaurant this thoroughly? The answer is yes—as long as the restaurant gives me a weekly paycheck. I used to work at Giovanni's as a waiter. And as a former employee, I know the behind-the-scene's secret of this restaurant's success. Her name is Savaria Schipani, but nobody calls her that. We just call her Mama.

You may never get the chance to meet this tireless 73-year-old Italian woman. Mama arrives early in the morning and leaves before lunch. In those hours she prepares the lasagna, the spaghetti sauce . . . and even finds time to bake the employees a rum cake. Yet no matter what Mama cooks, I always taste the same ingredient—care.

Besides having Mama in the kitchen, this restaurant also has another asset—a romantic decor. Giovanni's is filled with Old World charm. There's Venetian chairs, colorful murals of Italy, a terra cotta floor, hand-forged iron chandeliers, and a huge copper-hooded fireplace.

Just before this book went to press, I ran test No. 187—Mama-made lasagna. Good as ever. Mama's cooking is something I could eat day and night, and I realized there was only one sure way of doing that. But she said no. Mama keeps telling me I'm a nice boy, but I'm just a little too old to be adopted.

Menu Specialties: ☐ Baked Lasagna ☐ Veal Scallopine (thin, tender veal scallops sauteed with wine and fresh mushrooms.) ☐ Filet Mignon (a big steak—a full 2½-inch-thick cut of choice beef.) ☐ Pizza (a light hand-spun crust, a fresh, spicy sauce, and high quality Wisconsin mozzarella and Monterey Jack cheese—that's a Giovanni's pizza. My favorite topping? Sausage. Whenever the scale gives the slightest indication there's less of me than the week before, I get the urge to fill in this room to grow with Giovanni's sausage pizza.) Starters: Minestrone (a hearty soup packed with a garden of fresh vegetables); Combination Salad (a large tossed salad topped with artichoke hearts, salami, and cherry tomatoes. Try the house Italian dressing.) **Prices:** Inexpensive to medium. **Basics:** 2420 Shattuck Ave. (near Channing), Berkeley. Tel: 843-6678. Hours: 11 am-1 am Sun.-Thurs.; 11 am-2 am Fri., Sat. On Sunday, brunch is served from 11 am-3 pm. Cards: MC, V. Full bar.

La Mexicana: Oakland
Mexican/A family-run place that even makes tortillas by hand

No one would call the enchilada a fancy dish, but lately we've found it served in restaurants that dress themselves up in Latin plushorama. It's sort of like putting whipped cream on a hot dog. What's worse, these glossy places tend to use ready-made products, whereas a family-run restaurant like La Mexicana prepares their food the way it's made in a Yucatan village—by hand.

At La Mexicana, even the tortillas are made from scratch. A Mexican lady has been hired solely for this job. And she makes the tortillas just the way the Aztecs did over 600 years ago. She begins by pouring a sack of corn into a huge kettle of boiling water. When the corn is soft, she grinds it into a roughly-textured dough. Next, she places the course dough on a *metate,* a small stone table. Slowly, she smooths the dough out with a *mano*—a stone rolling pin. Now the dough is ready to be shaped into a tortilla and put on the grill. She grabs a handful of dough, dips it in water, and starts slapping the dough like she was James Cagney working over a member of a rival gang. You can hear this noise in the dining room, and it's a reliable indication that the main part of your enchilada is only a "wap" away from completion.

Menu Specialties: ☐ Enchilada al Horno (a thick, fresh, four star tortilla stuffed with homemade chorizo sausage. Topped with Monterey Jack cheese and a long-simmered crimson sauce—a sauce with the kind of deep, full flavor that results when "care" is part of the recipe. To sum it up, La Mexicana makes the best enchiladas in the Bay Area.) ☐ Chicken Enchilada (this one is filled with big, flavorful pieces of fresh chicken and topped with La Mexicana's fine sauce.) ☐ Chile Relleno (an 11-inch-long Anaheim pepper is stuffed with high quality Monterey Jack from the Cheese Factory in Pleasanton. Then it's dipped in egg batter and fried. Topped with a fresh, tasty tomato sauce.)

Dishes include: Spanish rice, refried beans, and two *made-minutes-ago* corn tortillas. **Prices:** Inexpensive. **Decor:** Four walls. Period. But the place is spotlessly clean and has a friendly, comfortable atmosphere. **Basics:** 3930 East 14th St. (near 39th Ave., about three-fourths of a mile from Montgomery Wards), Oakland. Tel: 532-9362. Hours: Noon-8 pm Wed.-Sun. Closed Mon., Tues. No cards. Beer only.

Emil Villa's: Oakland
Rod's Hickory Pit: El Cerrito
Barbecued Spareribs/Modest prices and homemade pies

See the two hands you're holding this book with? Rod's Hickory Pit and Emil Villa's want to put them to work. These two restaurants feature oak-barbecued spareribs, an item you just have to roll up your sleeves and attack with both hands.

When it comes to cooking spareribs, Emil Villa's and Rod's follow the old Southern method. This calls for the services of a seasoned veteran called a "pitman." Armed with a five-foot fork, the pitman carefully spears some spareribs from a tub of marinating spices and places the meat inside a brick barbecue pit filled with smoldering oak-wood logs. Clouds of smoke drift from the oakwood logs and sneak up to the ribs as quietly as a Kentucky sheriff approaching a moonshiner's still. Slowly, the fragrant oakwood smoke invades every fiber of the meat, coating the outside of the ribs with a thin, tasty, ebony crust.

When the pitman's trained eye tells him that the ribs are done, the meat is quickly pulled from the barbecue, sliced into a fan of succulent ribs, topped with a mild barbecue sauce, and delivered to your table along with a generous side of crisp French fries. And we guarantee when those meaty spareribs are set in front of you, your hands will reach for them at 60 m.p.h.

Another plus at Emil Villa's and Rod's is the prices. Very neighborly. Both places charge $4.50 for their sparerib platter. Why, at this price, you'll have enough change left to get one of the house's homemade pies. At Rod's, it could be a just-baked cherry pie, and at Emil Villa's it could be a fresh peach pie topped with an avalanche of whipped cream.

Emil Villa's: □ Oak-Barbecued Spareribs (the ribs are served with large, hand-cut French fries and toasted buns.) Dessert: Nine kinds of homemade pies are featured daily. When strawberries are in season, this is the place to be. Their 5-inch-high strawberry whipped cream pie is what homemade pies are all about. **Prices:** Inexpensive. **Decor:** A simple-looking, sun-lit dining room with counter service and a maze of wooden booths—each booth has a view of the "pitman" and his oak-wood barbecue pit. Note: Emil Villa's has fathered three other locations, but the sons don't quite compare with Dad. **Basics:** 4392 Telegraph Ave. (at 44th St.), Oakland. Tel: 654-0915. Hours: 11 am-8:45 pm daily. No cards. Wine and beer. Parking lot.

Rod's Hickory Pit: □ Oak-Barbecued Spareribs (the ribs are served with French fries and toasted sesame buns.) Dessert: Besides house-baked pies, Rod's also features an excellent chiffon-like cheesecake. **Prices:** Inexpensive. **Decor:** A well-lit place with comfortable booths and counter service. The restaurant has a sort of Fifties atmosphere. The Fonz would like it here. **Basics:** 11498 San Pablo Ave. (near Potrero, in the Golden Gate Lanes), El Cerrito. Tel: 234-3992. Hours: Open 24 hours a day, seven days a week. No cards. Full bar. Parking lot.

Fugetsu: Berkeley
Japanese/Relaxing Oriental setting

If you like Japanese food . . . oh, are you in luck. An ancient Japanese saying states that each time you eat sukiyaki, you'll live 75 days longer. If this saying is true, Fugetsu is the place to go. Their sukiyaki is the kind you'll enjoy having often. And we figure if you become a believer of this saying, you probably will be having it often. After all, eating sukiyaki has one advantage over a doctor's advice on how to live longer: it certainly is a lot easier than jogging.

Fugetsu also has other dishes worth ordering. The tempura, chicken teriyaki, and salmon misoyaki are all handled with skill. And Fugetsu serves them in an atmosphere as Japanese as the dishes themselves. Between the food and the decor, Fugetsu is a good all-round restaurant—especially when you're in the mood for three dozen orders of sukiyaki. Three dozen? Yes. How else are you going to live to be 162?

Menu Specialties: □ Chicken Sukiyaki (what an inventory! Tender nuggets of chicken breast, spinach, napa cabbage, fresh mushrooms, bamboo shoots, tofu bean cake, and Japanese noodles in a slightly sweet soy broth laced with sake rice wine.) □ Salmon Misoyaki (fresh broiled salmon brushed with a rich brown sauce flavored with 7 different spices imported from Japan.) □ Shrimp Tempura (shrimp and a garden of fresh vegetables dipped in an air-light Japanese batter and deep fried. Served with a tempura dipping sauce spiced with fresh ginger.) □ Chicken Teriyaki (moist, tender pieces of chicken covered with a dark, reddish brown teriyaki sauce that tastes 100% authentic and 100% good.)

Dinner includes: Miso bean soup, sunomono salad (bean sprouts and bay shrimp in a sweet Japanese vinaigrette), rice, and the owner's own blend of green tea. **Prices:** Medium. **Basics:** 1776 Shattuck Ave. (3½ blocks from University), Berkeley. Tel: 548-1776. Hours: 5-9:30 pm Tues.-Sat.; 5-9 pm Sun. Closed Mon. Cards: MC, V. Wine and beer.

Chez Daniel: Alameda
French/Small charm-filled bistro with small prices

How'd you like to trade places with restaurateur Daniel Pont? While you're trying to decide, maybe a description of Daniel's typical day would be helpful.

At 7 a.m. each morning Daniel Pont drives to the wharf area of San Francisco to select his fish. Then it's off to a small bakery in the Marina District to pick up his French bread. And by 9 a.m. Pont is on his way across the Bay Bridge. His destination is the Farmers market in Alameda. Once there, he starts walking around the displays of fruit and vegetables like he was an FBI agent searching for clues in an especially hard case. He spends about an hour at the market, and then he drives over to the butcher to get his meat.

Finally, around 11:15 a.m. he arrives at his restaurant. Daniel's next three hours are spent in the kitchen helping his chef—there are vegetables to cut, meats to trim, fish to bone, and sauces to stir. After everything is proceeding well, Daniel goes to the dining room. To relax? No, to set the tables.

By 4:55 p.m. Daniel is ready to greet his customers. He is dressed in a beautifully tailored European suit. For the next six hours Daniel will assume the role of a host and a waiter. He will also be required to be a diplomat and an accomplished mind reader.

Hopefully by 11 p.m. Daniel will be able to leave his small bistro. After all, he has to get up at 6 a.m. tomorrow morning. Oh, yes. If you'd like to trade places with Daniel Pont, just give him a call. He could probably use a vacation.

Along with everything else, Daniel also manages to keep his prices very reasonable. On a complete dinner with soup, salad, and dessert, filet of sole Grenobloise and chicken with tarragon sauce are both $6.00, and leg of lamb Maison is $6.50. And the dessert is usually a light, flaky apple tart. Which is appreciated. We were at a French restaurant recently where the pastries were so heavy, it took two strong men to lift a strawberry tart off the pastry tray and put it on our table.

Menu Specialties: □ Filet of Sole Grenobloise (English sole poached in white wine, clam juice, and herbs, and topped with a sauce of sweet butter and capers.) □ Chicken L'Estragon (tender, plump chicken in a light, fragrant tarragon-flavored sauce.) □ Lamb Maison (leg of lamb roasted with butter and garlic.) □ Scallops au Noilly (scallops sauteed in Noilly Prat vermouth with lemon and herbs.)

Dinner includes . . . 4 courses: Soup (maybe potato-leek or watercress soup), butter lettuce salad, main course with a fresh vegetable, and dessert. **Prices:** Inexpensive to medium. **Decor:** A romantic, ten-table dining room with a rose and a candle-lamp on each table. **Basics:** 2319 Central Ave. (near Park), Alameda. Tel: 522-7500. Hours: 5-9:30 pm Tues.-Sat. Closed Sun., Mon. Cards: MC, V. Wine and beer.

The Great
American Restaurant: Oakland
Homecooking/4-course dinners at anti-inflation prices

Kitchen recruitment

Once he's in the kitchen, this restaurant's chef is like a U.S. Army drill sergeant with a basic training company. Every day begins the same way. As soon as he arrives, the chef reviews what his assistant's selective service system has drafted for the Great American's menu. Like in the Army, the inductees come from all over—hams that were raised in the South; potatoes fresh from Idaho farms; some California surfer-types called clams, and a few scared recruits from Petaluma who admit being chicken. After taking a headcount, the chef barks out his orders.

"Attention, this is the duty roster for tonight. Hams will report for grill detail; clams will work together on the chowder brigade; chickens will be camouflaged with bread crumbs for pan-fried patrol; and potatoes are assigned to the mashing unit. Yeah, I know these are hard missions. But back home you had it easy. This is your chance to make something out of yourself. All right, now listen. When the clock reads 1900, I want you all to assemble on the tables in the dining room for field inspection by the customers. Okay, break rank and move out!"

The chef then hears a quivering voice, "Do you want to see us later tonight?"

The chef gives out a snarl, "No! In fact, I doubt if I'll ever see you again."

Menu Specialties: ☐ Ham Steak (an inch-thick slice of hickory-smoked ham grilled in butter and served with a flavorful Kentucky-style gravy.) ☐ Fried Chicken (fresh Petaluma chicken seasoned, breaded, and cooked according to an Arkansas recipe that's been in the chef's family for years.) ☐ The Daily Specials (Mon.—Yankee pot roast; Wed.—chicken 'n' dumplings; Thurs.—roast pork with cornbread stuffing; Sat.—roast leg of lamb.) Note: The Great American Restaurant has something that no customer ever gets tired of seeing—reasonable prices. The dishes we described above are $6.25 to $7.45 on the complete dinner. Dinner includes . . . 4 courses: Soup (maybe Boston clam chowder or split pea with ham), homemade honey bran muffins, tossed salad, main course with fresh vegetable and *real* mashed potatoes, and a just-baked, cobbler-like dessert called Apple Brown Betty. **Prices:** Inexpensive to medium. **Decor:** A friendly-looking place with captain's chairs and cream-colored walls hung with a collection of old-time hand-sewn quilts. The most interesting one dates back to the Thirties. This 7 × 5 foot quilt is made completely out of men's ties—it was put together by a prostitute during the Depression who used ties her clients absent-mindedly left behind. **Basics:** 5305 College Ave. (near Bryant), Oakland. Tel: 655-8780. Hours: 5-10 pm daily. Cards: MC, V. Wine and beer.

"You see, my friend, here at Le Marquis the chef really cares if the customers are enjoying the food."

At Le Marquis in Lafayette, there's a man with genuine concern in the kitchen

Chef-owner Robert Guerguy's cooking career started with an apprenticeship in the south of France. He was 15 years old. He then went on to cook at the "Summer" and "Winter" Casinos in Cannes, the Negresco Hotel in Nice, and a private club in the Bahamas, where the list of dinner guests included Brigitte Bardot and Queen Elizabeth. And all this experience has its advantages. Cooking is like making love—the more you do it, the better you get.

Chef Guerguy considers each of his dishes a personal statement. For example, his chicken Ma Facon comes with a rich brown sauce that's based on a stock Guerguy simmers a full 36 hours. And when he makes the sauce for his filet mignon, he uses an imported St. Emilion wine from the Bordeaux region of France. Then there's his Boudin aux Fruits de Mer. This is a Guerguy creation. You're served an air-light seafood quenelle studded with pieces of scallop, prawns, clams, and salmon in a sauce of sweet butter, white wine, lemon, and fresh sorrel.

The man in Le Marquis' kitchen is a true professional. For years, Chef Guerguy has even carried around his own set of knives. Of course, that's nothing. Once, in a tough section of Chicago, we found a restaurant that was really professional. Not only did the chef carry around his own set of knives, so did most of the customers.

Menu Specialties: □ Boudin aux Fruits de Mer □ Chicken Ma Facon (tender chicken crowned with a deeply-flavored sauce that's laced with fresh artichoke hearts, and black and green olives.) □ Filet of Beef St. Emilion (a thick filet mignon in a dark, classically prepared bordelaise sauce made with St. Emilion wine.) □ Salmon en Croute (encased in a light, flaky pastry crust is a filet of salmon on a bed of spinach. Served with a little pitcher of beurre blanc sauce that's the color of sunbeams.)

Dinner includes . . . 3 courses: Soup (maybe cream of asparagus or Guerguy's special almond soup), a butter lettuce salad, and main course with an elegant broccoli purée and fresh, sauteed carrots. **Prices:** Medium to a step above medium. **Decor:** In the dining room there's candlelit tables, plants in copper pots, and beautiful nineteenth century French prints. **Basics:** 3524 Mt. Diablo Blvd. (near 1st St.), Lafayette. Tel: 284-4422. Hours: 5:30-9:30 pm Tues.-Thurs., Sun.; 5:30-10:30 pm Fri., Sat. Closed Mon. Reservations suggested on weekends. Cards: MC, V. Wine and beer.

Marcello's: Orinda
Italian/Special 3-course dinners, romantic setting

Chef-owner Pierangelo Bigotti has made a special effort to create an attractive looking restaurant. In the softly-lit dining room, there are pale gold tablecloths, comfortable highback armchairs, chianti-red carpets, and paintings by Italian artists lining the wood-paneled walls. It's an inviting atmosphere. But what's more important, Bigotti realizes this isn't enough. Every night, Bigotti also makes a special effort in the kitchen.

Bigotti does everything he can to make his food good. He buys milk-fed veal. Grows some of his own herbs. Makes homemade pasta for his cannelloni. And after he puts the cannelloni in the oven, he constantly keeps his eye on it—Bigotti probably wishes he could sit in the oven and watch the cannelloni bake. But besides concern, Bigotti has something that's even more important. Bigotti has talent. It shows in the flavor of his prosciutto-stuffed breast of chicken, his golden-sauced prawns Medici, and his liqueur-rich Porcospino layer cake. And when a waiter puts a plate of Bigotti's homemade linguini and clams in front of you, the aroma alone could hypnotize.

Even the concept of Marcello's dinners shows special effort. On Marcello's 3-course dinner, instead of soup and salad, you're offered crab Fiorentina as a first course, and Bigotti's cannelloni as a second course. More work for the chef? Sure. But Pierangelo doesn't seem to mind the extra work. It's all part of his attitude. When Pierangelo Bigotti leaves the kitchen each night, you can be sure that he's given his restaurant 100 percent of his energy—which, contrary to what your employer might suggest, is all you can give.

Menu Specialties: □ Breast of Chicken Pier (a boneless chicken breast stuffed with prosciutto ham and Monterey Jack cheese, and seasoned with a quartet of Italian herbs, including sage and thyme from chef Bigotti's garden. Then topped with Bigotti's sherry-mushroom sauce.) □ Veal Scallopine (tender, milk-fed veal sauteed in Marsala wine with shallots, rosemary, and fresh mushrooms until a flavorful sauce results.) □ Scampi a la Medici (for this dish, Bigotti uses special Icelandic prawns—these shellfish have a sweet, delicate flavor somewhat similar to lobster meat. The prawns are served in a golden sauce of butter, dry sauterne, fresh garlic, and lemon juice.) □ Veal Saltimbocca Romana (veal scallops topped with paper-thin slices of prosciutto ham and melted Teleme cheese from Sonoma, and framed in a fragrant brown sauce that tastes as rich as it looks.)

Dinner includes . . . 3 courses: Crab Fiorentina (Dungeness crab topped with a blend of Italian herbs, bread crumbs, and parmesan cheese, and served in a scallop shell), cannelloni Romana (homemade pasta wrapped around a fine veal and chicken stuffing, and topped with Monterey Jack cheese, bechamel sauce, and some marinara sauce), main course with fresh vegetables sauteed Italian style, and coffee.

If you want to center your dinner around pasta: □ Linguini a la Vongole (one of the best versions of linguini and clams we've had. Chef Bigotti takes imported baby clams and sautes them in olive oil with herbs, shallots, white wine, and fresh garlic. Then he adds some of his homemade linguini pasta and tosses everything together. Sound simple to make? It isn't. Unless the ingredients are flawlessly combined and the chef's timing is perfect, the dish won't come out right. Recipes don't really help much in cooking linguini and clams. You just have to *know*. Bigotti knows.)

Dessert: Porcospino (a spongecake flavored with a mixture of expresso and seven liqueurs, including Kahlua and Mescollanza, and topped with a thick, fudge-like frosting.) **Prices:** Medium. **Basics:** 1 Orinda Way (near the intersection of Camino Pablo and Santa Maria Way, close to the Orinda exit off Highway 24), Orinda. Tel: 254-5433. Hours: 11 am-2 pm, 5-10:30 pm Mon.-Fri.; 5:30-10:30 pm Sat. Closed Sun. Reservations necessary. Cards: MC, V. Full bar. Parking lot.

La Paz: Moraga
Latin American/In the dining room, a piano-playing host

Mr. Castro Ascarrunz . . . please stand up. We've decided not to tell the people about your restaurant. Instead, we're going to let you do it.

"I'll try. Standing here like this makes me feel a little n-n-nervous. Maybe a glass of water . . . ahhh, you've put sangría in the water pitcher . . . carumba! Strong stuff. Tastes like someone's doing a flamenco dance on my tongue. Ah, yes, now I feel better."

"Okay, let me start with my background. I'm from Bolivia. My father owned a small hotel near the tin mines of Uncía. When I was six, he put me to work in the hotel's dining room. Later, my father went on to become a Bolivian congressman, and I went on to earn two Bachelor's degrees and one Master's degree. But over the years, I've learned that my real interest lies in the restaurant business."

"At La Paz, I do everything—oversee the kitchen, greet customers, wait on tables, pour wine, and whenever I can, I play the piano in the dining room and sing Bolivian love songs."

"By the way, how do you like my place? The pottery on the shelves comes from South America, the tapestries are from Mexico, and those hand-crafted tin plates over there are from my own country, Bolivia. The candlelight is also my idea—a touch of romance, that is good for a dining room. But no, my amigos, I don't forget. You come to eat. And I have many things to offer. My food is Latin American. I feature crab enchiladas, steak in a South American wine sauce, and prawns Criollos simmered with fresh tomatoes, green peppers, mushrooms, and sherry."

"I try to give my customers as much as I can. Each dinner includes a papaya appetizer, a bowl of Bolivian mountain barley soup, and a large salad. But more important, I try to bring my customers happiness. How? Easy, by keeping my prices down."

Menu Specialties: □ Prawns Criollos □ Crab Enchiladas (the enchiladas are stuffed with Dungeness crab and two cheeses—Monterey Jack and Mexican Cotica cheese. Topped with sour cream and a mild, oregano-seasoned red sauce.) □ Steak La Paz (a broiled filet mignon topped with a South American sauce made with tomatoes, sherry, and mushrooms.) □ Torta (a layered creation made with beef, guacamole, Monterey Jack cheese, and a fresh red sauce.)
Dinner includes . . . 4 courses: Fresh fruit appetizer, Bolivian mountain barley soup, salad, main course with two vegetables, and coffee. **Prices:** Inexpensive to medium. **Basics:** 360 Park St. (near the intersection of Rheem Blvd. and Moraga Rd.), Moraga. Tel: 376-2452. Hours: 5:30-10 pm Wed.-Sun. Closed Mon., Tues. Reservations suggested on weekends. Cards: MC, V. Full bar.

Believe It? or Don't!

Well known bad check artist, Ollie Kugel, once DISGUISED HIMSELF AS A DUCK in an attempt to pass a bum check for his meal at the **MANDARIN VILLAGE** Restaurant.

好食

ANSLEY

Baron Sigfried - in order to get a free dinner from the **MANDARIN VILLAGE** Restaurant - ALLOWED HIMSELF TO BE SHOT 155 FEET FROM A CANNON

Irving Seymour Dove never learned to fly and was FORCED TO HITCH HIKE every time he felt like going to the **MANDARIN VILLAGE** for dinner.

EGAD! KAFF KAFF

Mandarin Village's Specialties: ☐ Mongolian Barbecued Beef (slices of choice beef kept for six hours in a garlic and ginger flavored marinade, then put in a very hot wok and quickly stir-fried for the proper amount of time by a cook who understands, as the Chinese say, "huo-huo," or fire-timing.) ☐ Princess Chicken (boneless pieces of chicken marinated in mild spices, lightly rolled in water chestnut flour, deep-fried, and finally toss-cooked with snow peas and cloud ear mushrooms.) □ Manchurian Beef (beef slices dusted with Chinese Five Spice powder and stir-fried in a rich Chinese wine sauce until the sauce gently clings to each slice of beef.)

□ Sizzling Rice Shrimp (a dish that talks back. At the table, your waiter pours a mixture of moist shrimp and peas in wine sauce over a platter of sizzling hot, deep-fried rice cakes, causing the dish to go "ssssssss.") □ General Tso Chicken (pieces of tender chicken breast stir-fried in a Szechwanese sauce that's seasoned with homemade red pepper paste. But have no fear. The chef strictly follows an ancient bit of Chinese cooking wisdom: the purpose of hot spices are to stimulate the palate, not paralyze it.) **Prices:** Inexpensive to medium. **Decor:** A light, airy room with gold tablecloths, red cloth napkins, and bamboo-patterned wallpaper. **Basics:** 3594 Mt. Diablo Blvd. (near Moraga Rd.), Lafayette. Tel: 283-2141. Hours: 4:30-9:30 pm daily. Cards: MC, V. No alcohol (customers are permitted to bring in their own wine and beer).

Barbacoa Chajonju: Castro Valley
Barbecue/Two proud hard-working ladies in the kitchen

This is the Castro Valley-Hayward area's premier barbecue establishment. They top their spareribs and chicken with the kind of barbecue sauce that's good enough to start a conversation. The sauce contains 20 different ingredients, including tomatoes, onions, and garlic that owner Nathel Buford grows herself. It takes 30 minutes just to blend the ingredients together, and another three hours to simmer the sauce.

But Nathel usually doesn't get involved in this process. The lady who actually makes the sauce is Mrs. Buford's mother, Dorothy Glover. She also makes homemade sweet potato pie for the restaurant. Mrs. Glover says she uses a simple, classic recipe for the pie, but as far as the barbecue sauce is concerned, that's her "secret." All we're allowed to say is that you take two cups of—"beep"—blend in one ounce of—"beep"—then you . . .

Menu Specialties: □ Barbecued Spareribs □ Barbecued Chicken (both are cooked in a gas oven over hickory chips and served with Mrs. Glover's barbecue sauce.) Dishes include potato salad and barbecued beans. Dessert: Sweet potato pie. **Prices:** Inexpensive. **Decor:** A small cottage-like building with a homey, comfortable dining room. **Basics:** 20669 Santa Maria Ave. (at Castro Valley Blvd.), Castro Valley. Tel: 581-2961. Hours: 5-10 pm Sun.-Thurs.; 5-11 pm Fri., Sat. Closed Mon. Cards: MC, V. Wine and beer. Parking lot in back.

Loreto's: Danville
Italian/An inviting, family-run pasta house

Loreto's is a unique restaurant. It not only has six kinds of homemade pasta . . . it even has a pasta machine that's homemade.

Assunta DiLoreto, a hard-working woman from a small village outside Rome, made pasta by hand until she was 71. And she taught her son, Loreto DiLoreto, everything she knew. What did Loreto do after learning this skill? He became a general contractor and opened a machine shop in San Leandro. But then one day, years later, Loreto experienced the "aha!" phenomenon. His idea was to take what his mother had taught him about making pasta and adapt it to modern technology. Loreto built himself a pasta machine.

It took Loreto 9 months to make the machine. The result was a counter-sized, stainless steel machine that's so original, there's a patent pending. But more important, when it was finished, Loreto, his wife Mary, and his son Tony, opened a pasta house.

We enjoy Loreto's homemade pasta. Maybe a little too much. Sometimes we eat our pasta so fast, they're probably thinking about putting racing stripes on our forks. But at Loreto's, it's easy to get carried away. There are fresh tagliatelle egg noodles crowned with Mrs. DiLoreto's meat-thick, herb-fragrant Bolognese tomato sauce; giant two-inch-wide ravioli bulging with a rich ricotta cheese stuffing; and baked lasagna layered with two sauces, two cheeses, and bits of Italian sausage. And even the sausage is made at the restaurant. Sure, it's a lot of extra work. But when the DiLoreto family took the Homemade Oath, they meant it.

Menu Specialties: ☐ Tagliatelle Bolognese ☐ Ravioli ☐ Baked Lasagna ☐ Fettucine Alfredo (egg-rich noodles tossed in an elegant blend of butter, cream, and freshly-grated parmesan cheese.) ☐ Tagliarini with Tomato Sauce (Italian pear-shaped tomatoes and a pot full of secrets are simmered for 8 hours, and then an honest ladle of this sauce is used to top Mr. DiLoreto's "made-today" tagliarini pasta.) ☐ Cannelloni (Mary DiLoreto takes thin sheets of pasta, rolls them around a tasty, herb-seasoned meat stuffing, tops the dish with some of her red sauce, a little of her white sauce, a layer of freshly-grated Monterey Jack cheese, and then bakes the dish in the oven.)
Starters: Salad Loreto (crisp greens well-tossed in a fine dressing that's made with olive oil, red wine vinegar, and ten different herbs.)
Prices: Inexpensive. **Decor:** A friendly-looking place with white stucco walls trimmed with wood, a modern wall-type fireplace, and flower-print tablecloths in the colors of the Italian flag—green, white, and red.
Basics: 426 Diablo Rd. (in the Green Valley Shopping Center, near the Diablo Rd. exit off Highway 680), Danville. Tel: 820-1711. Hours: 11:30 am-2:30 pm, 5-11 pm Tues.-Fri.; 5:30-11 pm Sat.; 4-9 pm Sun. Closed Mon. Cards: MC, V. Full bar.

Oscar's Bistro: Hayward
Continental/4-course dinners in a white cottage

Our initial visit to a restaurant sometimes requires that we have the optimism of a Hollywood agent. Basically, we're food talent scouts—always checking out tips we get in hopes of making a "real discovery." It was this kind of search that brought us to Hayward, not exactly a dining mecca. There we found Oscar's Bistro.

From the outside, Oscar's looks like the type of plain-looking cottage that John Steinbeck described in *East of Eden*. Inside, however, it turned out to have a Continental decor, white tablecloths, and waiters in tuxedos. Still, the big surprise came when we ordered dinner. First we received a crisp butter lettuce salad. Immediately, its dressing announced that a huge cast of herbs were used in the production. Then came a dish of tagliarini noodles with a buttery clam sauce. It sang with flavor.

Finally, the veal Farci arrived—a plate of near white veal stuffed with a blend of romano, Monterey, and parmesan cheese, finely chopped spinach, and sausage. A great act. We could just picture Humphrey Bogart sitting there in a clay-colored trench coat, looking at the veal with his classic tough-guy squint, and asking, "Say, what's a dish like you doing in a place like this?"

Menu Specialties: ☐ Veal Farci (stuffed veal served with a dark brown sauce made from fresh mushrooms, butter, and burgundy wine.) ☐ Tournedos Sautees Champignons (two center-cut filet mignons sauteed in butter, smothered with mushrooms, and topped with a rich, golden yellow bearnaise sauce.) ☐ Chicken Dijonnaise (a panorama of flavors results when the chef sautes a tender, boned breast of chicken in sherry, brandy, shallots, Dijon mustard, and bits of ham.) ☐ Lobster Thermidor (tender lobster meat sauteed with butter, mushrooms, cream, and brandy. Then baked in a natural bowl—the lobster's bright red shell.)

Dinner includes . . . 4 courses: A tossed salad (butter lettuce, homemade croutons, and scallions in an olive oil and vinegar dressing flavored with 15 herbs), tagliarini in a tasty clam sauce, main course with two vegetables (maybe scalloped potatoes in a Wisconsin cheddar cheese sauce, and stuffed zucchini), and French cognac pudding. **Prices:** Medium to a step above medium. **Basics:** 21181 Foothill Blvd. (near Mattox), Hayward. Tel: 538-3522. Hours: 6-9:30 pm Tues.-Thurs.; 6-10:30 pm Fri., Sat. Closed Sun., Mon. Reservations necessary on weekends. Cards: AE, MC, V. Wine and beer. Parking lot.

Banchero's: Hayward
Italian/Huge, multi-course meals at prices that amaze

Mr. Banchero is a price magician—this gentleman features meals with "How does he do it?" prices. At his restaurant, Mr. Banchero can make a 6-course dinner appear on your table for $4.10.

As soon as you're seated at Banchero's, a waitress will quickly take your order and leave to get your first course. Seconds later . . . she's back! It's as if someone had shot her out of the kitchen with a catapult. The lady knows you're hungry. She'll be bringing you a huge tureen of soup and a basket stacked with sourdough. Next, she'll give you a large bowl of salad in an Italian dressing, and an appetizer tray filled with two kinds of salami, black and green olives, pepperoncini, marinated vegetables, and anchovies.

Ah, look! Here comes the waitress again with a dish of spaghetti and ravioli. The main course? No, just a little something to get you ready for the main course. She'll be back later with a platter of chicken cacciatora, fresh zucchini, and roasted potatoes. After that, she'll bring you some tangerine sherbet and coffee.

Would you like to know how Banchero's manages to serve a 6-course dinner for $4.10? So would we.

Menu Specialties: ☐ Chicken Cacciatora (chicken in a wine-flavored tomato sauce laced with bell peppers, onions, and black olives.) ☐ New York Steak or Rib Eye Steak (the price magician is at work here, too. Both steak dinners are just $5.40.)

Dinner includes . . . 6 courses: Soup, salad, a six-item appetizer tray, two pastas, main course with fresh vegetable and potatoes, coffee, and dessert. Note: The kitchen isn't sinless . . . occasionally a course or two may take a downhill turn. But at these prices, it's easy to forgive. **Prices:** Inexpensive. **Decor:** A big, plain-looking place with booths upholstered in Army-tan vinyl. But it's a comfortable dining room with a friendly staff. **Basics:** 20102 Mission Blvd. (near East Lewelling), Hayward. Tel: 276-7355. Hours: 4-9 pm Tues.-Thurs.; 4-9:30 pm Fri., Sat.; 1-9 pm Sun. Closed Mon. No cards. Full bar. Parking lot.

Broiler Fish House: San Pablo
Seafood/Net gains for a small investment

Time magazine reported that during the peak of the 1973 beef shortage, President Nixon rose from a seafood dinner at a Florida restaurant and paused next to a customer who was deliberating over the various expensive meats on the menu. Nixon leaned over like he was going into a huddle with the Washington Redskins and advised: "It's patriotic to eat fish."

Although most people remember Nixon's Watergate quotes, this is the one chef Louis Iribarne remembers best. Right after Nixon made this statement, a wave of "patriotic" eaters flooded Louis' seafood restaurant.

Many of these people became regular customers. They discovered Louis Iribarne is a man who gives his seafood special attention. Louis stuffs the turbot with deviled crab, prepares a cioppino that would earn him the respect of any Italian fisherman, and bakes his sea bass in so much wine, they shouldn't let minors order the dish. Louis even gives his Boston clam chowder a flavor boost by using live Little Necks from Discovery Bay, Washington. But Louis doesn't charge a lot for this special attention: the chowder is 75¢ and most of Louis' dinners are in the $5.50 to $6.50 range.

The Broiler Fish House is always filled with regulars, and we're positive it's the cooking and the prices that attracts them. Customers certainly don't come here for the atmosphere. The only atmosphere at the Broiler Fish House is the kind that's 20% oxygen and 80% nitrogen.

Menu Specialties: □ Filet of Turbot (between two white filet strips is a tasty stuffing of deviled crab. Baked in butter and wine.) □ Sea Bass, Creole Style (baked in a sauce of tomatoes, green peppers, mushrooms, and white wine.) □ Swordfish, Salmon, Halibut (all three are simply broiled, allowing their delicate flavor to be gently coaxed out by the basic combination of fish and fire.)

□ Crab Cioppino (you're served a bowl almost the size of the Houston Astrodome. Inside the bowl: a spicy Italian tomato sauce, some Pacific clams, and lots of fresh Dungeness crab in shell. The waitress ties a bib around your neck and you . . . plunge in! Only served Mon.-Thurs.) □ Eastern Pearl Scallops (the scallops are dipped in a bread crumb batter and then deep fried to a golden brown.)

Dinner includes: A romaine, chicory, and garbanzo bean salad with special house dressing, hot rolls, and main course with Basque rice or a moist baked potato. Starters: Boston clam chowder. **Prices:** Inexpensive to medium. **Basics:** 13740 San Pablo Ave. (about half a mile from the intersection of San Pablo Dam Rd. and San Pablo Ave.), San Pablo. Tel: 234-9665. Hours: 4-11 pm Mon.-Sat.; 3-10 pm Sun. Cards: MC, V. Full bar. Parking lot.

Juanita's: Vallejo
Prime rib, 2½ lbs. an order/The hostess, a legend in progress

Juanita has the body of Mother Goose, the personality of Mae West, and the voice of an Army drill sergeant. This combination has made her eligible for a unique occupation—the job of being a character. And she's good at it. This lady is what restaurant legends are made of.

Juanita had a definite reason for opening a restaurant. "I love catering to men," she told us, "and the only way I can do it legally is feed 'em." And Juanita does it right. She serves a 2½ pound cut of prime rib for dinner. "And honey, that ain't all," Juanita always reminds us. Dinner also includes a buffet—a giant spread of stuffed eggs, olives, ten different salads, three kinds of fruit, hot muffins, and country ham. With Juanita around, the plenty never ceases.

When Juanita isn't looking after the buffet, she can usually be found walking around the dining room in a volcanic-red Hawaiian muumuu. She shifts among the tables, always talking, constantly laughing, and occasionally firing off a smoking hot salvo of four-letter words. But this never shocks anyone. Or fools them, either. Everyone knows that Juanita is about as tough as cotton candy. Yes, Juanita is special. And that's why everybody likes her. A whole lot.

The locations of Juanita's restaurants have always been as unusual as the woman herself. She's served dinners on a dry-docked Sausalito ferryboat, an El Verano chicken farm, and when she ran the Fetters Hotel, she even served dinners *in her bedroom*. When Juanita said, "Come and get it," you had to think twice.

Juanita's latest restaurant is located in a two-story Victorian house that was built in 1898. Inside, the dining room has been filled with Juanita's amazing collection of antiques. And it looks like Juanita's here to stay. She recently told us, "Honey, this shack and me are permanent partners." And when Juanita said that, her voice was so loud, the ashtrays started to dance.

The Menu: ☐ The Prime Rib—a full 2½ pound cut of meat. ☐ The Dinner for Two: A couple can first visit the buffet and then share one of those huge cuts of prime rib.

146

Dinner includes . . . the 20-item buffet: On the first pass, you can weigh down your plate with a spicy tomato and zucchini salad, some Swiss cheese, black olives, and a slice-it-yourself piece of country ham. On the second pass, you might try a scoop of fresh potato salad, peaches, some marinated red beans and onions, cheddar cheese, and a tossed green salad topped with Juanita's blue cheese dressing. On the third pass . . . well, you get the idea.

Buffet Fans, Take Note: The buffet is available separately if this is where you want to center your attention. **Prices:** A wide range, so we'll quote the prices here. The 2½ pound Prime Rib Dinner including the buffet, $12.95. The Dinner for Two (one 2½ pound cut of prime rib plus buffet privileges for two), $9 per person. The Buffet by itself, $6. **Basics:** 437 Virginia St. (near Sonoma), Vallejo. Tel: (707) 553-1666. Hours: 6 am-11 pm daily. Cards: MC, V. Full bar.

Washington House Cafe: Benicia
Homemade Lunches/Located in a 139-year-old hotel

During the Thirties, there were so many prostitutes in Benicia, some say that they used to walk around the town's main street with mattresses on their backs. The town's hookers even paid for the municipal swimming pool. And the center of activity during this period was an ancient gabled structure built in 1840 called the Washington Hotel. Later, in 1950, the prostitutes were railroaded out of town by a Bible-quoting sheriff who was determined to clean up Benicia's moral landscape. The sheriff boarded up the hotel, and for the next 18 years, this sexual amusement park lay vacant.

In 1968, two women reopened the Washington Hotel; only this time around, the ladies were there strictly to demonstrate their kitchen skills. And there is indisputable proof that they are very good cooks. Business is even better now than before.

Menu Specialties: □ Open wide and meet the Washington Cafe's sandwiches: Baked crab and melted Monterey Jack cheese on a French roll, $3.95; Sonoma Valley cheddar cheese and bacon on black rye, $2.45; sliced turkey and imported Finnish cheese on sourdough bread spread with Russian dressing, $2.65. All sandwiches include a salad and a 3-fruit garnish. □ Fruit Salad (on a green lawn of romaine are sliced bananas, strawberries, apples, papayas, pineapple, and an igloo of rainbow sherbet. Topped with a honey-lemon dressing . . . yes, a salad gone Hollywood.), $2.75. Attention Early Californians: Sunday brunch is served. End the weekend with blueberry walnut waffles, papaya juice, bacon, and Italian roast coffee. **Basics:** 333 1st St. (at D St.), Benicia. Tel: (707) 745-9908. Hours: 11 am-6 pm Fri.-Sun. Closed Mon.-Thurs. Cards: MC, V. Beer only.

Short Takes

Fat Albert's
Thick hamburgers and the best apple pie in the East Bay

Some restaurant owners try to do a few things right. But not Fat Albert. He tries to do everything right. Fat Albert grinds his own hamburger, and bakes his own homemade buns. And when he puts one of those thick hamburger patties on the broiler, he treats it like it was a ten dollar steak. His menu states, "If it's not right, do me a favor . . . send it back!" Hamburger, $1.75.

Fat Albert's also has some other assets: great homemade soup (maybe black bean and ham), 60¢; totally greaseless, crisp French fries made from fresh potatoes, 60¢ an order (enough for two people); and an American classic—fresh homemade apple pie, a huge hunk, 90¢. How good is the apple pie? After the first bite, you hear drums and flutes. After the second bite, you see Washington crossing the Delaware.

Basics: 1346 Grove St. (at Rose), Berkeley. Tel: 526-2260. Hours: 7 am-11 pm daily. Wine and beer.

Genova
The best Italian delicatessen in the East Bay

Genova is stocked from floor to ceiling with Italian goods. The walls look like they're made out of olive oil cans. And behind the deli case, there's an A-Z assortment of Italian luncheon items from antipasto to Zampino sausage.

For starters, try a sandwich. Grab a sourdough roll from one of Genova's bread bins, and say to the counterman, "Fill it up." Suddenly the counterman starts handling stacks of salami and mozzarella like he was a blackjack dealer in Reno. Zip, zip, zip. A thick deck of Italian meats and cheeses forms on your roll. The counterman then gives you this "custom-dealt" sandwich and you give him $1.50. Also, you might ask the man for some Antipasto (a mixture of six fresh, crisp vegetables in a spicy red dressing), ½ pint, 99¢; or a slice of artichoke torta (an Italian vegetable pie), 50¢. Take-out only.

Basics: 4937 Telegraph Ave. (near 50th St., next to Vern's super-market), Oakland. Tel: 652-7401. Hours: 9 am-6:30 pm Mon.-Sat.; 8 am-5 pm Sun. Wine and beer.

Nordic House
Scandinavian deli offering 18-item smorgasbord lunches

In the back of this delicatessen there's a bright, homey-looking lunch room that features our favorite kind of amusement—a meal that's a roller coaster ride of flavors. For $3.15, the Nordic's 18-item smorgasbord includes Danish Havarti cheese, thinly sliced ham, Norwegian flatbread, a lettuce salad with real Danish blue cheese dressing, smoked sausage, sour cream potato salad, Scandinavian pickle relish, Danish paté, Finnish biscuits, and asparagus and pea salad. And for your main course, try the Swedish meatballs and lingonberries.

Basics: 3421 Telegraph Ave. (near 34th St.), Oakland. Tel: 653-3882. Hours: 11 am-3 pm Mon.-Fri. for lunch (deli: 9 am-5 pm Mon.-Sat.). Closed Sun. Wine and beer. Parking lot in back.

McCallum's
The best ice cream parlor in the East Bay

It's said that Americans eat enough ice cream each year to fill the Grand Canyon. Would you like to help America reach the canyon rim early this year? Then go to McCallum's and order their butter pecan. Once you start eating McCallum's butter pecan, it's hard to stop. This may be the best ice cream in California. And that isn't just our opinion. McCallum's butter pecan (75¢) has won the gold medal at the California State Fair for the last 20 years.

Of course, there are some other reasons to visit McCallum's—like their port-spiked Bordeaux cherry ice cream (50¢), and their frozen berry ice (50¢). And then there's McCallum's sundaes. We always order the caramel-marshmallow ($1.50), or the hot fudge sundae avalanched with real whipped cream ($1.50). These sundaes even save us money. They're so rich, we usually spend the next day on a very strict diet—air.

Basics: 1825 Solano Ave. (near Colusa), Berkeley. Tel: 525-3510. Hours: 11 am-11 pm Sun.-Thurs.; 10 am-midnight Fri., Sat.

Curds & Whey Deli:
A place with 46 different sandwiches to choose from

This establishment has a you-name-it selection of quality sandwich ingredients: German salami, smoked turkey, Russian bologna, Pennsylvania Dutch bologna, Norwegian Noekkelost cheese, Thuringer sausage, homemade herb-cream cheese, and more. In total, 46 made-to-order sandwiches are available ($1.50-$1.70). And each sandwich comes with lettuce, fresh sliced tomatoes, spiced mayonnaise, and your

149

choice of seven kinds of bread and rolls. But that's not all. This deli also features French potato salad (½ pint, 75¢) and Egyptian eggplant salad (½ pint, 95¢). Well, well . . . a delicatessen with Russian, German, American, and Middle Eastern items in the same display case. Can world peace be far behind? Take-out only.

Basics: 6311 College Ave. (near Claremont), Oakland. Tel: 652-6311. Hours: 10 am-6 pm Mon.-Sat. Closed Sun. Wine and beer.

Granata's
Hand-spun pizza topped with house-made Italian sausage

Granata's is located in an out-of-the-way, half-residential, half-industrial neighborhood, and the interior, although filled with plenty of comfortable booths, has a plain 1950 feel. So you wonder: "What brings people here?" Then the pizza arrives, and after your first slice you stop wondering. You'd be happy eating this kind of pizza in a small, dark closet. Granata's hand-spun pizzas have a fresh, authentic Italian flavor. You tell yourself, "Yeah, this is what pizza is supposed to taste like."

Pizza topped with Granata's house-made Italian sausage: small, $2.45; medium, $3.85; large, $4.40. Or for about the same price, you can have your pizza topped with either salami, pepperoni, mushrooms, black olives, or a very tasty linguica sausage.

Basics: 2730 9th St. (at Pardee—take San Pablo Ave. to Pardee and turn toward the bay), Berkeley. Tel: 845-9571. Hours: 11:30 am-3 pm Tues.-Fri.; 4-10 pm Tues.-Thurs., Sun.; 4-midnight Fri., Sat. Closed Mon. Cards: MC, V. Full bar. Parking lot.

Yorkshire
The best fish & chips in the East Bay

The fish & chips at the Yorkshire are prepared by a cheery English lady who calls everyone "Luv." And it's not just her accent that's authentic. The owner's family operated a fish & chips shop in Yorkshire, England for 25 years, and the recipe they used all those years has successfully made the transition from Great Britain to "the Colonies." At this tiny, twelve-seat Berkeley shop, you're served moist, flaky filets of Icelandic whitefish jacketed in a golden crust that's perfectly light and crisp. Fish & chips, $1.70. Along with your order try a Schweppe's ginger beer, 40¢.

Basics: 1984 Shattuck Ave. (near University), Berkeley. Tel: 841-7743. Hours: 11 am-9 pm Mon.-Sat. Closed Sun.

G.B. Ratto International Grocer
Custom-made sandwiches and after lunch a world tour

G.B. Ratto is located in a time-buffed Victorian building. Inside, there's a huge sunlit dining room, international flags, 25 tables with checkered tablecloths, and a display case filled with quality luncheon meats and cheeses—including excellent wine-cured salami.

The Weigh-In: When you reach the display case, the counterman grabs a crusty sourdough roll and asks you how you'd like it landscaped. A typical answer: "I'll take a slice of coppa ham, two slices of provolone cheese, and six slices of that great salami. No, make it eight. Ah, better make it ten. Well . . . " The counterman then takes the meats and cheeses you've ordered and weighs them. A generously stacked sandwich is about $1.50. With your sandwich? Try a Brazilian guarana fruit soda pop, 50¢. Good stuff.

Food Disneyland: After lunch, take a stroll through the grocery section. Fascinating! There are 80 kinds of cheese, 110 different spices, 30 kinds of imported pasta, 6 kinds of olives, Portuguese fava beans, Scottish kippers, African palm oil, and even Greek chewing gum. And you might get to meet the Egyptian consul. He shops here.

Basics: 821 Washington St. (at 9th St.), Oakland. Tel: 832-6503. Hours: 11 am-2 pm Mon.-Fri. for lunch (grocery store: 8 am-5 pm Mon.-Sat.). Closed Sun. Wine and beer. Parking lot.

Cocolat
The best pastry shop in the East Bay

After being trained in the art of pastry-making in Paris, Alice Medrich spent a couple of years baking for a food specialty house in Berkeley. Then, she decided to open her own French pastry shop. Alice found a location on Shattuck Avenue in Berkeley, and at 9:01 a.m., on December 5, 1976, she opened for business. By noon, every pastry in the place had been sold. When a pastry chef is as talented as Alice, word gets around fast.

Gateau Diabolo (a fantastically rich chocolate-almond cake with a creamy chocolate center. Topped with pure whipped cream.) *Noisettine* (a cognac-flavored French butter spongecake with three layers of coffee-buttercream laced with toasted hazelnuts.) *Helene* (an air-light genoise cake flavored with Myer's rum and hand-squeezed orange juice, and layered with homemade apricot preserves, coconut, and whipped cream.) All cakes are $1.00 a slice. No question—Alice is a major West Coast distributor of calories. Take-out only.

Basics: 1481 Shattuck Ave. (near Vine), Berkeley. Tel: 843-3265. Hours: 10 am-6 pm Tues.-Sat. Closed Sun., Mon.

Chris'
The best hot dogs in the East Bay

In 1935, Chris' had their hot dogs made especially for them by a small local supplier. And today, this same supplier is still making hot dogs for Chris'. The hot dogs (95¢) are juicy, eight-inch-long, Coney Island-style dogs that are packed with honest old-fashioned flavor. Also, between your hot dog and the bun, Chris' puts three just-sliced tomato wedges, some chopped onions, relish, and a specially blended mustard.

Over the years Chris' hot dogs have made a lot of friends. Including Clint Eastwood. According to owner Connie Foster, he stops by when he's in the area. Mr. Eastwood, did you ever think about using this place in a *Dirty Harry* movie? What a scene: a stripped-down green Ford crashes through Chris' front wall. Dirty Harry gets out of the car, gives the counterman his steely-eyed look and says, "Sorry, buddy, I thought this was a drive-in." Harry then . . .

Basics: 4366 Broadway (near Mather), Oakland. Tel: 652-9538. Hours: 9 am-1 am daily. Parking lot.

Mama's Royal Cafe
Light, fluffy three-egg omelets and great coffee

Mama's offers 18 kinds of omelets, including a ham and New York cheddar cheese omelet ($3.25), mushroom and tomato omelet ($3.20), and bacon and Monterey Jack cheese omelet ($3.20). For escorts, the omelets come with a four-fruit garnish (sometimes even mango or papaya), raisin-nut toast, and home fries cooked with fresh tomato bits and green onions, and topped with sour cream. The coffee (35¢) is a great Columbian-French roast and it's served with pure whipping cream. The setting? A former 1940-style chop suey cafe with its pagoda-style trim still intact. And for breakfast music there's FM rock. No, places like Mama's don't just happen—California creates them.

Basics: 4012 Broadway (near 40th St.), Oakland. Tel: 547-9561. Hours: 8 am-9 pm Tues.-Fri.; 9 am-9 pm Sat.; 9 am-3 pm Sun. Closed Mon. Wine and beer.

Mary B. Best
Homemade ice cream in a variety of unique flavors

This is an ice cream shop with a Hollywood touch—they feature flavors in Technicolor. Although their flavors rotate, you might find Buena Vista coffee ice cream laced with Irish whiskey, West Indian papaya sherbet, brandied apricot ice cream, strawberries Romanoff ice cream spiked with orange liqueur, or a Jamaican banana ice cream studded with bits of mango and coconut. Yes, Mary B. Best is offering something all of us occasionally need: a 67¢ thrill. That's what a big scoop of ice cream costs here.

Basics: 3794 Grand Ave. (near Boulevard Way), Oakland. Tel: 451-6059. Hours: 12:30-8:30 pm Tues.-Sat.; 12:30-5:30 pm Sun. Closed Mon.

Roaring Camp Cafe
Imaginative lunch specialties and flavor-packed soups

After you've finished one of owner Tari Bowman's lunches, you'll look at her and yell a four-letter word—"good!" Poker Flat (a puff pastry turnover stuffed with Italian sausage, ground beef, and mushrooms, and topped with a Swiss cheese sauce), $4.25. Chutneyed Chicken (a slice of squaw bread is the foundation for a mixture of chicken, grapes, and walnuts that's topped with a rich curry sauce and melted Jack cheese. Served with homemade peach-pineapple chutney.), $3.75. Both dishes come with salad.

Soup and Salad Combination (Tari's soups are masterworks: depending on the day, maybe spinach-clam soup, cheddar cheese-leek soup, or cream of artichoke with sherry. Served with a fresh salad tossed in the house green goddess dressing.), $2.50. The setting: Roaring Camp is located in a beautifully restored Victorian house that's a few doors away from where the famous writer Bret Harte lived.

Basics: 571 5th St. (near Clay), Oakland. Tel: 451-0863. Hours: 11:30 am-2:30 pm Mon.-Sat.; a variety of coffee drinks and pastries are served until 4 p.m. Closed Sun. Cards: MC, V. Wine and beer.

The Red Onion
Big hamburgers and five kinds of homemade pie

Tired of those hamburgers you can see through? Try one of Jim Jeffords' big, juicy grilled burgers. He uses thick patties of lean, custom-ground beef and tops each hamburger with a small mountain made of fresh tomato slices, crisp lettuce, red onions, mustard, and mayonnaise. "Home on the Range" is more than just the name of a song, for Mr. Jeffords it's a way of life. The Jeffords Hamburger, $1.60. But Jim doesn't spend all of his time standing next to a hot grill. He spends part of his day standing next to a hot oven. Jim bakes five kinds of pie daily, including peach, walnut, and lemon meringue. The pies are 85¢ a slice.

Basics: 11900 San Pablo Ave. (two blocks south of MacDonald Ave.), El Cerrito. Tel: 236-9462. Hours: 11 am-9 pm daily. Parking lot.

Melo's
Thick-crusted pizza made in the old country tradition

Carmello Piccolo has taught his cooks how to make pizza the right way. They take a mound of fresh dough, hand-pound it, give it a few frisbee-like spins, and then dress it with a basil-scented tomato sauce, an overcoat of Wisconsin mozzarella, and a top hat of house-made Sicilian-style sausage. The result is a thick, crusty, properly dressed pizza with a reputation for being well liked. Sausage Pizza: small, $3.00; medium, $4.25; large, $5.50. Combination Pizza (sausage, pepperoni, salami, mushrooms, ham, linguica, and bell peppers), small, $4.25; medium, $6.00; large, $7.50.

Basics: 1558 Contra Costa Blvd. (near Beth, six blocks from the Sun Valley Shopping Center), Pleasant Hill. Tel: 687-1880. Hours: 4-11 pm Sun.-Thurs.; 4 pm-1 am Fri., Sat. Wine and beer. Parking lot.

Rocky's
A champion in the heavyweight sandwich division

The slogan here is "heavyweight sandwiches." And that's exactly what you get. By the time the counter girl is through piling a huge French roll with Italian meats, cheese, lettuce, tomato, pickles, pepperoncini, and onions, the sandwich you just ordered is almost the size of a boxing glove. What now? Take a seat in one of Rocky's custom-crafted wooden booths, stop for a second to gaze at the stained glass window-portraits of famous champions like Joe Louis and Rocky Marciano, and then begin the fight to finish your sandwich.

Rocky's sandwiches are $1.69-$1.95, and our favorites are mortadella, Genoa salami, and provolone cheese; a sandwich of coppa ham, Monterey Jack cheese, and salami; and Rocky's Poor Boy, which is a little of everything. Note: Rocky has some hot sandwiches on the menu, but we don't feel that they're up to the standards of the other sandwiches.

Basics: 15848 Hesperian Blvd. (near Grant), San Lorenzo. Tel: 276-5133. Hours: 11 am-7 pm daily. Wine and beer.

MARIN COUNTY

SIR FRANCIS, THE NATIVES LOOK FRIENDLY.

SCENIC LOTS AVAILABLE

Included in This Section

Page 159
One of the best Mexican restaurants in the Bay Area.

Page 164
A Mill Valley restaurant with moderate prices
and a roof that ''rolls back.''

Page 168
Old-fashioned 5-course Italian dinners
in a 1920 roadhouse.

Page 173
Modestly priced homecooked Scandinavian dinners
in a tree-shaded cottage.

Canzona's: Larkspur
Italian/Small, chef-owned trattoria, modest prices

There is another element besides air and water that few human beings can do without for long periods of time—Italian food. Chef Riccardo Capra realized this. So he opened a small, trattoria-style restaurant in the tree-shaded town of Larkspur. As a community service. When the people of Marin County are gripped by an uncontrollable craving for Italian food, all they have to do is head for Canzona's. Whatever it is they want, Riccardo has: veal scallopine rich with fresh mushrooms, chicken cacciatora, and even seafood cioppino, San Polomatese style. This is Riccardo's specialty. You receive a huge bowl that's filled to high tide with a spicy tomato broth packed with crab legs, scallops, clams, and prawns that are almost as big as gondolas. Plus with all of these dishes the price is right: the cioppino is $6.25, the cacciatora is $3.95, and the scallopine is $5.25.

Riccardo personally makes everything on the menu except the pasta. But that's okay. What Riccardo doesn't do, Mama does. Riccardo's mother, Anna, makes the homemade fettucine egg noodles for the restaurant. And after eating Mrs. Capra's pasta, you're going to discover something—Riccardo is one lucky bambino.

Menu Specialties: ☐ Crab Cioppino ☐ Veal Scallopine with Fresh Mushrooms ☐ Chicken Cacciatora (chicken sauteed with artichoke hearts, green peppers, zucchini, and black olives. Topped with an oregano-flavored tomato sauce.) ☐ Laganelle Molisane (Signora Anna's homemade egg noodles in an ivory-colored cream sauce honeycombed with prosciutto ham and mushrooms and punctuated with fresh peas.) ☐ Veal Piccata (tender scallops in a lemon-wine sauce dotted with capers.)

Meat and seafood dishes include fresh seasonal vegetables sauteed Italian-style, rice, and homemade focaccia—a flat, pizza-like bread sprinkled with bits of green onions. Pasta includes the focaccia only. **Prices:** Inexpensive to medium. **Decor:** A small dining room with a Mediterranean look—white stucco walls, arched, brick-rimmed windows, copper pans on display, and an expresso machine in one corner. **Basics:** 455 Magnolia Ave. (near King), Larkspur. Tel: 924-3332. Hours: 11:30 am-2:30 pm Tues.-Fri.; 5-10 pm Tues.-Thurs., Sun.; 5-11 pm Fri., Sat. Closed Mon. Cards: MC, V. Wine and beer. Parking lot.

Taverna Yiasou: San Rafael
Greek/3-course dinners in candlelit cafe

At Greek banquets around 230 A.D., guests didn't use plates or silverware. According to the writer Athenaeus, everyone grabbed food directly from the steaming hot serving platters with their hands. When the food was good, a Greek had to work quickly to get his share. But greedy eaters had a special way of dealing with this problem. Prior to a banquet, these gluttons would soak their hands in scalding hot water. The purpose of this exercise was to condition their hands, making it easier for them to grab sizzling morsels of food while the other diners were waiting for the dishes to cool.

Today, it would be hard to find men that would resort to such practices. Unless you knew us better . . . ouch! That water's hot. Ooo. Ah. Ow! Honest, we don't mind dipping our hands in a pot of boiling water. Listen, what's a little suffering? We're going to the Taverna Yiasou tonight with a party of eight and we want our share. The food's that good. In our opinion, this restaurant serves the best Greek food in the Bay Area. And they serve it at very fair prices—most of their 3-course dinners are in the $6 to $7 range.

The professional restaurant men were wrong. Originally they predicted that the Taverna's owner, Beth Taylor, would tumble into the pit of failure. At first, that's the way it seemed. Beth opened the Yiasou with absolutely no restaurant experience. And that's not all. She wasn't even Greek—she was American. But Beth survived because she had one valuable asset: a fierce determination to be faithful to the Greeks in preparing their food. No wonder she's filled her taverna with people since 1966.

Beth's baklava tells the story. This dessert of walnuts, honey, and film-thin pastry layers is so difficult to make, most Greek restaurants purchase it from commercial bakeries. By the time this machine-made baklava reaches your table, it's usually so old, it deserves to be on Social Security. Not at Taverna Yiasou. This classic Greek dessert is baked *daily* in Beth's kitchen.

Menu Specialties: □ Moussaka (the national dish of Greece. A casserole dish of alternating layers of ground lamb and eggplant built up as carefully as a classical Greek temple. Topped with a roof of rich imported Kasseri cheese . . . and served with columns of creamy nutmeg-scented white sauce dripping down the sides.) □ Psito Lamb Riganato (a meaty lamb shank baked in a sauce made from plump fresh tomatoes and herbs. Topped with chunks of imported Greek feta cheese. A cut and grip dish. After you've cut most of the meat from the bone, you grip it as if you were Ulysses and gnaw away happily.) □ Dolmades (stuffed grape leaves. Four rolls generously filled with ground lamb, feta cheese, rice, and pine nuts; covered with a brownish-red sauce that whispers the presence of lemon. For this dish, Beth uses

Fresno grape leaves. The Fresno packer that supplies them grows grapes *just for the leaves.*)

Dinner includes . . . 3 courses: Mezethakia (peasant salad. Lettuce mixed with green pepper rings, celery, and homemade croutons, and topped with an olive oil and lemon dressing. Served with feta cheese, Greek olives, Satziki yogurt dip, Skordalia potato dip . . . and a side dish of chilled dipping vegetables.), lamb and chicken broth soup packed with 10 different vegetables, a basket of Koulouria (sweet ring bread coated with sesame seeds), and main course with rice and a sauced artichoke bottom.

Dessert: Homemade Baklava (a masterpiece of 20 filo pastry layers, chopped walnuts, and honey.) **Prices:** Inexpensive to medium. **Decor:** A small, homey, festively-decorated cafe with candles on each table, and Greek bazouki music playing in the background. **Basics:** 48 North San Pedro Rd. (near the North San Pedro exit off Highway 101, across from the Marin Civic Center), San Rafael. Tel: 479-2991. Hours: 6-9:30 pm Thurs.-Sat. Reservations necessary. Cards: MC, V. Wine and beer. Parking lot.

Mayflower Inn: San Rafael
English Cooking/Transplanted London pub

At the Mayflower Inn you'll find authentic English cooking. And you'll find it, as an Englishman might say, "at conservative prices, Guv'nor." At the Mayflower most of the entrees are around $3.25 and the desserts are 75¢.

The Inn's menu features a collection of London pub specialties, including fish & chips, and two different types of hearty, baked-at-your-command meat pies. The most popular pie is the crescent-shaped Cornish pasty—a flaky, golden-brown pastry filled with corned beef, garden vegetables, and topped with an honest ladle of rich pan gravy. Then there's the Inn's desserts . . . mince pie, fresh orange cake, and the sherry trifle—a pound cake covered with a path of strawberry jam, showered with sherry, and decked with peaches, custard, and whipped cream.

Menu Specialties: ☐ Cornish Pasty ☐ Steak & Kidney Pie (a butter-dough pie shell houses a filling of lean pieces of steak and kidney in a flavorful gravy. Served steaming hot from the oven. One of these pies and an icy mug of Watney's Lager beer from the Mayflower's tap is what an Englishman would call "a fine pub meal.") ☐ Fish & Chips (a classic . . . done right. The crust—crisp and greaseless. The fish—Icelandic whitefish. And the waitress goes between fryer and table like a baseball player stealing third.)

Dishes include large, hand-cut French fries (or as the English say, "chips"), and, sob, canned peas. Observation: There's a reason why the Jolly Green Giant is always laughing. He gets to stand around with his hands on his hips while the little people have to work like crazy canning vegetables. **Desserts:** Sherry trifle, mince pie, orange cake. **Prices:** Inexpensive. **Decor:** The Mayflower has all of the props necessary to make it look like a British pub: a fireplace, family crests on the walls, and pewter mugs dangling over the bar. **Basics:** 1533 4th St. (near E St.), San Rafael. Tel: 456-1011. Hours: 11 am-2 pm Mon.-Fri.; 5-9 pm Sun.-Thurs.; 5-10 pm Fri., Sat. No cards. Wine and beer.

Ramona's: San Rafael
Mexican/The owner, a lady who has been cooking for 42 years

The year is 1937. The place is Lindsay, California. You're sitting in a small Mexican restaurant wondering if you can get the recipe for the fine chicken Mole you've just finished. Across the room you spot this little Mexican girl with a hoop skirt, pigtails, and dimples almost as big as foxholes. In a loud voice you call out, "Hey, kid, who's the owner around here?" She quietly walks over to you and peeps, "Me."

Ramona opened her first restaurant in 1937. She was 14 years old. And over the last 42 years, she's learned a lot. We consider her present place in San Rafael one of the best Mexican restaurants in the Bay Area. It has nothing in common with the hundreds of local taco cafes which seem to specialize in premeditated indigestion. Instead of relying on the hot sauce bottle to give her food character, Ramona puts her dishes together with the help of a vast reservoir of experience that's been filling up since she was a teenager.

The dazzling flavor of Ramona's chicken Mole is no accident. The dish has over 40 different ingredients, including three peppers which Ramona must travel to Mexico to get. It takes Ramona 20 hours to make the Mole. But each minute pays off. The chicken Mole is as rich as a Tampico gambler with a pair of loaded dice . . . as spicy as a bullfighter's language after he trips over his cape . . . and as interesting as the love life of an Acapulco bar girl.

Menu Specialties: ☐ Chicken Mole (among the many ingredients in Ramona's Mole sauce are ancho peppers, mulato peppers, sesame seeds, almonds, raisins, cinnamon, and cloves. When the sauce is finished, it's an unbelievably rich shade of dark brown. Then this sauce is poured over chicken that has been boiled in a liquid containing tomatoes, onions, and epazote—a fragrant Mexican herb which Ramona grows in flower pots around her house.) □ Chalupas (four-inch-long tortilla boats hand-shaped out of masa cornmeal. The boat is filled with Ramona's homemade chorizo sausage, topped with cheese, and baked.) □ Arroz Con Pollo (on your platter is a huge, steaming mound of yellow rice topped with strips of pimentos and black olives. The color of the rice, not to mention the unique flavor of the dish, comes from the world's most expensive spice—saffron. Used in generous amounts. Peeking through this mound of rice are pieces of linguica sausage, green olives, capers, and artichoke hearts. And in the middle is the prize— moist pieces of chicken flavored with wine.)

□ Panuchos (a tortilla foundation supports a thick layer of imported Yucatan black beans, a layer of flavorful pork strips, and a topping of onion circles that have been marinated in a pineapple vinegar Ramona makes herself.) □ Ramona also does the "Standards." All are excellent. The Green Enchiladas are even better than that.

Starters: Tossed Green Salad (with Ramona's special dressing. What's in it? We couldn't find out. One-time customer Hugh Hefner couldn't find out. Probably the CIA couldn't find out.) **Prices:** Inexpensive. **Decor:** A small dining room with a hacienda decor and tables inlaid with Mexican tile. **Basics:** 1025 C St. (near 4th St.), San Rafael. Tel: 454-0761. Hours: 11:30 am-2:30 pm Tues.-Fri.; 5-10 pm Tues.-Thurs., Sun.; 5-11 pm Fri., Sat. Closed Mon. No cards. Wine and beer.

Rice Table: San Rafael
Indonesian/An exotic 12-dish feast for $6.95

Indonesia has been the world's spice cabinet since the days of the Roman Empire. To reach the Roman market in 93 A.D., Indonesian outrigger canoes carrying nutmeg and cloves made a 4,500 mile voyage across treacherous seas that kept many a crew's nerve endings on red alert.

Centuries later, the Dutch decided to "come to where the flavor is" and colonized many of the 3,000 tropical islands that make up Indonesia. Before long, the Dutch discovered the Indonesian genius for spices and quickly developed a taste for Indonesian food. The dishes the Dutch liked best were served at gigantic colonial feasts called rijstaffels. During the days of Dutch imperialism, the rijstaffel dishes were brought out by a single file line of barefoot natives dressed in skirts made of banana leaves. Each man carried one dish, and according to a journal of 1805, "a rijstaffel required 23 men and a boy to serve."

The Rice Table in San Rafael gives the rijstaffel the *Reader's*

Digest treatment and serves an abridged 12-dish version of this meal for $6.95. Still, what a feast! One waiter presents you with a kaleidoscope of dishes, including bright green Atjar vegetables; Kerrie Ajam chicken in a crimson-colored curry sauce; pink shrimp chips; Smoor beef squares glistening with an ebony-colored sauce; yellow saffron rice; and charcoal-brown pork Satay covered with a tan peanut sauce and served on bamboo skewers. The only color to approach with caution is the red pepper Banjak dip. A little too much of this dip, and you may embarrass others in your party by screaming.

The Menu: A 12-dish rijstaffel dinner starts with . . . *Krupuk* (deep-fried shrimp chips festively tinted pink and orange. With the Krupuk come three Indonesian dipping sauces.) Next comes *Sup Sajur* (Indonesian soup with a split pea base) . . . followed by *Lumpia* (an Indonesian egg roll stuffed with pork and shrimp) . . . while you nibble the Lumpia, you're brought *Asinan Toge* (an Indonesian vegetable salad.)

Now the next seven dishes are served—all at once. The inventory: *Kerrie Ajam* (Indonesian curry—chicken breasts in a rich curry sauce based on pure coconut milk), *Satay* (Indonesian shish kebab—pork chunks left for eight hours in a spicy marinade and charcoal broiled), *Frikadel* (Indonesian meatballs—moist and spicy), *Smoor* (beef squares sauteed with butter, soy sauce, and a lemony tropical spice from Indonesia), *Bihun Goreng* (Indonesian chow mein—rice noodles, vegetables, and shrimp fried together), *Atjar* (Indonesian marinated vegetables with a flavor that's gently tart), *Nasi Kuning* (yellow rice cooked with saffron. Served with roasted and shredded coconut. Sprinkle at will.)

Finally, dinner ends with dessert—*Pisang Goreng* (Indonesian banana fritters—sweet, hot, and good.) **Prices:** Medium. **Decor:** Inside, there's lots of bamboo, Buddhas, and incense. The dining room looks a little like a 1940 South Seas movie set—during dinner, you almost expect someone named "Trader Horn" to walk up and offer to take you to the lost treasures of King Wuruk. But instead of Trader Horn, you'll get to meet the restaurant's owner—Mrs. Hool, a friendly Indonesian lady who first learned to speak English by reading the labels of spice boxes in a supermarket. **Basics:** 1617 4th St. (near G St.), San Rafael. Tel: 456-1808. Hours: 5:30-10 pm Thurs.-Sat.; 5-9 pm Sun. Closed Mon.-Wed. Reservations necessary on weekends. Cards: MC, V. Wine and beer.

464 Magnolia

Clark Gable would have liked this place

On one of Clark Gable's visits to San Francisco, he was asked by a young reporter what brought him to the City. Gable replied, "Oh, you might say Valdostana."

"Is she beautiful?" the reporter slyly asked.

"Beautiful, yes. A woman, no. Valdostana is the name of a veal dish served at an Italian restaurant located just off Columbus Avenue."

This wasn't the first time that Clark Gable came here to eat. He tried to dine in the San Francisco area whenever he could. Gable felt that restaurants in this area had a "special quality."

Clark Gable would have liked 464 Magnolia. It has that "special quality." Owner Mike Goldstein and a handful of other Bay Area chefs have pioneered a new kind of restaurant where the menu continually explores the world of food. Variety is this restaurant's trademark—at 464 Magnolia, Mike offers a different menu each night. Last year, he featured over 300 different dishes.

Now, let's take a tour of some of Mike's most recent menus. From Italy came the inspiration for Mike's veal birds Florentine stuffed with spinach and Mediterranean herbs; from France came the inspiration for his sole Cardinal—fresh petrale sole rolled around a salmon mousse and kissed with a cream-rich Cardinal sauce. And from the farms of Sonoma County, U.S.A., came the duckling Mike used to prepare his roast duckling in a black currant-liqueur laced bigarade sauce. Mike's menu also travels to the other side of the world. Recently, he prepared roast marinated Chinese pork loins with spiced pears and apple sweet and sour sauce.

Sometimes, Mike's inspiration comes from inside. Two of his most recent creations were abalone stuffed with baby shrimp and slivered brazil nuts, and roast rack of lamb crusted with Italian Asiago cheese and almonds. But remember, these are just examples. This chef has an active imagination that refuses to stand still.

Mike's restaurant is located in the tree-shaded town of Larkspur. The friendly feeling of this small town extends into 464's dining room, where you'll find fresh flowers, burgundy tablecloths, oceans of Oriental rugs, and a skylight overhead.

In the front of the dining room, there's an antique oak table. On it, there's a book. A very important book. It contains Mike's mailing list. At the beginning of each month, Mike sends his customers a mailer which describes some of the dishes he plans to feature on upcoming menus. If you'd like to receive one of these mailers, just put your name on the list when you visit 464 Magnolia. Then look for Mike's dinners. They'll be in your mailbox.

The Menu: There are usually five to seven main courses served each night, and 464 Magnolia is happy to tell you what the list of dishes will be for any given evening. So give 'em a call. With a restaurant like 464, if you like seafood, you might as well be there on the night when Mike is featuring fresh southern California sea bass. Or if you like creative cooking, you might as well be there when Mike features his chicken Hollywood.

Dinner includes . . . 3 courses: Appetizer (choice of four each night—maybe stuffed mushrooms, marinated scallops, or a fresh artichoke with homemade mayonnaise), just-baked whole wheat rolls, spinach salad with a spicy vinaigrette, and main course with three fresh vegetables. Dessert: Five homemade desserts are offered each night— maybe a walnut torte with buttercream frosting, Grand Marnier liqueur custard studded with currants and pieces of apricots, or lemon mousse topped with fresh blueberries. **Prices:** Medium to a step above medium. **Basics:** 464 Magnolia Ave. (near Ward), Larkspur. Tel: 924-6831. Hours: 6-10 pm Tues.-Thurs., Sun.; 6-11 pm Fri., Sat. Brunch on Sat. and Sun. from 10 am-2 pm. Closed Mon. Reservations necessary on weekends. Cards: MC, V. Wine and beer.

Davood's: Mill Valley
Middle Eastern/Impressive decor & moderate prices

At Davood's the food and the atmosphere are good. Davood's also has something else—something that makes the food and the atmosphere seem even nicer. The prices are moderate. This is one restaurant where you won't get a Jesse James check—a bill that takes everything you've got.

Davood Kohanzadeh is Persian, and the menu reflects his background. Davood prepares stuffed breast of chicken saffron; marinated Joojeh kebabs; and a gently-spiced lamb dish layered with eggplant and imported cheese. Then there's Davood's curries. Although curries are mainly associated with India, they also appear in Persia. And curry is our favorite dish at Davood's. His curries are flavored with 12 different hand-ground spices, and served with Checkered Demon chutney—a flavorful mango chutney that Davood makes himself. But while these dishes are authentically Persian, Davood gives them some California escorts. Each of these dishes comes with a crusty homemade bread, a cantaloupe slice garnish, and a butter-sauteed mixture of seven, San Joaquin Valley-fresh vegetables. Oh, yes. For dessert, Davood features an all-American walnut pie.

Davood's restaurant is located at the base of Mt. Tamalpais, in the quaint, tree-shaded town of Mill Valley. And the restaurant blends in well with its location. Everything in the dining room has been custom-made from natural wood. The effect is impressive, and things get even more impressive when you look up. Part of the roof rests on a motorized track, and can actually be "rolled back." How nice when you discover that the dining room has a 6-mile-high ceiling painted sky blue.

Menu Specialties: □ Joojeh Chicken Kebab (once the lemony marinade has been allowed to work some Persian magic, the chicken pieces are skewered and charcoal broiled.) □ Eggplant Casserole (layers of lamb and eggplant in a fresh, basil-scented tomato sauce with a top layer of melted Swiss Emmentaler cheese.) □ Curries (Davood's golden-colored Persian curries—rich, fresh, and fragrant. Choice of lamb, chicken, or prawn curry.) □ Breast of Chicken Saffron (a boned breast of chicken stuffed with fresh mushrooms and rice, then roasted with saffron butter.)

Dinner includes: A large salad in an herb vinaigrette, homemade bread, main course with a party of seven fresh vegetables, rice pilaf, and fresh fruit wedge. Dessert: Walnut pie. **Prices:** Medium. **Basics:** 22 Miller Ave. (near Throckmorton), Mill Valley. Tel: 388-2000. Hours: 11 am-10 pm Sun.-Thurs.; 11 am-11 pm Fri., Sat. Cards: MC, V. Wine and beer.

Soupcon: Sausalito
Creative Cooking/Small, colorful, side street cafe

SPECIAL TREATMENT
a short play

SCENE I: *Monday morning at Riera and Smith's office. A worried looking man arrives and Riera greets him:* "Hello, Mr. Jones. Good to see you again. My, you look a little pale. What seems to be the problem? *(Mr. Jones softly mumbles something.)* Oh, you say that you're constantly getting bad meals in restaurants, and it gives you a headache to pay the check? Well, it sounds to me like you've come down with 'diner's ailment.' In cases like this, you don't have much choice. Mr. Jones, you need to see a Food Specialist. I suggest you make an appointment with Karen Brennan immediately. She practices at the Soupcon Cafe."

SCENE II: *That evening at the Soupcon—a small, colorfully decorated cafe on a side street in Sausalito. Inside, Karen Brennan, a friendly lady with an honest smile, looks up as Mr. Jones enters. Karen welcomes him:* "You're Mr. Jones, I presume. I'm Karen Brennan. Go ahead, loosen your tie. My office is very informal. Doesn't the floral print wallpaper and Casablanca-style fan lift your spirits? Yes, I know my office is small. Seven tables to be exact. But I try to fit in everyone who needs help."

SCENE III: *Ten minutes later. Karen pats Mr. Jones on the back and says:* "Well, Mr. Jones, after diagnosing your problem, I'm sure that the following treatment will work wonders. Each night, I'll start you off with a different soup . . . maybe a shrimp bisque, or a Hungarian vegetable soup. Then, I'll fortify you with a main course, possibly prawns Malabar, or short ribs braised in English ale. By the way, most of my prescriptions are flavored with herbs from my own garden. You see, I've studied herbology. Finally, your therapy each night will end on a sweet note. It could be my brandy-pecan pie, my Brazilian coffee-chocolate cake, or my banana cream pie that, believe it or not, Mr. Jones, is six inches high. I use a special baking method. *(By now, Mr. Jones' eyes are shining like two searchlights at the grand opening of a furniture store.)* And don't worry, Mr. Jones. My services are moderately priced, and this treatment won't bother you at all. Why, some patients, I'm told, secretly don't want the therapy to end."

CURTAIN

Menu Specialties: □ Prawns Malabar (large, moist Gulf prawns in a garlic-scented herb butter sauce laced with green onions and black olives.) ☐ Chicken Katherine Fletcher (chicken breast topped with melted Monterey Jack cheese, a paper-thin slice of ham and a buttery wine sauce. Served on a bed of avocado.) ☐ Scallops Pattersquash Island (big, tender scallops in a light cream sauce flavored with white wine and sherry.) ☐ The Soupcon Special (maybe pork chops with an apple and bread crumb stuffing, veal Strasbourg, or ale-braised beef short ribs.)

Dinner includes: Soup (maybe a potato and cheddar cheese soup, oyster-spinach soup, or a Sally Stanford favorite called "Booney Bean"—a white bean soup spiked with rum), or salad (a huge wedge of crisp lettuce topped with a thick blue cheese dressing), hot garlic bread, and main course with fresh zucchini and rice.

Dessert: Maybe chocolate bourbon cake avalanched with whipped cream, a custard-filled peach cinnamon Kuchen pie, or strawberry Charlotte (a molded cake with a filling of fresh strawberries and crushed almonds, and a crust of ladyfinger cookies.) **Prices:** Medium. **Basics:** 49 Caledonia Ave. (near Pine, one block off Bridgeway), Sausalito. Tel: 332-9752. Hours: 11:30 am-2:30 pm, 5:30-10 pm Mon.-Sat. Closed Sun. Reservations necessary. No cards. Wine and beer.

La Marmite: San Rafael
French/Candlelit setting, moderate prices

Many restaurants seem to cater to a specific target group, but that's certainly not true here. Instead, La Marmite has been stretched into a restaurant for all reasons. The menu attracts purists who demand authentic French cooking; the prices are moderate enough to bring in families out for a special occasion; and the candlelight lures the couples who require a suitably romantic place for nutritional foreplay.

La Marmite's owner has chosen to hold his restaurant together with the strongest adhesive available—good food. Chef Yves Larguinat is very skilled in the art of making sauces and his customers seem to take advantage of this fact. Sometimes a table tends to look like a color wheel—the white tablecloth serving as a background for plates of salmon in a yellow hollandaise sauce, steak in a wine-red bordelaise sauce, duck in a dark orange bigarade sauce, and veal in a golden Dijonnaise sauce.

Yves realizes that it's the little things that make a successful dinner. He buys 7-year-old French wine vinegar for his salad dressing, boils his carrots in bottled spring water, and has his bread made from his own recipe at the Bordenaves bakery in San Rafael. Yves' perfectionist attitude is probably a result of his training. From age 14 to 28, he underwent a long, strict apprenticeship in Lyon and Biarritz. In France, great chefs warn their apprentices right from the start to keep one thing in mind—accidents happen in the bedroom, not in the kitchen.

166

Menu Specialties: ☐ Rack of Lamb Provencale (rack of lamb marinated for 5 days in olive oil and a $14-per-pound blend of herbs imported from France. The lamb is then brushed with Dijon mustard and garlicked sourdough crumbs, and then slowly roasted. The lamb is carved at your table. Serves two.) ☐ Filet of Beef en Croute (a butter-sauteed filet mignon is placed on a bed of peppercorns and topped with a mushroom duxelle. Then, it's completely enclosed in a pastry shell and baked. Served with a Madeira wine sauce.) ☐ Chicken Vin Vieux (fresh, boneless Santa Rosa chicken marinated for 3 days in burgundy wine and spices. On the chosen night, the chicken is sauteed in its own marinade along with bacon slices, pearl onions, and fresh mushrooms.)

The Final Touch: Yves has an artist's concern for visuals . . . the lamb is served tableside with a sprig of flaming rosemary, which is dropped still smoldering into the sauce for flavor . . . the chicken is topped with a heart-shaped piece of parsley-coated toast . . . and the filet mignon is garnished with potatoes that Yves carves into rose-like shapes and tints pink and orange. The potatoes are so "original," we take them home with us. No, not to show our friends. After the potatoes have been framed, we sell them to wealthy matrons as pop-art.

Dinner includes . . . 3 courses: Soup (maybe cream of watercress or a seafood bisque flavored with Pernod liqueur), butter lettuce salad with sliced mushrooms and hearts of palm, main course with two vegetables (maybe French-cut green beans and an herb-stuffed tomato Provencale.) **Prices:** Medium. **Decor:** Candlelight . . . cocoa brown walls, white tablecloths, fresh flowers on each table, and tall crystal wine goblets everywhere. Also, there's fine, friendly service, and as a fringe benefit, the tables are extravagantly spaced out, offering each party an extra margin of privacy. **Basics:** 909 Lincoln Ave. (near 3rd St.), San Rafael. Tel: 456-4020. Hours: 6-10:30 pm Tues.-Sun. Closed Mon. Reservations strongly suggested on weekends. Cards: MC, V. Wine and beer.

Galli's: Ignacio
Located in a classic 1920 roadhouse
Inside? Italian dinners. Big ones. Frank Galli style.

Galli's is an institution. Founded almost six decades ago. But if you want to enjoy one of Galli's 5-course Italian dinners, you must be willing to play two little games.

Game I is called "The Wait." Your instructions: Open the screen door of this tree-shaded roadhouse and march across the dining room. Don't look at the plain yellow walls lined with brass coat hooks or the old oak sideboard sitting in the corner. Keep walking. Turn left by the ancient juke box stocked with Mills Brothers records. Sit down at the elbow-polished bar. Look at the gray-haired Italian man wearing the Hawaiian shirt. This is Frank Galli.

After Frank has determined how many people there are in your party, he'll turn around and ring a bell like he's reporting a fire. Don't question this ritual; just relax and watch the hula girls on Frank's Hawaiian shirt sway back and forth as he mixes you a drink. Wait. Be patient. Before you know it, Frank will casually tell you that your table is ready. As your party is leaving the bar, Frank will probably say, "Best table in the house, folks." Ignore this remark. Frank tells this to everybody.

When you reach your table, it will be completely carpeted with food. How did it get there? As soon as the waitress heard the clang of Frank's bell, she started to load your table with an army of little plates of salami, coppa ham, green olives, marinated red beans, Galli's special "senza nome" relish, pepperoncini . . . well, the table sort of looks like the display case in an Italian delicatessen. And in front of every seat at the table, you'll also find one of Galli's special salads. It contains a harvest of 15 different vegetables, including artichoke hearts, tomatoes, asparagus, zucchini, bell peppers, and broccoli. You feel healthy just looking at it.

Your next move is to eat everything in sight. Then, after you've popped the last olive in your mouth you remember. Those were just the appetizers. There's still four courses to go: a bowl of steaming hot homemade soup, a plate of spaghetti in an excellent rosemary-scented meat sauce, then the main course, maybe Galli's chicken cacciatora or one of his thick, well-aged sirloin steaks, and after that, a dish of fruit-studded spumoni ice cream for dessert.

Finally, dinner is over. You've spent the last hour spooning, carving, and forking your way through one of Galli's 5-course Italian dinners. Now it's time to play Game II. This one's called "Try and Get Up." Good luck.

Menu Specialties: □ Chicken Cacciatora (moist, tender pieces of chicken in a fresh herb-flavored sauce that's dense with mushrooms.) □ Galli's Sirloin Steak (Frank Galli's steaks are thick, tender, and weigh "at least" eighteen ounces. Sometimes more. Galli cuts his own steaks and he says, "I don't measure my steaks with a scale. I use my eyes." And Galli has a generous way of looking at things.) □ Veal Scallopine (veal scallops are sauteed with dry sherry, sauterne, button mushrooms, and onions until a light, tasty pan-sauce is created.) □ Beef Ignacio (two tender medallions of filet mignon topped with Galli's Italian wine sauce and whole fresh mushrooms. Served on a bed of genuine wild rice from Minnesota.)

Dinner includes . . . 5 courses: A parade of appetizers and Galli's 15-vegetable salad, soup, spaghetti, main course with roasted potatoes and green beans, coffee, and spumoni ice cream. Honor Thy Pasta: Instead of spaghetti, you can have Galloni's for 50¢ extra. What are Galloni's? Frank Galli's version of ravioli—huge pasta squares bulging with one of the best ravioli fillings we've had locally. If you're wondering about the name, it wasn't Frank's idea. Many years ago, Galli served this ravioli to a Roman Catholic priest who felt they were so special, he renamed them "Galloni's." Note: Galloni's are available as a main course on the complete dinner. **Prices:** Medium to a step above medium. **Basics:** 350 Ignacio Blvd. (near the Ignacio Blvd. exit off Highway 101), Ignacio—7 miles north of San Rafael. Tel: 883-9911. Hours: 5:30-10 pm Wed.-Sat.; 4-9 pm Sun. Closed Mon., Tues. All major cards. Full bar. Parking lot.

"Start dancin', kid. Let's see how good you are."

Yankee Lobsterman

*They feature live New England lobsters,
and at prices that are definitely a tough act to beat*

John Polando sells live New England lobsters and he's very qualified for the job. He spent his youth on a small boat that was based in Marblehead, a 350-year-old fishing village on the coast of Massachusettes. John is an ex-lobster fisherman. And Marblehead is still his source of supply. Twice a week, John's sister in Marblehead sends him a shipment of lobsters by air freight. The system is so refined that from the time the lobsters are hauled in from the Atlantic to the time they're put in this restaurant's tanks, only 12 hours have passed.

The lobsters arrive packed in insulated containers cushioned with seaweed. And it's a sure bet the lobsters in those containers are the pick of the catch. John's sister grew up in Marblehead and knows most of the local fishermen by name, so naturally she gets the best they have.

Once at the restaurant, the live lobsters are put in clear Plexiglas tanks that are visible from the dining room. These are specially designed, custom-built tanks. Lobsters require a tank that's kept at a

170

constant 42 degrees and filtered with fresh seawater. We can almost hear Polando now: "Tom, do me a favor. Take this bucket, run down to the ocean . . ."

Now it's your turn to participate. You look in the tank and make your choice. Fifteen minutes later, a steaming hot, bright red lobster is placed on your table. And what's in front of you is the pride of America. *Homarus americanus*, or New England lobster, is considered the finest species of lobster in the world. In fact, the legislature of Massachusetts considers this shellfish such a native of our land that, by law, only American citizens can fish for lobsters. But Massachusetts legislators aren't the only ones who consider this shellfish special. Once, when a shipment of 40,000 pounds of lobster was trucked from Boston to New York, it was accompanied by shotgun-carrying guards.

But despite the New England lobster's status, John manages to sell his lobsters for a lot less than his competition. A 1½ pound lobster at most restaurants is $14; at John's it's $9. There are two reasons why John is able to do this. First, there's his "Marblehead connection." Second, rather than maintain an atmosphere of silver service and polished crystal, he serves New England lobster the way it should be served—clambake style. This means you eat at picnic tables on paper plates. Lobster is meant to be eaten with the hands. At John's, you do. The only thing that John doesn't supply is the sand.

Menu Specialties: ☐ Live New England Lobster (you have your pick of any lobster from 14 ounces to 5 pounds! The cost is $5.50 per pound plus $1 for cooking.) ☐ Ipswich Clams (these New England clams have a sweet, gentle flavor that makes them a true delicacy. The restaurant gets them in live and then steams them to order. The cost is $2.29 per pound. For about 18 clams you'll pay $3.50.) ☐ The Clambake Special (a 1 pound New England lobster, 12 Ipswich clams, corn-on-the-cob, a cup of Ipswich clam juice, and hot Bordenaves French bread, at a price of $10.) **Prices:** Medium to a step above medium. **Basics:** East Sir Francis Drake Blvd., in the Larkspur Landing Shopping Center (across from the Larkspur ferry terminal, near the Richmond-San Rafael exit off Highway 101), Larkspur. Tel: 461-9191. Hours: 11 am-9:30 pm daily. Cards: MC, V. Wine and beer.

The Royal Mandarin: San Rafael
Chinese/Menu tours the mainland, a 200-dish journey

The cuisine of China is made up of an endless variety of dishes. And time has had a lot to do with it. The art of Chinese cooking dates back over 4,000 years. But considering the limited chow mein menus found at some places, you'd think Chinese cuisine was invented last Tuesday. At the Royal Mandarin, however, it's a different story. This restaurant gives you the opportunity to explore a menu that offers over 200 dishes from mainland China.

Owner Peter Tien's background accounts for the variety of dishes on his menu. Before he came to the United States, Mr. Tien owned a restaurant on the island of Taiwan. Many of the chefs who work in Taiwan's restaurants are immigrants from mainland China, 90 miles away. In fact, Taiwan boasts chefs from every major province of China. In this atmosphere, Mr. Tien was able to learn many different styles of Chinese cooking. And what Mr. Tien learned in Taiwan is what's on his menu in San Rafael.

At the Royal Mandarin, the menu tours China. From the remote farming province of Hunan, Mr. Tien features General Cho chicken, a hearty, country-style dish named after the famous military leader of western China; from the port city of Shanghai on the East China Sea, he offers crab in a rich, ginger-laced brown bean sauce; and from the mountainous province of Szechwan, he features spicy Chung King beef on a bed of crisp, snow white rice noodles.

Mr. Tien's menu also offers a unique dish from the ancient city of Peking—sizzling rice shrimp. When you order this specialty, the waiter appears at your table holding two platters. In one hand is a plate of golden, deep-fried rice cakes; in the other hand is a plate of steaming hot shrimp and Chinese vegetables in a light, mildly-seasoned sauce. As the waiter pours the shrimp mixture over the sizzling hot rice cakes, the dish goes *sssss*. Yes, a dish with a voice. Who knows? Maybe someday the Chinese will invent a dish that says hello.

Menu Specialties: ☐ Sizzling Rice Shrimp ☐ Chung King Beef (tender, well-trimmed ribbons of beef, each slice coated with a rich, mahogany-colored sauce. Served on a bed of crisp, snow white rice noodles.) ☐ General Cho Chicken (the menu says it's "Diced Chicken Breast with Special Sauce." And the menu is very accurate—the dish's spicy sherry and ginger-scented sauce is special.)

☐ Crab in Brown Bean Sauce (you're served a whole, fresh, cracked Dungeness crab in shell, coated with a brown bean sauce laced with green peppers, water chestnuts, and bamboo shoots. At this point, the audience is asked to participate. The Royal Mandarin's crab in shell is a "use-your-hands" dish. After your performance, small, moistened towels are provided.) ☐ Sweet & Sour Pork, Southern Style (bite-size pieces of crisp, batter-coated pork with onions, tomatoes, and pineapple in a ruby-colored sauce flavored with the juices of oranges and lemons.)

☐Pork with Peking Sauce (more audience participation. You get a plate of julienned pork strips and black mushrooms in plum sauce, a stack of paper-thin rice flour pancakes, and a set of instructions from the waiter: "Take some pork, wrap in pancake, eat with fingers.") **Prices:** Inexpensive to medium. **Decor:** There are dragon designs on the walls, pagoda-style arches, bamboo screens, and a fresh flower on each table. **Basics:** 234 Northgate One Shopping Center (near the Terra Linda exit off Highway 101), San Rafael. Tel: 472-5676. Hours: 11:30 am-9:30 pm Mon.-Thurs.; 11:30 am-10 pm Fri., Sat.; 4-9:30 pm Sun. Cards: MC, V. Full bar.

Old Viking: Lagunitas
Scandinavian/Mr. Mattsson's cottage in the woods

Matts Mattsson's Scandinavian dishes have a homecooked quality. And we're not the only ones who think so. One night we were sitting next to this gentleman who, by the sound of his accent, was obviously Scandinavian. When Mr. Mattsson asked the gentleman how he liked his meal, he replied, "This is the kind of homecooking I wish I'd gotten at home."

Mr. Mattsson's prices are as pleasing as his food. His Swedish-style short ribs of beef are $6.50, Kottbullar meatballs with lingonberries are $5, and his pan-fried veal cutlet with a Scandinavian mushroom sauce is $7.25. And these prices include your choice of either a hearty soup or a tossed salad with Matts' Danish blue cheese dressing. But

173

before you have your first course, you might think about letting Matts fix you a "Viking"—a unique blended wine cocktail that's Matts' own creation.

Matts has a two-part day. He spends his afternoons in the kitchen helping his wife and he spends his evenings in the dining room taking care of his customers. Matts makes a good host. To watch Matts greet a guest, you get the impression he's just been reunited with a friend from the old country.

For the location of his restaurant, Matts found a quaint cottage in the scenic town of Lagunitas, a thickly-wooded refuge that's a twenty minute drive from San Rafael. Many artists and writers have fled to this quiet village for the same reason that Matts came here. Lagunitas is one of the few communities left that can boast of having more trees than street lights.

Menu Specialties: □ Kottbullar (a dozen small, moist, flavorful meatballs sauteed in butter and topped with a rich brown sauce. Served with imported lingonberries.) □ Short Ribs of Beef, Swedish Style (slowly braised until the meat almost falls off the bones and a fragrant natural gravy is produced.) □ Jagar Schnitzel (a tender, butter-fried veal cutlet with a golden brown, bread crumb crust. Served with Mrs. Mattsson's fresh mushroom sauce.)

Dinner includes: Soup (maybe Swedish yellow pea soup or Danish vegetable soup), or the Old Viking salad, a breadbasket filled with a variety of Scandinavian breads (everything from Swedish orange loaf to Norwegian flatbread), and main course with dill potato balls and imported Belgian baby carrots glazed with honey. Dessert: Homemade Swedish applecake with vanilla sauce. **Prices:** Inexpensive to medium. **Basics:** 7303 Sir Francis Drake Blvd., Lagunitas—11 miles from San Rafael. Tel: 488-9928. Hours: 5:30-10 pm Mon., Tues., Thurs.-Sat.; 4-9 pm Sun. Closed Wed. (During the summer they remain open on Wed.) Reservations suggested. No cards. Wine and beer.

Lorenzo's: San Anselmo
Italian/Romantic, New York-style trattoria

Marco Civarello was worried. The shipment had arrived at the San Francisco International Airport early that morning, and it still hadn't been delivered. Finally, a flatbed truck pulled up carrying a 2,500-pound steel container. Marco's container. As he went out to inspect it, Marco's eyes began to glow like the Star-of-Bethlehem. What could be inside? Hijacked gold bullion? Stolen art treasures? Counterfeiting equipment? Wait! As he opens the door, gray smoke begins to drift out. A bomb? Nope. Not a chance. Inside, packed in smoking dry ice, there's a huge assortment of New York cheese, ravioli, and Long Island clams.

On a regular basis, Marco's friend and business associate in New York, Vincent Lorenzo, personally packs a huge steel container with food items he's collected from some of New York's best specialty shops, and ships it to Marco by cargo jet. A typical shipment might include wheels of East Coast mozzarella and provolone cheese, fresh Atlantic clams, silver dollar-sized ravioli filled with ricotta cheese, and a rum and pistachio flavored Italian ice cream.

It's said that New York-style Italian food has a distinctive flavor. And Lorenzo's dishes certainly support that viewpoint. Lorenzo's veal saltimbocca, layered with New York mozzarella and New York prosciutto ham, is more than just excellent—it's unlike any other version we've had locally. There's a memory in every bite.

Lorenzo's even offers a little of New York in its decor. The candlelight, brickwork, custom-made wine racks, red tablecloths, and white roses all combine to give this small restaurant the feel of a romantic Manhattan trattoria. And finally, there's the service: very good. This is one place where you won't have to wave your tablecloth to get your waiter's attention.

Menu Specialties: □ Veal Saltimbocca (veal is the flagship of Lorenzo's menu. They buy only milk-fed Iowa veal, and prepare it six different ways. Our favorite is the Saltimbocca—tender white veal scallops layered with New York mozzarella and paper-thin slices of prosciutto ham, and set on a bed of butter-sauteed spinach. Served in a wine sauce flavored with fresh sage.) □ Shrimp Marinara (large, plump shrimp in a Neapolitan tomato sauce with the kind of deep flavor that results when care is part of the recipe.) □ Chicken Rollatine (two butter-tender rolled chicken breasts bulging with a spicy Italian stuffing that includes provolone cheese from New York. Topped with a chestnut-colored wine sauce and a fortune in fresh mushrooms.)

□ New York Ravioli (generously stuffed with creamy ricotta cheese. Served in a thick, spicy meat sauce.) □ Mostaccioli with Broccoli (our favorite pasta dish at Lorenzo's. The mostaccioli and pieces of emerald-green broccoli are married to a silk-smooth, ivory-colored sauce based on cream, Italian herbs, and two New York cheeses.)

Meat and seafood dishes include a mixed green salad and fresh zucchini in a garlic-butter sauce. Pastas include the salad. Starters: Baked Clams (Long Island clams baked with a very tasty Italian bread crumb stuffing. Lorenzo gets up at 3 a.m. to buy these clams at the Fulton Fish Market in New York, so they can be on the plane by 9 a.m. And improvements in this system are being made all the time. Lorenzo is presently trying to teach the clams how to buy their own airline tickets.)

Desserts: Cremolata (rum and pistachio-flavored Italian ice cream); Italian Lemon Cheesecake (made with New York ricotta cheese); Chocolate Granita (a New York Italian ice with a deep chocolate flavor. Similar to a sherbet.) **Prices:** Medium to a step above medium. **Basics:** 729 Sir Francis Drake Blvd. (near Red Hill Ave.), San Anselmo. Tel: 453-2552. Hours: 5-10 pm Sun.-Thurs.; 5-11 pm Fri., Sat. Closed Mon. Reservations necessary on weekends. Cards: AE, MC, V. Wine and beer.

Short Takes

Taqueria de Marin
The best tacos and burritos in the county

We always felt that somewhere in the mountains of Mexico, there's a wise old man who knows the way to make perfect tacos and burritos. And now we suspect something else—the Taqueria's cook has talked to that man. At the Taqueria, cook Rafael Cisneros uses fresh-ground spices and marinated top sirloin strips for his tacos and burritos. He makes his own chorizo sausage. He prepares the refried beans for his tacos and burritos twice a day, and his sauce of fresh chopped tomatoes and cilantro three times a day. Plus the ingredients are never assembled until he gets your order, and then it's done right before your eyes.

When one of those tacos or burritos are set on the counter, everyone always says the same thing—"Let me at it." Specialties: Carne Asada Taco filled with strips of marinated, broiled sirloin, $1.20; Burrito stuffed with house-made chorizo sausage, $1.35; Carnitas Burrito (a burrito bulging with pork chunks in a fresh red sauce), $1.35.

Basics: 1001 Sir Francis Drake Blvd. (at College), Kentfield. Tel: 453-5811. Hours: 10 am-10 pm daily. Parking lot.

Golden Egg Omelet House
Omelets made with eggs that just left the farm

If there was an omelet building code, the Golden Egg's omelets would certainly be considered up to code. The omelets are cloud-light. They're cooked in real butter. They're filled with tasty ingredients. And they're made with eggs that can honestly be called "farm fresh." A Petaluma farmer supplies this place with all their eggs.

The Golden Egg offers 40 kinds of omelets, including a bacon, tomato, and Swiss cheese omelet, $2.75; ham and cheddar cheese omelet, $2.55; sauteed mushrooms and fresh spinach omelet, $2.65; and an Italian sausage, fresh zucchini, and Monterey Jack cheese omelet, $2.75. The decor: although surrounded by industrial buildings, the Golden Egg is a little oasis of natural wood, indoor plants, and burgundy-colored chairs. It's a sunlit dining room that seems to say "Good Morning."

Basics: 85 Woodland Ave. (at Irwin), San Rafael. Tel: 454-9591. Hours: 6 am-3 pm Mon.-Fri.; 7 am-3 pm Sat.; 8 am-3 pm Sun. Wine and beer. Parking lot.

The Royal Frankfurter
The best hot dogs north of the Golden Gate Bridge

Owner Calvin Wong is Chinese, but his hot dogs are All-American. He features old-fashioned kosher franks that are shipped to him directly from Brooklyn, New York. Calvin bundles the dogs in fresh Italian sesame rolls, and has a condiment island that's stocked with three kinds of mustard, two relishes, and hot sauerkraut. But since Calvin Wong is Chinese, there are a couple of Oriental touches. This is probably the only hot dog stand in America that offers Chinese-style mustard and Jasmine tea. Kosher franks, 90¢.

Basics: 811 4th St. (near Lincoln), San Rafael. Tel: 456-5485. Hours: Noon-6 pm Mon.-Sat. Closed Sun.

Cat's Cradle
A bakery-cafe with the best pastries in Marin County

The Cat's Cradle is a cheerful-looking establishment with a six-table dining area that faces a row of pastry cases. And one look at those pastry cases and you'll start moving your tongue back and forth across your lips like a windshield wiper. Inside you'll see . . .

- Blueberry nut squares and the richest Napoleons in Northern California.
- Chocolate rum balls and Bavarian custard tarts with a pistachio filling.
- Marzipan apple strips and whipped cream eclairs with a black velvet chocolate icing.

In total those pastry cases represent 24 feet of temptation. Oh, yes, you might also keep in mind that the Cat's Cradle is a good place to go for a light breakfast. From 7 a.m. until 11 a.m. each day they feature an assortment of fresh-from-the-oven Danish and croissants. The pastries are 45¢-75¢, the Danish are 45¢ to 55¢, and the croissants are 40¢.

Basics: 1125 Magnolia Ave. (near Murray), Larkspur. Tel: 461-0744. Hours: 7 am-6 pm Tues.-Sat. Closed Sun., Mon.

THE PENINSULA

Included in This Section

Des Alpes: Palo Alto
European Cooking/3-course dinners, modest prices

With all the restaurants around today, sometimes the hunt for a decent meal can turn into a game of culinary Russian roulette. In the Russian game, you may end up with a bullet in your head; in this version, the danger is lead in your stomach. One way to beat this game is to keep going to a place that you know is good. And that's why many people return again and again to Des Alpes.

But it's not just the food that brings them back. It's the prices. When you dine at Des Alpes, you don't have to stop at the bank first. Most of Des Alpes' 3-course dinners are in the $6 range, and include a homemade soup or crisp green salad, the main course with a fresh vegetable and a moist baked potato, and dessert.

Although the name of his restaurant is Swiss, chef Heinz Selig believes in a kitchen without a country. Each night, Heinz can be seen bent over his stove preparing Italian chicken Toscana, German beef Roulade, and Maryland corn chowder. Since fish is Heinz's specialty, he also offers two fresh seafood dishes nightly. For dessert, Heinz serves ice cream. But not just any ice cream—ice cream he makes himself. This is pure ice cream, which makes it different from the grocery-store product. Today, there are so many chemical additives in supermarket ice cream, you could probably put a quart of the stuff in your gas tank and get better mileage.

Menu Specialties: □ Chicken Toscana (the chicken is cooked with fresh mushrooms, green peppers, artichoke hearts, black olives, tomatoes, and white wine.) □ Beef Roulade (thin beef strips rolled around a filling of bacon and sweet onions, and braised in a distinctive wine sauce.) □ Capon Excelsior (a boned breast stuffed with mushroom duxelles, breaded with sourdough crumbs, and baked. Served with a port wine sauce.) □ Fresh Seafood Des Alpes (Heinz always keeps a pot of flavorful poaching liquid and some lemony hollandaise sauce ready for whatever fresh fish might be available—maybe filet of sole, sea bass, or salmon. By the way, the next time you're thinking about ordering salmon remember this: salmon is considered an aphrodisiac. Does this sound strange? Not if you think about it. Listen, when's the last time you swam 1,000 miles upstream for some sex?)

Dinner includes . . . 3 courses: Soup (maybe cream of cauliflower or Philadelphia pepperpot), or a mixed green salad in chef Selig's house dressing, main course with fresh zucchini sauteed with butter and a baked potato, coffee, and homemade ice cream (maybe blueberry or fresh strawberry.) **Prices:** Inexpensive. **Decor:** A small, friendly-looking dining room with red tablecloths, fresh daisies, and walnut-paneled walls hung with polished brass skillets. **Basics:** 201 California Ave. (at Park), Palo Alto. Tel: 326-4112. Hours: 11:30 am-2 pm Tues.-Fri.; 6-9:30 pm Tues.-Thurs.; 5:30-10 pm Fri., Sat. Closed Sun., Mon. Cards: MC, V. Wine and beer.

Wah Yen: San Mateo
Chinese/Owned by a Hong Kong cooking master

Some tourists returning from China insist that our Chinese restaurants are better than the ones on the mainland. To hear these people talk, any day now the Chinese ambassador will be caught somewhere ordering 8,000,000,000 won ton to go. Maybe they're right. Anyhow, if Peking's envoy is ever discovered making such an order, there's a good chance he'll be found at the Wah Yen. The reason is very simple. Chef Kom Leong, who came here many years ago from Hong Kong, is a true master of the Chinese kitchen.

Like most artists, chef Leong works alone. In this small, comfortable restaurant, Leong's family handles the dining room, and Leong handles the kitchen. And, as usual, when a dish is prepared by a restaurant's owner, it shows. There are few places that can match chef Leong's uniquely flavored beefsteaks Chinese-style or his mushroom-laced Wah Yen chicken.

The Wah Yen chicken especially benefits from chef Leong's quality standards. This man trims his meats with the eye of a sculptor and picks his mushrooms with the eye of a jeweler. Each morning Leong spends a full hour at a local hothouse, hand-picking the mushrooms he'll use that night.

Other dishes, like his prawns in blackbean sauce, benefit from his knowledge of Chinese herbs. To make this fragrant blackbean sauce, Leong blends together 12 different ingredients—all of them secret. Leong learned his trade in Hong Kong, where chefs follow a strict code of ethics: nothing is written down, and beginning chefs vow never to reveal the recipes they are taught—*not even to their own family*.

Menu Specialties: ☐ Wah Yen Chicken ☐ Wah Yen Beef ☐ Gulf Prawns, Blackbean Sauce ☐ Beefsteaks Chinese-Style (you're presented a platter ringed with a fence of pineapple slices and cherries . . . a subtle hint that you're getting something special. And you are. In the middle are thinly sliced pieces of New York steak draped with a mahogany-colored sauce as individual as your fingerprints. This sauce is Leong's own creation.) ☐ Sweet & Sour Filets of Fish (pieces of fresh Bodega Bay rock cod with a golden brown crust in a sweet & sour sauce that glows like liquid rubies.) ☐ Szechwan Pork (in a fascinating Chinese pepper sauce. Wham! The flavor hits you. And as tiny wisps of smoke leave your ears, you say, "I like it.")

☐ Fried Won Ton (a nice appetizer. These Chinese ravioli are stuffed right, fried right, and sauced right.) ☐ Yang Chow Fried Rice (the barbecued pork, shrimp, green onions, and rice all come out moist and tender because chef Leong cooks them very quickly in a very hot wok. And the way a good Chinese chef tests the heat of his wok is by listening. He drops some rice into the wok and the sizzling sound that's made tells him if the wok is the right temperature. Of course, a Chinese chef needs good ears. After all, you can't tell people, "Quiet! Can't you see I'm listening to the rice?") **Prices:** Inexpensive to medium. **Basics:** 211 South San Mateo Dr. (near East 3rd Ave.), San Mateo. Tel: 343-1144. Hours: 11:30 am-9 pm Mon.-Sat. Closed Sun. Reservations necessary on weekends. Cards: MC, V. Wine and beer.

La Bonne Auberge: San Mateo
French/Moderately-priced 4-course dinners at the Perugia's

The salt and pepper shakers at La Bonne Auberge feel useless. They should. They're rarely given a chance to add anything to chef Philippe Perugia's meals. When a dish leaves the kitchen, chef Philippe has already spiced it to perfection. With some dishes, it's as if he hand-seasoned each molecule.

Of course, Philippe isn't the first French chef to be a perfectionist. According to a newspaper report of 1887, there was a chef in Paris, Augustin Saboureau, who wouldn't let his customers salt and pepper their own food. If a diner was bold enough to demand extra seasoning, a frowning Augustin would leave the kitchen and personally salt and pepper the dish . . . using a set of jewel-encrusted shakers he carried on a chain around his neck.

Unlike Augustin, Philippe doesn't have any time to leave the kitchen. There's too much to do. His salmon with green peppercorn butter is not a dish that can be made quickly. It's also a slow process making a classic bordelaise sauce for his steaks and a Madeira sauce for his richly stuffed veal Cordon Bleu. But the extra work hasn't influenced Philippe's decisions in the area of prices. La Bonne Auberge's meals are all moderately priced—on the 4-course dinner, veal is $6.50, salmon is $7.00, and the steak is $8.00.

Since Philippe can't be in the dining room, he's left it in good hands—his wife's. Huguette Perugia greets each party as if they were arriving at her home and her natural Gallic friendliness, coupled with the rustic French countryside decor, work together to make you feel relaxed and comfortable. Philippe doesn't even have to visit the dining room to hear what people have to say about his food. With the first bite of his salmon, customers usually let out an *mmmmmm* noise that's so loud, it sounds like the Mormon Tabernacle Choir beginning a hymn.

182

Menu Specialties: ☐ Steak Bordelaise ☐ Filet of Salmon (fresh King salmon from Oregon—poached in a wine and herb-perfumed court bouillon until the bouillon's flavor hugs every morsel of salmon. The salmon is then crowned with an unusual sauce made from butter and hand-crushed green peppercorns from Madagascar.) ☐ Veal Cordon Bleu (veal scallops stuffed with Gruyere cheese and a paper-thin slice of ham, breaded, and then sauteed. Finally, the crisp brown envelope of veal is sealed with a rich sauce containing Spanish Madeira wine and sent out to you—with an aroma that says you're receiving a Special Delivery.) ☐ Scallops St. Jacques (you're served a huge seashell shaped like Marie Antoinette's fan. On the surface: a bronze-colored cheese crust. Below the surface: tender scallops in a cream-rich vermouth sauce.) ☐ Rack of Lamb La Bonne Auberge (rack of lamb in a sauce of pan juices, butter, white wine, and herbs. But not just any herbs: bay leaves and thyme that Philippe grows in his own garden.)

Dinner includes . . . 4 courses: A family-style tureen of soup (maybe potato-leek or a long-simmered stockpot vegetable), butter lettuce salad with a fine house dressing, main course with two vegetables (maybe broccoli with Mornay sauce and eggplant and zucchini ratatouille), and for dessert, vanilla mousse. **Prices:** Medium. **Basics:** 2075 South El Camino Real (at 21st Ave.), San Mateo. Tel: 341-2525. Hours: 5:30-10 pm Wed.-Sat.; 5-9 pm Sun. Closed Mon., Tues. Reservations necessary on weekends. Cards: MC, V. Wine and beer.

Estrellita's: Los Altos
Mexican/Handmade burritos that span the plate

A Mexican lady stops at your table. She looks like a character in a Steinbeck novel. Silently, she places a burrito in front of you. As you look down at the plate, your eyes widen to the size of frisbees. The burrito is huge! It stretches across the entire plate—it's a long, rolled, handmade tortilla . . . bulging with chicken and topped with a generous handful of mild green chiles, white and yellow cheeses, and a sauce that speaks with a true Mexican accent.

The lady who served you the burrito was the owner, Mrs. Bustamente. For the last 18 years, she's been serving people the kind of dishes you can't get everywhere—the kind that are made with honest ingredients and hard work. But she has help. At this humble-looking restaurant there is a staff of 10 women.

Besides the homecooked flavor of her dishes, Mrs. Bustamente's restaurant has another likeable characteristic: while the portions are large, the prices are small.

Menu Specialties: ☐ The Giant Burrito (filled with either chicken or hand-shredded center-cut beef.) ☐ Tamale (100% authentic, right down to the fact that Mrs. Bustamente shucks, boils, and grinds her own corn to make the masa dough. The tamale is packed with chicken, steamed in a cornhusk, and topped with a mild red chile sauce.)

☐ Beef and Chorizo Enchilada (a fresh corn tortilla rolled around a filling of beef and chorizo sausage. Topped with chopped onions, melted Monterey Jack and cheddar cheese, and Mrs. Bustamente's long-simmered red sauce.) **Prices:** Inexpensive. **Decor:** Concentrate on the food. The decor is . . . missing. Plain walls, plain tables. The closest thing to decoration is a 1956 pay phone on the wall. **Basics:** 971 North San Antonio Rd. (one block from the El Camino), Los Altos. Tel: 948-9865. Hours: 11 am-2 pm, 5-9 pm Tues.-Sat. Closed Sun., Mon. No cards. Wine and beer.

London House: Palo Alto
English Cooking/10 kinds of homemade cake daily

English tearooms have always been considered sort of saloons for ladies, with a special appeal to eighty-year-old matrons who wear those crinkly chiffon dresses you can see through but don't want to. According to the owner of the London House, Sheila Barnes, this is a misconception. Sheila notes that in England, both men and women patronize tearooms and she hopes that her tearoom in Palo Alto will attract the same balance of customers. Yes, Mrs. Barnes wants a co-ed tearoom.

The atmosphere of the London House would please anyone. With its arched walkways, stucco walls, tile floors, and coat of arms over the fireplace, this restaurant looks like a Spanish villa that was redecorated by a British ambassador. And the food is just as pleasing. There are English steak pies, chicken peach casseroles, and a variety of interesting sandwiches.

And then, mmmm, come the desserts. The London House makes the best desserts on the Peninsula. Depending on what day it is, there might be cinnamon apple cake with lemon butter frosting; orange, date, and walnut cake with brandy frosting; or English Eccles cake filled with currants and topped with a brown sugar sauce. But whatever they have, one thing's for sure—when the dessert cart rolls by, will powers collapse and lips start smacking.

Menu Specialties: *Lunch:* ☐ Sandwiches—chablis-poached salmon mixed with sour cream . . . a sandwich of English Stilton blue cheese flavored with port wine . . . a sandwich of chicken salad made with nine ingredients including walnuts and apples. Yes . . . unusual sandwiches. Not bad, considering the English are usually accused of being so conservative they iron their shoelaces. ☐ Imported English Crumpets (like muffins, only better. Topped with melted cheddar cheese studded with minced ham.) *Dinner:* ☐ Steak & Mushroom Pie ☐ Chicken Peach Casserole ☐ Cornish Pasty (a large, crescent-shaped pastry shell with a richly flavored beef filling.) Items above include salad. Dessert: 10 different cakes are featured daily. **Prices:** Inexpensive. **Basics:** 630 Ramona St. (one block off University), Palo Alto. Tel: 321-0778. Hours: 11 am-11 pm Tues.-Sat. Closed Sun., Mon. Cards: MC, V. Full bar.

The Antique: Palo Alto
Chicago-Style Pizza/The favorite of Alfonso Capone

During a Chicago bootleg war with "Bugs" Moran, Al Capone took a big risk and left his Cicero stronghold to eat at a pizzeria in Moran's territory. Why? Al loved Chicago-style pizza and this place served the best pies in town. Of course, when Capone visited his favorite pizzeria, he came "prepared." While Al and a showgirl sat there eating pizza, the front and back doors were being watched by a couple of Capone's men armed with submachine guns.

Is Chicago pizza worth those kind of risks? Judge for yourself. At the Antique in Palo Alto, it's the specialty of the house.

When you visit the Antique, you'll discover that Chicago-style pizza is a little different from the version we've all been eating for years. With this kind of pizza, the cheese and meat go on *first*. Then the pie is topped with an oregano-scented blanket of whole plum tomatoes. But the biggest difference is in the way it's cooked. Chicago pizza is baked in a deep, cast-iron pan. By using a pan, the pie comes out of the oven with a thick, flaky crust that's a full two inches high at the edges. It's sort of the skyscraper of pizza crusts.

Menu Specialty: ☐ Chicago-Style Sausage Pizza (the pie is brought to your table in the cast-iron pan it was baked in.) **Prices:** Inexpensive. **Decor:** You sit in big, comfortable booths, and you're surrounded by a collection of interesting antiques. Also, there's outdoor dining on an umbrella-shaded patio. **Basics:** 2700 El Camino Real (at Page Mill Road), Palo Alto. Tel: 329-0870. Hours: 11 am-10 pm Mon.-Thurs.; noon-12:30 am Fri., Sat.; 3:30-10 pm Sun. Cards: MC, V. Wine and beer. Parking lot.

"We'll take two orders of salmon, please."

At Monti's restaurant
the specialty is fresh seafood

For 26 years, Monti Montalbano ran a fish market in Redwood City. Then, one day in 1972, Monti had an idea. He put a few tables in the back of his fish market, bought a stove, and announced that he was ready to cook anything in the market's display cases. Monti had himself a restaurant. And the place became so successful that, in 1977, he moved to his present location — a fine looking restaurant in Menlo Park decorated with oak paneling, antiques, checkered tablecloths, and hurricane lanterns.

But Monti isn't making you pay for the move. His petrale sole, for example, is a reasonable $5.50, and his salmon is $6.25. Or for $6.50, Monti will serve you his crab cioppino — a huge bowl containing Dungeness crab legs in shell, Cherrystone clams, and bay shrimp in a Sicilian-style tomato sauce. The bowl is filled with so much seafood, you begin to feel like you just bought Fisherman's Wharf.

At Monti's, you'll be able to taste a tang-of-the-ocean freshness in everything. Each morning at 6 a.m., Monti goes to the wharf area of San Francisco and gets what he needs for the day. And when Monti gets there, he knows what to buy. Purchasing a good piece of fish requires a trained eye, and Monti is a living encyclopedia of seafood knowledge. He'll even try to tell you how a fish thinks. Monti sounds so believable, you feel like taking a peek behind his ears to see if you can spot any gills.

186

Menu Specialties: □ Crab Cioppino □ Filet of Petrale (fresh snow-white filets dipped in a seasoned egg batter and sauteed with white wine, sherry, and lemon.) □ Salmon, Swordfish or Red Snapper (all three are sauteed with wine and butter . . . it's a simple preparation that allows their delicate flavors to be gently coaxed out.)

□ Rex Sole or Sand Dabs Meuniere (boned filets in a lemon-butter sauce. Both fish are caught just outside the Golden Gate.) □ Combination Seafood Platter (oysters, scallops, sole, and prawns deep fried to a crisp golden brown.) Dishes include sauteed zucchini and French fries. **Prices:** Inexpensive to medium. **Basics:** 1706 El Camino Real (near Buckthorn), Menlo Park. Tel: 321-3724. Hours: 11 am-11 pm Mon.-Fri.; 5-11 pm Sat.; 4-10 pm Sun. Cards: MC, V. Full bar. Parking lot.

Galano's: Sunnyvale
Italian/Old World chef, modest prices

Charles Atlas can change the shape of your midsection in two months. Mike Galano's cooking can do it in one hour. Galano features a hearty brand of home-style Italian cooking. Chef Galano makes homemade lasagna, a thick vegetable-packed minestrone, beef Rolladine stuffed with prosciutto ham, and veal Bocconcino sauteed with Italian herbs and topped with melted cheese.

On the ocean side of Galano's menu our favorite dish is the filet of sole stuffed with crab, shrimp, and spinach. And twice a month, Galano puts four or five kinds of shellfish into a pot along with a fresh tomato sauce, and announces that he's throwing a cioppino feed. But no matter what Galano makes, you'll taste an authentic Old World flavor. And there's a reason. Galano is an Old World chef. For 11 years, Mike was chef at the famous Tramontano Hotel in Sorrento, Italy.

Galano doesn't charge you much to rearrange your shape. Most of his entrees, including soup or salad, and spaghetti, are in the $5.35 to $6.95 range. Or you can have a pasta dinner for around $3.95.

It's also Galano's policy to serve food as soon as it comes off the stove. So give your food a chance to cool off. We remember one man who didn't. His lasagna was still bubbling hot when he started to eat it. After one bite, the man let out such a scream, all of the workers at the General Motors plant in Fremont knocked off for lunch.

Menu Specialties: □ Veal Bocconcino □ Beef Rolladine (thinly-sliced New York steak rolled around a stuffing of prosciutto ham and Swiss cheese. Then sauteed in olive oil and burgundy wine, and topped with a mushroom sauce.) □ Filet of Sole Fiorentina (stuffed with crab, shrimp, and spinach, topped with romano cheese, fresh mushrooms, and a lemon-sauterne sauce, and baked.) □ Lasagna Sorrentina (a deck of homemade egg noodles—between the pasta cards are alternating layers of meat sauce and four cheeses: ricotta, mozzarella, aged romano, and parmesan.)

Dinner includes: Soup (a minestrone simmered for 12 hours with 7-10 seasonal vegetables), or salad (crisp lettuce, kidney beans and garbanzo beans tossed in a dressing made with olive oil, herbs, and a wine vinegar Galano makes himself from C.K. Mondavi jug wine), homemade rolls, and main course (except lasagna) with spaghetti. **Prices:** Inexpensive to medium. **Decor:** A casual, sunny, cheerful room with Italian plaques lining the walls. Galano's son acts as the host and does a good job of making everyone feel at home. **Basics:** 1635 Hollenbeck Ave. (at Homestead, in Loehmann Plaza, about 2½ miles from the El Camino Real), Sunnyvale. Tel: (408) 738-1120. Hours: 11 am-2:30 pm, 5-10 pm Mon.-Fri.; 4-10 pm Sat.; 2-9 pm Sun. Cards: MC, V. Full bar.

Alpine Inn: Burlingame
Swiss-German/Husband cooks, wife serves

There's a reason why the big restaurant chains resort to frozen food items and conveyor-belt cooking techniques—they're busy places, they just don't have the time to prepare things by the slower, more traditional methods. But at the Alpine Inn, chef Werner Bertram has time. Time to marinate his beef sauerbraten for one week. Time to make homemade spatzle dumplings and trim his own veal. Time to prepare fresh vegetables. And time to create a rich sauce for his filet of sole Cardinale. What the big chains don't have time to do, Bertram does.

This is the way things are done when the chef is European-trained instead of chain-trained. Chef Bertram began his apprenticeship at the age of 16 in Bonn, Germany, and apparently Bertram was a good student. At the end of his apprenticeship, he was asked to join the team of chefs who went to the Bonn villa of Chancellor Adenauer to prepare dinners for visiting government officials and heads of state. And for this kind of work, you have to be qualified in more ways than one. When President John F. Kennedy had dinner at the Bonn villa, Bertram was thoroughly investigated by the Secret Service.

Since then, Bertram's stovecraft has led him to jobs in a number of places, including a major hotel, a country club, and a large seaside restaurant. But eventually Bertram decided that he didn't want to spend the rest of his life in a large kitchen. He wanted to spend it in a small kitchen. So he and his wife opened the Alpine Inn. At the Inn, Bertram handles the cooking and his wife Heidi handles the service. And besides being a small, personal operation, there's also something else that makes the Inn appealing—reasonable prices. Most of the Alpine Inn's 3-course dinners are $6.25 to $7.50.

On our last visit to the Alpine Inn, we spotted a friend of ours. His presence was a tribute to the restaurant. He wouldn't be at the Alpine

Inn unless the food and prices represented real value. And he's the kind of man you just can't fool. He's a lawyer by profession, and they say he's so sharp, he could get Stevie Wonder a driver's license.

Menu Specialties: ☐ Sauerbraten (a choice cut of beef is first marinated for one full week, then slowly roasted, sliced "to order," and topped with a flavorful dark brown sauce with a gently tart backtaste. Served with homemade spatzle dumplings and chef Bertram's fresh red cabbage.) ☐ Veal Zurcher Geschnetzeltes (one of Switzerland's most famous dishes—thin, hand-cut strips of sauteed veal in a rich, shallot-accented cream sauce that's thick with fresh mushrooms. Served with homemade spatzle dumplings.) ☐ Filet of Sole Cardinale (fresh filet of English sole poached in a white wine court bouillon and then topped with a cognac-flavored lobster sauce.) ☐ Chicken Breast Alpine Inn (a distinctively stuffed breast of chicken in a light, fragrant mushroom sauce.)

Dinner includes . . . 3 courses: Soup (maybe German vegetable soup or potato-leek soup), salad (butter lettuce in a very tasty house dressing), and main course with fresh vegetable. **Prices:** Inexpensive to medium. **Decor:** Inside the small restaurant there's fresh flowers, candlelight, crisp linen, pictures of the Swiss Alps, and a tapestry depicting a 19th century German village. **Basics:** 401 Primrose Rd. (near Burlingame Ave., in the Library Plaza), Burlingame. Tel: 347-5733. Hours: 5:30-10 pm Tues.-Sat.; 4:30-9 pm Sun. Closed Mon. Cards: MC, V. Wine and beer.

L'Escargot: Burlingame
French/Candlelit bistro with moderate prices

The Case of
the Missing Chef

It all began one dark, misty night at 3 a.m. My colleague, Sherlock Holmes, had just found a way of getting into the restaurant and called me over. "Watson, the kitchen window's been left unlocked." Holmes climbed in first. I followed.

We didn't consider this break-in a gentlemanly thing to do, but we were here at the request of our clients—Riera and Smith. These men had received a vague report of the arrival of a good chef in the area, but could learn no more. The local townspeople were withholding information for fear it would be difficult getting a table if news of the chef's skill became general knowledge. Riera and Smith had begged us to find this chef and it was their appeal that brought us here tonight.

Once we were inside the empty kitchen, Sherlock Holmes removed his deerstalker hat and his cape-backed overcoat and set to work.

"Watson, old chap, please fetch me a menu," the detective said.

I returned with the menu. Holmes gave it a quick glance and then started examining the kitchen. As I followed him around, I had the feeling that Holmes knew what he was looking for.

An hour later, the master detective was finished. Putting down his magnifying glass, Holmes said, "I've determined that the chef at L'Escargot uses fresh vegetables, makes his soups from scratch, and is skilled at sauteing his veal Louise."

"How can you be sure?" I inquired.

Sherlock Holmes gave me a studied look. "Elementary, my dear Watson, elementary. The vegetable paring knives are dull from extended use. The burners on the stove are slightly indented—obviously from the pressure of soup pots simmering on them for long hours. And none of the saute pans have any of those telltale scratch marks which are produced when a pan must be vigorously rubbed with scouring pads after something has burned on the cooking surface. I believe, old fellow, we've found our man."

"Amazing!" I cried.

"Furthermore, while you were gone," Holmes continued, "I heated up some beef bourguignon I found in the icebox. Delicious. Care for a bite, Watson?"

Menu Specialties: ☐ Veal Louise (veal scallops sauteed in butter and finished with a rich cream sauce that announces a trio of flavors—

190

white wine, brandy, and cognac.) ☐ Beef Bourguignon (beef, mushrooms, and onions simmered slowly in a hearty burgundy wine sauce.) ☐ Chicken Diable (a tender breast coated with a spicy sourdough bread crumb crust, and served with a dark brown diable sauce.) ☐ Medallion Elder (a medallion of beef sauteed in butter and topped with a golden bearnaise sauce and bits of fresh tomato.) ☐ Salmon Duglere (a salmon filet in a distinctive cream sauce laced with bay shrimp.)

Dinner includes: Soup (maybe asparagus or potato-leek), or salad with a very good house dressing, main course with two fresh vegetables, and coffee. Dessert: Soufflé Glace (a light frozen soufflé flavored with Grand Marnier liqueur.) **Prices:** Medium. **Decor:** Inside the bistro, there's a small candlelit dining room with friendly French waiters and copper pots hanging on the walls. **Basics:** 1137 California Dr. (near Broadway), Burlingame. Tel: 344-4144. Hours: 6-10 pm Tues.-Sat. Closed Sun., Mon. Reservations necessary. Cards: V. Wine and beer.

China First: Palo Alto
Chinese/Interesting specialties, Uncle Wang style

Along the El Camino Real there are over a hundred Chinese restaurants. And many of them have the same boring menus. We've always wondered why. Then one day we were reading the newspaper and . . . aha! It all became clear. According to the article, the Chao Kwan Company in Hong Kong specializes in restaurants—*to go*. You send them $250,000. And they ship you a prefabricated restaurant—complete with tables, Chinese lanterns, waiters' uniforms, chopsticks, and a 6 months' supply of food. By following the easy instruction sheet included with the shipment, your contractor can erect you a 5,000 square-foot Chinese restaurant in 15 days. Ah yes, very interesting. The next time we see an empty 20-foot-high packing crate sitting next to a new Chinese restaurant on the El Camino, we'll know not to eat there.

From the outside, China First looks like it could be a Chao Kwan product—just another average Chinese restaurant. But that's where the similarities end. The owner here, Uncle Wang, isn't your average Chinese chef. "Uncle" is a title that the Chinese reserve for experienced chefs, and Uncle Wang has certainly earned his title. His restaurant in Manhattan was judged 4 stars by the *New York Times*.

China First's menu features a number of dishes that earned Uncle Wang his reputation. Like his richly-seasoned sliced leg of lamb, Hunan-style, a dish that must be deep-fried and then wok-tossed—all in less than three minutes. Then there's his minced squab soup, served in a special bamboo cup. The cup flavors the broth, and can only be used twice.

Those are the "simple" dishes. To make his Lake Tung Ting shrimp, Uncle Wang has to go through six different steps. The shellfish must be salted, placed under a cold water shower, hand-patted dry, and then marinated in Shao-Hsing wine, egg whites, and spices. Next, they're stir-fried with matchsticks of peanut-fed ham, fresh snow peas, and ginger. Finally, they're taken off the fire and brushed with a few drops of sesame oil. But all this effort produces results. Uncle Wang's Tung Ting shrimp is a dish that will ripple your face with pleasure.

Menu Specialties: ☐ Lake Tung Ting Shrimp ☐ Sliced Leg of Lamb, Hunan Style (in a silk-smooth, ginger-fragrant sauce that's laced with green onions and bamboo shoots.) ☐ Szechwan Beef (strips of beef with yellow ears of Taiwan baby corn, orange carrot ribbons, and bright green pepper curls in a spicy, reddish-brown sauce with a mild Szechwan pepper backtaste.)

☐ Sliced Chicken with Sizzling Rice (in an ivory-colored sauce embroidered with jade green snow peas that Uncle Wang personally goes to Chinatown to get. When the dish arrives at your table, the waiter mixes in nutty-flavored sizzling rice cakes.) ☐ Shredded Pork with Garlic Sauce (matchsticks of pork quickly stir-fried with cloud ear mushrooms, chives, and a Chinese garlic sauce. Yes, our old friend garlic—the object of many a love/hate relationship.)

☐ Ingredient Fried Rice (a flavorful Szechwan-style blend of rice, ham, chicken, shrimp, and peas.) ☐ Minced Squab Soup (you get a small portion. But don't be alarmed. The deep, fascinating flavor will prove that it took a large portion of squab to make this dish.) **Prices:** Medium. **Decor:** A large place with hand-carved teakwood screens, Chinese silk paintings, and white tablecloths. And good service . . . even to the point where the waiters describe each dish as it's served. **Basics:** 675 El Camino Real (near University, next to Holiday Inn), Palo Alto. Tel: 326-3900. Hours: 11:30 am-2:30 pm, 5-9 pm Mon.-Thurs., Fri. and Sat. to 10 pm; 5-9 pm Sun. Cards: MC, V. Full bar. Parking lot in back.

Pine Brook Inn: Belmont
Continental/Tree-shaded building, moderate prices

At the Pine Brook Inn, owner-chef Klaus Zander features moderately-priced 3-course dinners. It's a dinner that will have your attention right from the start.

Dinner begins with a salad. And chef Zander gives you the chance to make this salad look like a float in the Rose Bowl Parade. It might contain anything from marinated green beans and mushrooms to a Pennsylvania Dutch mix of julienne meats and cheese. It all depends on you. For your first course, the waitress brings you a bowl of romaine tossed in an herb-flavored dressing and a miniature smorgasbord of side dishes. Along with the salad, you're served four different kinds of bread—homemade Kadota fig muffins, Russian rye, sesame rolls, and Armenian flat bread.

Next comes a Flädle beef consomme in an earthenware tureen. The flavor of this soup primarily depends on the accuracy of your waitress. Armed with a Spanish goatskin bota bag, your waitress stands five paces from the table and squirts an arch of sherry into the tureen.

Between the soup and the main course, take a good look at your surroundings. Besides the restaurant's setting, everywhere you look in the dining room there's plants; even the restaurant itself has been carefully built around a huge redwood tree. The decor and the food make this restaurant an example of a partnership that works. At the Pine Brook Inn, Klaus takes care of the kitchen, and Mother Nature takes care of the decor.

Menu Specialties: ☐ Roulade of Beef (thin slices of flank steak rolled around a bacon-flavored stuffing and simmered in a burgundy wine sauce.) ☐ The Coachman's Pan (a boneless breast of chicken sauteed in butter with fresh mushrooms and artichoke hearts. Topped with a brandy cream sauce.) ☐ Roast Sirloin of Beef in Saltcoat (the beef is completely jacketed in rock salt. As the meat roasts, the salt melts into a diamond-like crust, sealing in the meat's natural juices . . . surprisingly without making the beef salty.)

Dinner includes . . . 3 courses: A crisp, crouton-laced romaine salad and the mini smorgasbord, Flädle beef soup, a basket generously filled with four different breads including the unusual fig muffins, main course with sauteed asparagus and scalloped potatoes with melted cheddar cheese, and a complimentary glass of plum wine. Dessert: Innkeeper's Rumpot (five fresh fruits marinated in Bacardi rum and liqueurs . . . vitamins with muscle.) **Prices:** Medium.

Attention Early Californians: The Pine Brook offers Sunday brunch. It's a 15-item, have-as-much-as-you-want buffet . . . including blueberry pancakes, German sausage, apple Danish, Canadian bacon, spinach soufflé, Baron of Beef, and champagne ($6.75). **Basics:** 1015 Alameda De Las Pulgas (at Ralston, about 1½ miles from the El Camino Real), Belmont. Tel: 591-1735. Hours: 11:30 am-2:30 pm Mon.-Fri.; 6-10 pm Tues.-Thurs.; 6-10:30 pm Fri.; 5:30-10:30 pm Sat.; 10:30 am-2 pm (brunch), 5-9 pm Sun. Closed Mon. evening. Cards: MC, V. Full bar. Parking lot.

St. Michael's Alley: Palo Alto
Creative Cooking/20 new dishes every night

St. Michael's is very popular with Stanford professors and students. These people have discovered that St. Michael's always has a library of interesting dishes to check out. Wait! There's a Stanford couple at the door, now. The guy is wearing a lamb's wool sweater so thick it has to be vacuumed, and his date is wearing a neon-yellow dress and a Garbo hat. Greeting them is the owner, Vernon Gates, a gray-haired writer who once ran a coffeehouse that employed many of Ken Kesey's Merry Pranksters—the legendary chemists of author Tom Wolfe's *The Electric Kool-Aid Acid Test*.

Vern leads the couple over to an eight-foot-high blackboard where the daily menu is listed. On the blackboard there are 20 choices. Tonight, the entrees include Indonesian lamb curry, veal bourguignon, Cornish game hen, and petrale sole with basil. While his guests look over the selection, Vern notes that St. Michael's makes its own chutney for the curry, and bakes its own bread. Wait! Before the couple can decide what to order, a waiter erases one entree from the blackboard and chalks in another. Vern apologizes and explains that he not only changes the menu daily, but sometimes in the middle of dinner—in the name of freshness.

The couple from Stanford settled on St. Michael's version of bourguignon—veal chunks browned in Italian olive oil according to a French recipe, and then simmered in California zinfandel. Did they enjoy this cultural mix? Yes. There are no rules in cooking, only sins. And the biggest sin is dullness. But as this couple found out, no one will ever call St. Michael's chef a sinner.

Menu Specialties: Although the menu changes daily, at least 20 dishes are featured each night . . . everything from chicken curry to fresh swordfish—when they can get it. The following dishes, however, tend to appear with some regularity: ☐ Veal Bourguignon ☐ Cornish Game Hen (a whole hen stuffed with herb-seasoned rice, raisins, and nuts, then topped with a peach sauce that teases you with a gentle tartness and caresses you with a hint of sweetness.) ☐ Crab Creole (a pot is filled with crab, fresh mushrooms, and vegetables until it's as crowded as New Orleans during the Mardi Gras. Next, the pot is flavored with white wine and Louisiana herbs. Finally, everything is simmered together for hours.) ☐ Pork Roast, Sauce St. Michael's (the meat is rubbed with garlic and sage, then roasted. Topped with a sauce made from 3 different wines and 6 spices. What are they? Alas, St. Michael would say no more.)

Dinner includes: Soup (maybe U.S. Senate bean soup or split pea laced with pastrami), or a butter lettuce salad with cherry tomatoes and black olives, main course with fresh vegetable (maybe zucchini in a sour cream-dill sauce), and homemade bread (baked each day by a man who arrives at 6 a.m. just for this purpose. He then spends some long, hard hours mixing up one of his specialties—cracked whole wheat, egg bread, or basil bread.)

Loafers Beware: In our opinion, St. Michael's talented baker produces bread of Whittington quality. What's Whittington quality? In 14th century England, Lord Mayor Whittington passed laws regulating the quality of English bread. Only breads of a high quality were allowed to be sold. No excuses. Bakers who violated the quality code were locked in knee-high stocks with a loaf of their substandard bread hung around their necks. But these weren't the only bakers who had to face strict penalties. In the 17th century, German bakers who cheated their customers were put in a straw basket and dunked in the Rhine with a seesaw contraption. Oh, yes . . . the law specified that the baker had to pay for the rental of the seesaw. **Prices:** Medium. **Decor:** Inside, there's natural wood walls, director's chairs, Tiffany lamps, lots of hanging plants, and soft background music, which keeps both plants and diners happy. **Basics:** 800 Emerson St. (at Homer, three blocks off University), Palo Alto. Tel: 329-1727. Hours: 11 am-10 pm Mon.-Sat.; 5-10 pm Sun. No cards. Wine and beer. Street parking usually available.

Bay Window: Menlo Park
Continental/A small neighborhood place with outdoor dining

Opening statements to the court:

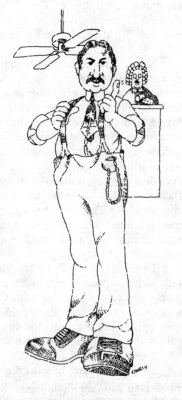

"Your Honor, in the case of the Bay Window, I'm going to prove beyond a shadow of a doubt that this is a restaurant worth knowing about. These are the facts.

First, let's look at the menu. The Bay Window has something for everybody. They feature a fresh fish of the day, beef bourguignon, Italian cannelloni, and chicken breast Divan topped with a sherry-cream sauce and cheddar cheese.

Fact number two. Their dinners are reasonably priced. Fresh fish is $4.95, cannelloni is $4.75, chicken Divan is $5.25, and beef bourguignon is $5.95. And dinner includes a homemade soup or a large tossed salad, an individual loaf of warm, crusty bread, garden fresh vegetables, and coffee.

Fact number three. The Bay Window has an inviting atmosphere. It's located in a Colonial-style red brick building, and inside, the dining room has sea-blue walls, comfortable booths, and striped pastel tablecloths. Plus the restaurant also has an oak tree-shaded patio that's used for outdoor dining.

In closing, your Honor, I would like to sum up this restaurant with a comment you made to me over and over again during our pretrial discussions at the Bay Window. As you yourself said each time I bought you and your wife dinner there, 'I can see this place has a lot to offer.'"

Menu Specialties: ☐ Chicken Divan ☐ Fish of the Day (the chef always has a saute pan ready for whatever is fish-market fresh. Usually featured—petrale sole, sea bass or red snapper.) ☐ Cannelloni (rolled pasta stuffed with a veal and spinach filling and topped with mozzarella, Monterey Jack, and parmesan cheese. Then a fresh tomato sauce is added and the cannelloni is baked.) □ Beef Bourguignon (chunks of beef simmered in a red wine sauce laced with pearl onions, fresh mushrooms, and smoked ham.)

Dinner includes: Soup (maybe cream of potato-leek or split pea), or salad (butter lettuce, cherry tomatoes and cucumbers tossed in the Bay Window's house dressing), an individual loaf of bread, fresh vegetable (maybe corn-on-the-cob or stuffed zucchini), and coffee. **Prices:** Inexpensive. **Basics:** 1026 Alma St. (near Ravenswood, one block off El Camino), Menlo Park. Tel: 326-6666. Hours: 11:30 am-2:15 pm, 5:30-8:30 pm Mon.-Fri.; noon-2:15 pm Sat. Closed Sat. evening and Sun. No cards. Wine and beer.

Estrada's: Daly City
Fried Chicken/The Colonel isn't the only one with a secret

Fried chicken. Along with apple pie, it's the co-captain of the team of food that the world recognizes as American. But this doesn't mean that fried chicken is completely free from foreign intervention. A Mexican restaurant in Daly City called Estrada's serves one of the best versions of fried chicken we've had locally. It's perfectly crisp and golden outside and moist and tender inside. What's their secret? Estrada's isn't saying. Maybe they're afraid the Colonel might find out.

The perfect partner for your chicken is the tostada Compuesta, a hot salad. Resting on a fried tortilla foundation is a layer of refried beans, a mild homemade chile sauce, freshly grated cheddar cheese, and a mound of crisp shredded lettuce. At the last minute, vinegar is sprinkled over the hot tostada. Clouds of steam float from the plate and give your face a free Turkish bath when this dish reaches your table.

Menu Specialties: Instructions for a chicken feast—have the waitress bring you two platters of *Estrada's Fried Chicken*, a mist-producing *Tostada Compuesta,* and a couple of bottles of *Dos Equis Beer.* With the table so set, gaze into the eyes of·your partner and say, "Let the finger-lickin' begin." **Prices:** Inexpensive. **Decor:** A large, comfortable room with wrought iron trim and soft lighting. There's no Mexican music, but after a few bottles of Dos Equis, you may hear some anyway. **Basics:** 7440 Mission St. (near San Pedro), Daly City. Tel: 755-1282. Hours: 4-10:30 pm Tues.-Sun. Closed Mon. No cards. Full bar. Parking lot.

Three Peninsula Pizzerias

They make it the right way

In the dining room, everything is peaceful and fairly quiet. Meanwhile, in the kitchen . . . Whap! Whump! Thud! Whap! It sounds like there's a fight going on. But it's just the sound of someone hand-pounding the pizza dough at Formico's, Jose's, and John's. It's extra work, but it's the only way to make a really good pizza. And making a good pizza is what these three places are all about.

Formico's, Jose's, and John's are our favorite pizzerias on the Peninsula. Each place is owned by a highly talented pizzacrafter. At Formico's, there's Vito, who makes thick-crusted New York-style pizza that's topped with his own homemade sausage. At Jose's, there's Jose Ibanez, a Cuban who's adapted some of his island's cooking methods to Italian pizza—with successful results. And at John's, there's Mr. Natale, who's been making pizza since 1943. And it shows. When Mr. Natale makes a pizza, he does it with style. He pounds the pizza dough like he was a heavyweight boxer; he tosses the dough into the air like he was an Olympic discus thrower; and he catches it like he was a major league baseball player fielding a fly ball.

John's Pizza: Salami or ham: small, $3.15; medium, $3.95; large, $4.65. Combination (salami, pepperoni, bell peppers, ham, and Italian fennel sausage), small, $4.65; medium, $5.45; large, $6.35. **Basics:** 484 El Camino Real (at Whipple), Redwood City. Tel: 364-1090. Hours: 4-midnight daily. Cards: MC, V. Wine and beer. Parking lot.

Formico's Pizza: Homemade sausage or black olive: small, $2.75; medium, $3.45; large, $4.30. Stromboli Pizza (mushrooms, pepperoni, salami, and sausage), small, $3.50; medium, $4.50; large, $5.50. **Basics:** 2115 St. Francis Dr. (near Embarcadero, just west of Highway 101, in the Edgewood Plaza), Palo Alto. Tel: 328-6532. Hours: 11 am-11 pm Mon.-Thurs.; 11 am-midnight Fri.; 4-midnight Sat. Closed Sun. No cards. Wine and beer.

Jose's Pizza: Mushroom: small, $2.90; medium, $4.50; large, $6.50. Jose's Special (pepperoni, mushrooms, and Spanish chorizo sausage), small, $3.50; medium, $6.15; large, $7.90. **Basics:** 2275 El Camino Real (near Cambridge), Palo Alto. Tel: 326-6522. Hours: 11:30 am-2:30 pm Tues.-Fri.; 5:30-10 pm Tues.-Sun. Closed Mon. Cards: MC, V. Wine and beer.

Le Pot-Au-Feu: Menlo Park
French/Moderately priced, chef-owned bistro

Discovering Le Pot-au-Feu was about as surprising as finding out that Santa's elves no longer make the toys, but get them by shoplifting. Le Pot-au-Feu is the kind of restaurant you'd expect to find along a vineyard-lined road in France. But instead, we found Le Pot-au-Feu in Menlo Park, U.S.A.

Le Pot-au-Feu's chef and owner, Jean Cornil, describes his bistro as "very casual." True. The walls are plastered with French wine labels; a couple of tables are shaded by Cinzano umbrellas; and when Jean opens a bottle of champagne, he sometimes shoots the cork into the ceiling.

The food here reflects Jean's straightforward attitude. He offers fresh Napa Valley chicken simmered in a hearty burgundy wine sauce with mushrooms and slivers of bacon, and Le Pot-au-Feu, the mainstay dish of the French housewife. To make this dish, Jean slowly cooks herb-seasoned briskets of beef in an earthenware pot brimming with a garden of fresh vegetables.

It's touches like these that make Le Pot-au-Feu the opposite of the stereotyped haughty French restaurant—where the maitre'd has a smile nailed to his face, suggests a bottle of chateau whateveritis, and is ready to do a somersault for a $20 bill.

Menu Specialties: ☐ Le Pot-au-Feu ☐ Chicken au Vin Napa Valley ☐ Duckling a la Orange (tender roast duckling topped with a classic orange sauce that has just the right sweet-tart balance.) ☐ Salmon en Croute (two slices of salmon with a layer of tarragon cream sauce in the middle. The salmon is then encased in a flaky pastry dough and molded into the shape of a fish! Beautiful. The baked salmon is served with beurre blanc—a chablis-butter sauce.) ☐ Beef Brochette aux Champignons (tender, well-trimmed pieces of filet mignon topped with fresh mushrooms sauteed in butter.)

Dinner includes . . . 3 courses: Soup (maybe cream of potato and leek or a country-style split pea soup), salad (butter lettuce and red leaf lettuce tossed in a light, tasty house dressing), and main course with two vegetables (maybe puree of fresh broccoli and sauteed potatoes.)
Prices: Medium. **Basics:** 1149 El Camino Real (near Santa Cruz), Menlo Park. Tel: 322-4343. Hours: 6-10 pm Tues.-Sat. Closed Sun., Mon. Cards: MC, V. Wine and beer. Parking lot in back.

Peking Duck: Mountain View
Chinese/The Imperial duck ceremony, an experience

Since the 1920s, jade buyers visiting the Orient have been warned by their firms to wear dark glasses whenever they make a purchase. Chinese jade dealers are known to watch a buyer's eyes to determine how much the buyer is willing to pay for a gem. This practice is based on the scientific fact that the pupils of the eyes widen when something pleases a person. See for yourself. Go to the Peking Duck restaurant with a hand mirror. Then taste their Peking duck and have a look. You'll notice that your pupils are almost the size of bowling balls.

This restaurant's Peking duck is an impressive dish—one that shouts its Chinese heritage. The kitchen's method of preparing Peking duck dates back almost 300 years to the Ch'ing dynasty. The plump, tender ducks are roasted s-l-o-w-l-y, according to an ancient recipe of the Imperial Palace, and then served in the traditional Peking manner. The first platter served contains squares of crisp, beautifully glazed skin, which the Chinese consider the best part of the duck. Next, comes some of the meat itself, carefully cut into bite-size pieces and accompanied by stacks of paper-thin Chinese pancakes and a special sauce that explodes with flavor. You put the pancake, sauce, and moist tender meat together and eat. And eat. The platters of meat keep coming from the kitchen until the entire duck has been carved and served. Whew! By the time you're finished, it's obvious that this dish involved a dizzying amount of work. But this is what tradition demands. The Chinese have been preparing Peking duck the same way for almost 300 years. No one's going to make any sudden changes now.

Menu Specialties: Peking duck isn't all this restaurant features. Other specialties: ☐ Jade Fountain Shrimp (this famous West China specialty needs two things: understanding hands to toss-cook the delicate shrimp, and a flavorful crimson sauce perfumed with wine. The chef supplies both.) ☐ Imperial Chicken (a lesson in contrasts—pieces of snow-white chicken breast and crisp, light brown water chestnuts framed against an ebony-colored sauce.) ☐ Chung King Pork (Chinese vegetables, bamboo shoots, and lean tender pork stir-fried in a sauce made with imported Szechwan red peppers. But don't worry, the chef is careful with the peppers; the dish is always a pleaser rather than a scorcher.)

☐ Peking Duck Dinner (includes: the Peking duck, shrimp chips, fresh winter melon soup, a platter of Peking vegetables—a stir-fried garden of broccoli, snow peas, green peppers, bamboo shoots, and carrots—rice, tea, cookies, and *one of the above dishes*. Note: The duck must be ordered one day in advance and there should be at least two people in your party.) **Prices:** Medium to a step above medium. **Decor:** A small dining room with bamboo screens, Chinese lanterns . . . and a nice Western touch—white tablecloths. **Basics:** 702 Villa St. (near

Castro), Mountain View. Tel: 968-1040. Hours: 11 am-2 pm, 5-9 pm
Mon.-Sat. Closed Sun. Cards: AE, MC, V. Wine and beer.

A Short History . . .

The Sandwich
Est. 1762

A sandwich is harder to make than you think. The world's first
working model wasn't put together until 1762.

The event took place at an aristocratic men's club in London. A
member of the club, an Earl named John Montagu, was a compulsive
gambler. As the sun began to rise one morning in 1762, Montagu had
just completed his 29th hour at the club's gaming tables without eating.
A platter of onion-sauced beef next to him was too messy to eat with his
hands and use of silverware would have taken his attention away from
the cards. Finally, dizzy with hunger, Montagu grabbed two pieces of
bread and used them like tongs to pick up the meat. Aha! He found he
could hold his cards with one hand and eat with the other. Rather than
call his discovery a "Montagu," he named it after his royal title. And
Montagu was the fourth Earl of Sandwich. (The Hawaiian Islands, once
called the Sandwich Islands, were also named after the Earl.)

Since 1762, the Earl of Sandwich's invention has come a long way.
Below, we've listed three sandwich shops that have made some good
improvements on the Earl's original working model.

Perfect Recipe—*19 sandwich combinations:* This place is a
something-for-everyone sandwich cafe. Their roll call of sandwiches
includes Danish ham and Norwegian Jarlsberg cheese; turkey with
cranberry and imported Swiss cheese; and a sandwich of hickory-
smoked roast beef with a tomato and horseradish-spiked cream cheese.
All sandwiches are $2.85. Sandwich partners: Italian vegetable salad
($1.35). Like some Peruvian coffee? At the Perfect Recipe, 18 kinds of
foreign coffee are available by the cup (40¢). **Decor:** In a shopping
center, but the decor helps you to forget . . . everywhere you look
there's natural wood walls, redwood tables, and hanging plants. All a
room like this needs to be totally natural is organic nails. **Basics:** 76
Stanford Shopping Center (near University), Palo Alto. Tel: 327-3890.
Hours: 9 am-10 pm Sun.-Wed.; 9 am-11:30 pm Thurs.-Sat.

Mayven Lane—*Jewish deli-style sandwiches:* Let's face it—some
places serve pastrami that's so dried out and tasteless, you're not sure if
it's pastrami or a page from the Dead Sea Scrolls. But not here. This
Jewish sandwich shop serves a deli-style pastrami sandwich that's a
moist, flavorful classic ($2.25). Also, there's kosher salami ($1.95),
and a chopped chicken liver sandwich ($1.95). Instead of a sandwich?

The owner, Mrs. Rosman, makes excellent blintzes—a Jewish crepe filled with two kinds of cheese and served with sour cream and strawberry preserves ($2.85). **Decor:** There's a blue and green village-scene mural, a striped canopy overhead, and sun yellow tables with chairs that look like little park benches. **Basics:** 1204 Broadway (near Laguna), Burlingame. Tel: 344-2193. Hours: 8 am-3 pm Mon., Wed.-Sun. Closed Tues. Wine and beer.

Togo's—*Huge Italian submarine sandwiches:* If you can fit your mouth around a watermelon, you should be able to handle one of Togo's sandwiches. They even have their French rolls custom-baked for them—regular rolls just aren't big enough for the kind of sandwiches that Togo's makes. And Togo's also thinks big when it comes to variety: 25 different Subs are offered. Our favorite? No. 16—Genoa salami, Coppacolla ham, provolone cheese, mortadella, and Cotto salami topped with lettuce, tomato, onions, pickles, and peppers ($1.40). **Decor:** A simple-looking, comfortable place with a self-service counter and plenty of room to sit back and attack your Sub. **Basics:** 4131 El Camino "Way" (near the intersection of El Camino Real and West Charleston), Palo Alto. Tel: 494-8223. Hours: 11 am-10 pm daily. Wine and beer. Parking lot.

Tino's: San Mateo
Italian-Continental/European atmosphere

Back East, there are many Mafia-run restaurants. When New Yorkers go to a Sicilian dinner house, they usually have to ask for bulletproof napkins. In California, we don't have this problem. Although Tino's is owned by three Sicilian brothers, a burst of fire here simply means that one of the Costantino brothers is preparing a dish on the brick cooking island in the middle of the dining room. And when one of the Brother's Costantino has his hand on a flaming saute pan, it's easy to see that there's years of experience in every flick of the wrist. These men learned their trade at papa Costantino's restaurant in Sicily and then worked at a number of major restaurants in Europe.

The bulk of what the Costantino brothers learned in their travels is now being applied at Tino's. Their chicken parmigiana, veal saltimbocca, and prawns Provencale all possess an authentic, hard-to-define European flavor. The brothers even make their own pasta—just the way papa Costantino taught them to do.

At Tino's, you'll also find that the service, like the crystal, is highly polished—another result of the Costantino's European training. Of course, their many years of training does create one drawback . . . experience doesn't come at cut-rate prices. If you go to Tino's with another couple, and there's any question about who's picking up the bill, be sure to reach for the check like it was a piece of broken glass.

Menu Specialties: □ Prawns Provencale (large, moist prawns in a sauce based on butter, tomatoes, garlic, and white wine.) □ Veal Saltimbocca (four tender veal scallops topped with paper-thin slices of prosciutto ham, and served in a rich, sage-flavored brown sauce.) □ Chicken Parmigiana (boned breast, coated with a sourdough crumb-egg batter and sauteed. Then topped with Telame cheese and baked in a fresh marinara sauce.)

Dinner includes: Soup (maybe onion soup topped with melted Gruyere cheese or a vegetable soup dense with the season's best), or salad (crisp romaine lettuce tossed in Tino's herb dressing), and main course with sauteed Italian vegetables and potatoes au gratin.

Starters: Pasta Costantino—the Costantino brothers went to Italy and purchased a special pasta-making machine. And they use it every day to make: Ravioli Bolognese; Tortellini (stuffed with meat and covered with a smooth cream sauce); and Lasagna Pasticciate (green spinach noodles layered with a white sauce, a red sauce, and two cheeses.)

Dessert: Profiterole (homemade pastry puffs filled with whipped cream and coated with a dark, rich chocolate sauce.) **Prices:** A step above medium to expensive. **Decor:** Two small rooms, light yellow walls, red drapes, white tablecloths, waiters in tuxedos . . . all in all, the decor makes you feel wealthier than you are. **Basics:** 1208 South El Camino Real (near 12th Ave.), San Mateo. Tel: 573-7555. Hours: 5-10 pm Tues.-Thurs., Sun.; 5-11 pm Fri., Sat. Closed Mon. Reservations suggested on weekends. Cards: MC, V. Full bar. Parking lot in back.

Shalimar: Sunnyvale
Indian/The house recipes, 1,000 years old

The recipes which the Shalimar's owner, Sharda Tawde, uses to prepare her curries are over 1,000 years old. Originally, these recipes were the closely-guarded secrets of Indian chefs serving royalty. But they eventually lost this privileged status. Competitive Indian cooks outside the royal kitchen learned how to duplicate these dishes down to the smallest detail by following T.S. Eliot's advice: "The amateur imitates, the pro steals."

And these recipes aren't all this restaurant has to offer. At the Shalimar, you'll be dining on dishes meant for royalty . . . but at prices meant for us common folks. The Shalimar's 4-course chicken or beef curry dinner is $5.25. Plus at Mrs. Tawde's restaurant, you'll also get something you can't buy at any price—the services of a cook who works like she really cares. Although she wears gold jewelry and a cinnamon-colored silk sari, Mrs. Tawde moves around the stove like a determined typhoon.

Menu Specialties: □ Chicken or Beef Curry (both meats are wedded to a mild curry sauce with a deep, rich, mysterious flavor. The sauce contains a 10-spice mix that's personally blended by Mrs. Tawde. Both curries are served with homemade pineapple chutney.)

Dinner includes . . . 4 courses: Samosas (golden-brown triangles filled with spicy ground beef), Pakoda (slices of zucchini dipped in a seasoned Indian batter and deep-fried. Served with homemade mint chutney.), main course with Indian-style vegetables and delicately cooked saffron rice, and Raita (a fruit salad of Mandarin oranges, bananas, and strawberries in a sour cream dressing.) **Prices:** Inexpensive. **Decor:** A small, modest-looking place with Indian sitar music playing in the background. The Taj Mahal, it isn't. Comfortable, it is. **Basics:** 1061 East El Camino Real (half a mile from the Lawrence Expressway), Sunnyvale. Tel: (408) 249-3332. Hours: 11:30 am-2 pm, 5:30-8 pm Tues.-Fri.; 6-9 pm Sat. Closed Sun., Mon. No cards. Wine and beer. Parking lot.

SAN JOSE

Fisherman's Village: Cupertino
Seafood/Chef-owned establishment with real "net" worth

If you wanted to get into Edwardo Del Rosario's dining room a few years ago, it would have cost you $1,500 per person. Of course, Edwardo had a special dining room. It had six diesel engines, and was able to reach Australia in two weeks. You see, for 10 years Edwardo was head chef on the luxury liner President Roosevelt.

Today, it's no longer necessary to go to sea for a taste of Edwardo's cooking. He now owns Fisherman's Village, a restaurant in Cupertino. And Edwardo's specialty is bringing the sea to you. He gets his oysters from the Eastern seaboard, his king crab from the icy bays of Alaska, and his plump, sweet prawns from the warm waters of the Gulf of Mexico. But don't get the idea that Edwardo has forgotten our local waters. Until he needs them, his halibut, sea bass, and petrale sole can be found swimming off the coast of California.

The seafood that Edwardo gets from his suppliers is very good. But that doesn't satisfy a chef like Edwardo Del Rosario. Before he gives it to you, he makes it even better. As you navigate through Edwardo's menu, you'll find oysters Rockefeller in a creamy Pernod-spiked Mornay sauce, sea bass Reggio in a fine Sicilian red sauce, petrale sole Marguery stuffed with shrimp, and crab legs Diavolo—with each leg wearing a golden, herb-flavored crust. Edwardo also prepares shellfish Louisiana Creole-style. And the dish that results is as interesting as a Dixie jazzman's past, as rich as a Mississippi gambler with a pair of loaded dice, and as spicy as the language of a Creole madam who's been shortchanged.

This restaurant gives you many indications that it's a seafood house. Outside, there's a red and white whaling boat on display. Inside, there are plush booths that overlook two huge aquariums holding a rainbow of tropical fish, including some very expensive—and deadly—Lion fish, which are said to be more poisonous than cobras. And in the kitchen there's Edwardo, surrounded by so much seafood it looks like he's planning to open up a new ocean.

Menu Specialties: □ Oysters Rockefeller □ Sea Bass Reggio □ Sole Marguery (fresh petrale sole stuffed with shrimp and oysters, and cloaked with a lemony cream sauce.) □ Crab Legs Diavolo □ Creole Shellfish (clams and shrimp in an "interesting," "rich," and "spicy" tomato-based New Orleans sauce.) □ Fettucine Vongole (thin ribbons of pasta and tender, moist baby clams in a flavorful, garlic-spiked sauce.)

□ Halibut Steak Cardinale (topped with mozzarella cheese and baked in a mushroom-dotted white wine-cream sauce.) □ Crab Cioppino Siciliano (you get a bib. An oyster fork. A shellfish cracking tool. And you get a giant tureen, filled to the brim with fresh Dungeness crab, Cherrystone clams, and Gulf prawns in a sauce of tomatoes, wine, and herbs. The Red Sea has come to you.)

Dishes include Italian-style sauteed vegetables and rigatoni Edwardo. Dessert: Sicilian Cannoli (a crisp pastry shell filled with a creamy mixture of ricotta, chocolate chips, candied fruit, and rum.) **Prices:** Medium. **Basics:** 19930 Stevens Creek Blvd. (near Blaney, about one mile from the DeAnza Blvd. exit off Highway 280), Cupertino. Tel: (408) 996-2332. Hours: 11:30 am-10:30 pm Mon.-Fri.; 4-11 pm Sat., Sun. Reservations suggested on weekends. All major cards. Full bar. Parking lot.

Cranberry House: Los Gatos
Old-Fashioned American Cooking/Williamsburg decor

The rebellion against "the American way" has affected every corner of society, but so far, the Cranberry House is still practicing old-fashioned Americanism in its kitchen. At the Cranberry House, they grind their own country sausage, make their own sweet watermelon pickles, marinate their Yankee pot roasts for a full 36 hours, and bake everything from banana nut bread to yeast rolls. By the time you finish your dinner with a slice of chocolate rum pie, you're ready to stand up, put your hand over your heart, and recite the Pledge of Allegiance.

The owner of the Cranberry House is Reed Whitelam, a hard-working gentleman who walks around wearing a bow tie and a wool cardigan. He looks like the corner grocer who used to sell you penny candy. Between trips to the market to hand-pick his vegetables, seafood, and meats, Reed has found the time to assemble an unusual collection of antique music boxes and clocks. So now Mr. Whitelam's dining room has two noticeable features—a Williamsburg decor and an interesting assortment of things that go tinkle, tweet, chirp, and cuckoo. He even has the world's first juke box, an ancient wooden machine that plays "big" hits—tin records two feet in diameter. Mr. Whitelam's collection interested Columbia Records so much, they came down and recorded a mechanical concert for an album. You might say that Reed Whitelam is the P.T. Barnum of the music box.

Menu Specialties: ☐ Maryland Baked Crab (crab meat cooked in a sherry-cream sauce.) ☐ Breast of Chicken (served with pan gravy and orange-flavored cranberry sauce.) ☐ Yankee Pot Roast ☐ Virginia Ham Steak (a butter-grilled ham steak garnished with pineapple.) ☐ Homemade Country Sausage with Cinnamon Applesauce ☐ Roast Prime Rib of Beef (you're served a moist, slowly roasted cut of beef with a flavor that's as American as baseball and John Wayne. Saturday only.) ☐ Roast Tom Turkey with Dressing (Sunday only.)

Dinner includes . . . 3 courses: Appetizer dish of sweet watermelon pickles, a basket of banana bread, yeast rolls, and pumpkin bread, soup (maybe chicken rice or navy bean), or salad, main course with fresh mashed potatoes and baked spinach, and dessert (maybe peanut pie, strawberry shortcake, or chocolate rum pie.) **Prices:** Inexpensive. **Basics:** 208 Bachman Ave. (near Santa Cruz Ave., two blocks off Highway 9), Los Gatos. Tel: (408) 354-3162 Hours: 11:30 am-2 pm, 5:30-9 pm Wed.-Sat.; noon-8 pm Sun. Closed Mon., Tues. Cards: MC, V. Full bar.

Emile's Swiss Affair: San Jose
Continental/Romantic setting and the best food in town

Chef Emile Mooser has a wall that talks. And it has a lot to say. At the entrance to Emile's restaurant, there's a wall filled with awards that Emile has won for his cooking. In the 28 years Emile has been cooking in the capitals of Europe, South America, Canada, and the United States, he's been showered with trophies, citations, plaques, and other awards, including the Antoine Carême medal. This medal, which Emile won in 1970, is awarded to only five chefs in the world each year.

And there have been other honors. When Emile was chef at the Windsor Hotel in Ontario, Canada, he was asked to prepare a dinner for the visiting Queen of England.

Emile's years of restaurant experience have taught him that if a chef's food is to be fully appreciated, it must be framed in the right atmosphere. At Emile's restaurant this means you'll find soft lights, snow-white tablecloths, fresh baby roses, and polished, hand-carved woodwork. The dining room seems to say, "slow down, relax, enjoy." And so does the service. At Emile's, there's a helpful, well-trained staff of friendly waiters who take an honest pride in the food they serve.

They have a right to be proud. In our opinion, this restaurant serves the best food in San Jose. Emile's menu is filled with a collection of interesting specialty dishes that he's perfected over the years, including a golden-colored prawn soup, a distinctive chicken Jerusalem with artichoke hearts and mushrooms, and Grenadins Trois Rois—medallions of beef, lamb, and veal with three different sauces.

Another one of Emile's specialties is Fruits de Mer en Croustade, a huge puff pastry boat filled with lobster meat, prawns, scallops, and fresh petrale quenelles, and crowned with a rich lobster sauce. We won't attempt to give this dish a rating. There's no need to. When chef Mooser finishes preparing the Fruits de Mer en Croustade, a tiny galaxy of ★★★ immediately forms over the dish.

Menu Specialties: ☐ Fruits de Mer en Croustade ☐ Grenadins Trois Rois (have you ever had one of those "I'm-going-to-order-everything-on-the-menu" fantasies? If you have, order this dish. It may not be "everything," but it's a good start. You're served three broiled

208

filets—beef, lamb, and veal—each topped with its own sauce. The beef comes with a classic bearnaise sauce; the lamb is christened with a finely-seasoned herb butter; and the veal is served with a silk-smooth Madeira sauce.) ☐ Chicken Saute Jerusalem (moist, tender pieces of chicken regally coated with an ivory-colored, white wine cream sauce laced with artichoke hearts, fresh mushrooms and bits of chives.)

☐ Veal Piccata Facon du Chef (this is one of Emile's creations. He takes milk-fed Wisconsin veal, dips it in egg and parmesan cheese, sautes it, and then serves the veal in a special sauce he created for the dish—a sauce that has more secrets than the Winchester Mystery House.) Dishes include two fresh vegetables (maybe zucchini sauteed with sweet basil, and broccoli in Mornay sauce.) Starters: Prawn Bisque (a rich, buttery, cream of prawn soup flavored with brandy.) **Prices:** Medium to expensive. **Basics:** 545 South 2nd St. (near East William), San Jose. Tel: (408) 289-1960. Hours: 5-9:30 pm Tues.-Thurs., Sun.; 5-10 pm Fri., Sat. Closed Mon. Reservations necessary. Cards: AE, MC, V. Wine and beer.

Foo-Loo-Soo: Campbell
Chinese/A small cafe with small prices

Foo-Loo-Soo's primary asset is that it's a small, personal operation. The owner, a friendly Chinese lady named Mrs. Hsu, does all the cooking herself. And when an owner is in the kitchen, the food always seems to benefit. At Foo-Loo-Soo, you can taste "pride" in every dish Mrs. Hsu makes. Of course, you'll also be tasting "experience." Mrs. Hsu has been a professional cook for the last 20 years.

Menu Specialties: ☐ Chicken with Water Chestnuts (well-trimmed pieces of chicken breast are toss-cooked with pieces of crunchy, fresh-tasting water chestnuts and strips of green pepper in a flavorful, mildly spicy sauce.) ☐ Shrimp with Cashew Nuts (shrimp, green onions, and roasted cashew nuts woven together in a light Chinese wine sauce with a gently sweet backtaste.) ☐ Shredded Pork with Hot Sauce (ribbons of tender pork, Chinese vegetables, and ginger stir-fried in a hot bean sauce. But don't worry about the sauce having more kick than a Kung-Fu instructor. The "heat" is kept well under control.)

☐ Beef with Oyster Sauce (tender, marinated strips of beef and fresh broccoli are stir-fried in, as Mrs. Hsu says, "the best brand of oyster sauce from Hong Kong.") **Prices:** Inexpensive. **Decor:** A small place that basically looks like an American coffee shop. Except for one thing. Foo-Loo-Soo also has a Chinese grocery section. On one side of the room, there's two rows of tables, and on the other side of the room there's some unplanned artwork—a colorful mosaic of shelves stocked with Chinese food items. **Basics:** 2895 South Bascom Ave. (near Camden, in the Victoria Plaza), Campbell. Tel: (408) 377-4830. Hours: 4-8 pm Wed.; noon-9 pm Thurs.-Mon. Closed Tues. Cards: MC, V.

Old Spaghetti Factory: San Jose
$2.95 pasta dinner + a fascinating decor = cheap thrill

This restaurant has let it be known that a certain undesirable element isn't welcome here. At the Old Spaghetti Factory, they don't allow inflation through the door. The average dinner here only costs $2.95 and includes a salad with blue cheese dressing, an individual loaf of sourdough bread with garlic butter, coffee, spumoni ice cream, and a big plate of spaghetti topped with a long-simmered meat sauce.

Needless to say, the Spaghetti Factory's low prices are a people magnet, so there is usually a Cecil B. De Mille-style crowd scene at the bar. On a Saturday night, there's usually a wait, but the time should go fast. It'll take you that long to absorb the surroundings. Housed in an old brick warehouse, the Spaghetti Factory is the pasta version of the Mad Hatter's Tea Party. As you scan the interior, you can't help but wonder: why are some of the tables made out of brass bed frames? Where did they get this gargoyle-green couch I'm sitting on? Oh, yes, what's a 1910 Birney streetcar doing parked *in the middle of the dining room?* And finally you'll wonder, as we did, who was the author of the note scratched on the old wooden telephone booth? The message read, "This is the weirdest restaurant we've found on your planet."

Menu Specialty: □ Spaghetti with Meat Sauce (a deep red sauce that's simmered for one full day. And if you're athletically inclined, remember this: according to *Guinness,* the world's record for eating spaghetti is 100 yards in 67.0 seconds.)

Dinner includes: Tossed green salad, a loaf of sourdough bread, main course, coffee, and spumoni ice cream. Liquid Assets: Drink your way around the world . . . 36 kinds of foreign beer are available. **Prices:** Inexpensive. **Basics:** 51 North San Pedro St. (near West Santa Clara), San Jose. Tel: (408) 288-7488. Hours: 5-10 pm Mon.-Thurs.; 5-11 pm Fri., Sat.; 4-10 pm Sun. No cards. Full bar.

Las Cazuelas: San Jose
Mexican/Authentic cooking and unusual specialties

As the side show barker once asked, "You looking for something different?" If you are, this is the place. Although Las Cazuelas offers the Standards, they also feature dishes that are rarely found at most Mexican restaurants. So step right up, folks! Las Cazuelas is offering you a peek into the inner soul of Mexican cooking.

Menu Specialties: □ Pescado Veracruzana (rock cod in a green olive and Jalapeño sauce.) □ Pollo en Almendrado (chicken in a tasty red sauce thick with crushed almonds. Although seldom seen here, this rich almond sauce is very popular in Mexico.) □ Enchiladas de Camaron (rolled tortillas filled with tiny bay shrimp and covered with a yellow roof of Quesito—a mild Mexican cheese. For a flavor contrast, the enchiladas are also landscaped with guacamole.) □ Chile Morita (pork chunks simmered in a sauce made from the Morita pod—a chile which is highly prized among the Mexicans.)

Items above include salad, or Spanish chicken soup, refried beans, and rice. Also on the table is a little bowl of marinated vegetables to nibble on. Very tasty . . . except for the red peppers in the mixture. We found them too hot. How hot were they? For a similar effect, try licking a blowtorch. **Prices:** Inexpensive. **Decor:** A plain but spotless cafe with a counter, big comfortable booths, and helpful service. **Basics:** 30 South 2nd St. (near East Santa Clara St.), San Jose. Tel: (408) 297-6370. Hours: 8 am-midnight Sun.-Thurs.; 8 am-3 am Fri., Sat. No cards. Wine and beer.

China House: San Jose
Chinese/Small dining room, Ming Dynasty decor

Tic. Tic. Tic. You glance at your watch. *Tic. Tic.* It seems like the chef is taking a long time with your dinner. You're becoming convinced that the chef is so slow, it must take him five minutes to blink. Then the food arrives. And you realize that you shouldn't have been so impatient.

Sure, the China House's chef takes a little extra time. But there's a reason. He gives each dish a little extra flavor. Most of the China House's dishes are cooked to order, including such time-consuming dishes as the China House's butterfly prawns. To make this dish, the chef takes large prawns, slits them, carefully inserts bacon, dips them in egg white, and finally stir-fries them in a tawny brown sauce.

Then there's the decor. At the China House, the small dining room is filled with Ming Dynasty relics the owner, Mrs. Lee, brought back from China. Mrs. Lee is also very helpful in answering your questions about Chinese cooking and its history. She seems aware of almost every development in the culinary history of China between 1300 B.C. and last Monday.

Menu Specialties: □ Butterfly Prawns □ China House Beef (tender beef slices in a dark brown sauce that's a Mrs. Lee original.) □ Mo Shiu Pork (pork, cloud ear mushrooms, and Chinese vegetables—all stir-fried together with plum sauce. This fragrant mixture is served with paper-thin Chinese pancakes. You roll the pancakes around a few spoonfuls of the mixture like you're making a giant enchilada . . . and eat.)

□ Phoenix Chicken (boneless chicken breast, sliced, stuffed with ham, battered, and wok-fried. Served on a bed of fresh jade-green vegetables with a picket fence of snow peas woven between the chicken slices.) Dessert: Tropical Ice Cream (coconut, mango, banana, or lichee—all made especially for Mrs. Lee.) **Prices:** Medium. **Basics:** 1163 South Saratoga-Sunnyvale Rd. (near Kentwood, in the Huntingdon Shopping Center), San Jose. Tel: (408) 255-1220. Hours: 11:30 am-2:30 pm Tues.-Fri.; 5:30-9:30 pm Tues.-Thurs., Sun.; 5-10:30 pm Fri., Sat. Closed Mon. Cards: MC, V. Full bar.

Genji: San Jose
Japanese/Teppan drama, chef plays lead

The most intriguing stage show in the Bay Area is not in San Francisco, but at a teppan-yaki table at the Genji. The audience for a typical evening's performance—usually four couples—is seated around the table. The producer, director, playwright, and star in this culinary drama is a Japanese chef who convincingly plays the role of a Japanese chef.

Act I sees a cast of zucchini, onions, bean sprouts, shrimp, chicken, and steak perform on a stainless steel grill sunken in the teppan-yaki table. The plot thickens as the chef mercilessly chops and pounds his supporting cast with uncanny speed and accuracy. sometimes pausing to throw in some spices over his shoulder. Our talented star of the show then allows the members of the cast to rest on the sizzling grill until they're a delicious, rich brown color. As a finale, he scoops them up and gracefully arranges them on lacquer plates for a curtain call. In keeping with the avante-garde trend in today's theatre, the audience is expected to participate in Act II by devouring the chef's supporting cast.

As this scene begins, the star says good night. Exit, stage right: the teppan-yaki chef—a man who handles a kitchen knife the way Errol Flynn handled a sword.

Menu Specialties: □ Chicken. Shrimp. New York Steak. You pick one. And it's cooked in front of you on the sizzling teppan grill. Before your eyes, it will be spiced, sake-wined, and sculptured into bite-size pieces by a lightning-fast teppan chef. Served with two dipping sauces: a spicy, gold-colored one, and a fragrant, dark brown ginger sauce.

Dinner includes . . . 4 courses: A teppan-cooked shrimp appetizer, Japanese suimono soup, a salad with Genji's house dressing, main course with teppan vegetables and rice, Japanese tea, and chilled Mandarin orange slices for dessert. **Prices:** Medium. **Basics:** 1335 North 1st St. (near Highway 17), San Jose. Tel: (408) 286-4120. Hours: 11:30 am-2 pm, 5-10 pm Mon.-Fri.; 5-10:30 pm Sat.; 5-9 pm Sun. Reservations suggested. All major cards. Full bar. Parking lot.

Restaurants in Weekend Places

THE COAST

Jerry's Farmhouse: Olema
Seafood/4-course dinners, very neighborly prices

City life. Are you tired of crowds, traffic jams, and the sound of birds coughing in the trees? Want to escape for a little while? Then head for Point Reyes, an area full of isolated beaches and cool, pine cone-carpeted forests.

After your appetite has been sharpened by the clean country air, we suggest you try Jerry's Farmhouse for dinner. This little restaurant is located in Olema—a tiny, cracker-barrel town with a population of 60.

The Farmhouse itself is a 1920-style, red clapboard building that looks like the kind of place you'd expect to find next to a Nebraska corn field. Jerry and his wife live upstairs, which probably accounts for the down home flavor of their food. Jerry's wife even bakes her own biscuits and makes her own homemade jam. And the prices are as down home as the cooking. Most of Jerry's 4-course dinners are in the $5.75 to $6.50 range.

When you visit the Farmhouse, ask Jerry to take you to the backyard and show you the rusty still house where they used to make whiskey back in the Twenties. Good stuff. According to a few old-timers, one sip and your eyebrows fell off.

Menu Specialties: □ Halibut (grilled in butter.) □ Rock Cod (brought in fresh from Bodega Bay, 20 miles away.) □ Pan-Fried Local Oysters (fresh from nearby Drake's Bay. And when they arrive, Jerry's so polite, he knocks on the shell before opening them.) □ Barbecued Half Chicken (roasted on a spit that's hand-cranked by Jerry's wife, Agnes.)
Dinner includes . . . 4 courses: Clam chowder, salad, Agnes' powder biscuits (served hot from the oven and ready for some jam made from blueberries grown in Jerry's backyard), main course with baked potato, coffee, and for dessert, a wedge of peach pie. **Prices:** Inexpensive. **Basics:** State Highway One, Olema—19 miles from San Rafael, 37 miles from San Francisco, Tel: (415) 663-1264. Hours: Noon-9 pm Tues.-Sun. Closed Mon. Cards: MC, V. Full bar.

Chez Madeleine: Point Reyes
French/Small country bistro with moderate prices

Just the two of you. Leaving town for the weekend. There you go, your car crawling over the hills of Marin toward the end of the continent. You're both quietly thinking about the romantic weekend ahead and it's making you breathe a little heavier than normal. In fact, the way you're breathing, the windows are getting so foggy you have to drive with the defroster on.

By the time the sun has set on the horizon you're in Point Reyes, ready for dinner. You're hoping to find a place that fits the mood, and when you pass by Chez Madeleine, something tells you to stop.

The place is small and inside there's a friendly-looking candlelit dining room with French music softly playing in the background. Since the owners still depend on roadside business, a hamburger is available, but it's served with a marchand de vin sauce. Also, there's no attendants mademoiselling the women here, just Madeleine, who serves you while her husband Roger stays in the kitchen preparing dishes like chicken Marengo and shrimp Armoricaine, all at moderate prices. When you put everything together, there's no question what this restaurant is—it's the kind of bistro a couple looks for after a romantic country drive.

Menu Specialties: ☐ Shrimp Armoricaine (shrimp in a rich sauce of brandy, tomatoes, and French herbs.) ☐ Chicken Marengo (fresh Santa Rosa chicken in a flavorful white wine sauce.) ☐ Filet of Sole Princesse (poached in wine and finished with a buttery cream sauce, mushrooms, bay shrimp, and Gruyere cheese.)

Dinner includes . . . 3 courses: French onion soup, salad, or a whole fresh artichoke (which you dip, leaf by leaf, in a tarragon-flavored dressing), and main course with sweet peas and pommes potatoes.

The Light Meal: Roger's Franco Burger (between two buns are 12 ounces of ground beef dripping with a marchand de vin sauce made from shallots, mushrooms, and red wine. Served with soup or salad.) The Franco Burger— a childhood favorite with French sex appeal . . . it's sort of like finding Mother Goose wearing a see-through blouse.
Prices: Medium. **Basics:** State Highway One, just south of Point Reyes Station—19 miles from San Rafael, 39 miles from San Francisco. Tel: (415) 663-8998. Hours: 5-9 pm Wed.-Fri.; 4-9 pm Sat., Sun. Closed Mon., Tues. Cards: MC, V. Wine and beer.

The Shore Bird: Princeton
Seafood & Steak/In an ocean front Cape Cod house

Time magazine once ran a photograph of Ted Kennedy at Hyannis Port. There was Ted, with a haircut that couldn't decide whether it was liberal or conservative, and such a bright smile, you could have photographed the guy in a closet without a flashcube. Behind Kennedy was his summer cottage, and the Shore Bird in Princeton could be its stand-in. Everything matches up, from the white picket fence to the view of a harbor dotted with fishing boats and sea gulls.

The Shore Bird may look like a home on the Nantucket Sound, but the menu is strictly Californian. Many of their dishes are supplied by an immediate neighbor—the Pacific Ocean. And the Shore Bird's neighbor is generous. The restaurant manages to offer at least three types of local fish each night.

For those seaside visitors who may not feel like a piece of halibut or petrale sole, the Shore Bird also offers the bedrock delicacy of the West—steak. And they know how to handle it. The beef is aged for 14 days, basted with vermouth as it broils, and is never allowed to linger over the charcoal longer than it should.

Menu Specialties: ☐ Top Sirloin Steak ☐ Catch-of-the-Day (red snapper, petrale sole, lingcod . . . whatever's f-r-e-s-h. All fish are basted with butter, charcoal broiled, and served with a homemade tartar sauce.) ☐ Whole Cracked Crab (a whole fresh Dungeness crab is steamed, cracked, and then brought to your table on a bed of ice. All that's left is for you to pick the sweet white meat from the shell. Served with the Shore Bird's seafood cocktail sauce.)

Dinner includes: Salad (you're served a generous amount of lettuce and cherry tomatoes in a huge stainless steel bowl. We mean huge. You could almost attach an outboard motor to the stern of the thing and take it water-skiing. Also placed on the table are three homemade dressings and croutons to use at will.), and fisherman's-style sourdough bread. Planning to dock at noon? Try a grilled crab and shrimp sandwich. **Prices:** Inexpensive to medium. **Basics:** 390 Capistrano Rd. (just off State Highway One), Princeton—4 miles from Half Moon Bay, 26 miles from San Francisco. Tel: (415) 728-5541. Hours: 11:30 am-3 pm daily (brunch is served on Sun.); 5:30-10 pm Mon.-Thurs.; 5-10:30 pm Fri., Sat.; 4-10 pm Sun. Cards: AE, MC, V. Full bar. Parking lot.

Zachary's: Santa Cruz
Southern Smoked Meats/Inviting wood and brick decor

The idea that spawned Zachary's was a simple one. Owner Mike Williams noticed that it was almost impossible to find good spareribs locally. Even when the authentic item could be found, the place was often located in a neighborhood where the kids were so tough, they stole hub caps off moving cars.

Since the states of the Confederacy know the most about preparing smoked meats, Mike decided to jump into his Ford van and head toward the Mason-Dixon line. When he got to Dixie, he stopped at every country cafe between Arkansas and North Carolina that smelled of hickory smoke and badgered the good ol' boy in the kitchen about his cooking methods.

When Mike returned, he was ready to open Zachary's. By using the notes he'd taken on his trip, Mike was able to build an important feature into his restaurant—an authentic southern smoke box. In this box the meats inhale smoke from a smoldering oakwood fire for at least four hours. When the time is up, the box has worked its magic . . . the meat and smoke have become one. Each piece of meat is jacketed with a glistening ebony crust. And all this effort seems to be paying off: judging from the business this place is doing, we don't think that Zachary's will ever have to quit smoking.

Menu Specialties: ☐ Eastern Pork Spareribs ☐ Prime Beef Short Ribs ☐ Half Chicken. All three are smoked and then brushed with a mild, tasty, southern-style barbecue sauce.

Dinner includes a salad (red leaf lettuce, mushrooms, and tomatoes), and main course with homemade baked beans. **Prices:** Inexpensive. **Decor:** Desert gold director's chairs, a guitarist that fills the room with soft sounds, and lots of natural wood, brick, and artwork. Southern comfort—California style. **Basics:** 819 Pacific Ave. (near Laurel, half a mile from the boardwalk), Santa Cruz. Tel: (408) 427-0646. Hours: 5:30-9:30 pm Sun.-Thurs.; 5:30-10 pm Fri., Sat. Cards: MC, V. Wine and beer.

Shadowbrook: Capitola
Steak/Romantic hillside chalet with its own cable car

Besides a waterbed with a three-speed vibrator, we don't know of a more romantic place to have dinner. The Shadowbrook is an old redwood chalet that sits halfway down a steep hill. From the windows you can see a creek where the water is emerald green and the rocks have fur coats made of moss. Nature is even allowed inside. The vines from the surrounding hillside have been permitted to sneak through the crevices in the building and curl their way up to the ceiling. The Shadowbrook also has some other romantic assets—a dining patio, a stone hearth as thick as a castle wall, and a hand-carved balcony that looks like it belongs on the stage of an Italian opera.

The Shadowbrook has even devised a romantic way of getting you from your car to the restaurant: at the top of the hill, they've stationed a bright-red cable car the size of two telephone booths. All night long, this car takes couples up and down the hill.

Not all of the Shadowbrook's food is as charming as the surroundings. The only item on the menu we recommend is steak. The beef is corn-fed Black Angus and it's carefully broiled over the charcoals. In the romance and steak department, the Shadowbrook does a good job. But when it comes to some of the other entrees on the menu, it's possible to receive the kiss of disappointment.

Menu Specialties: ☐ Top Sirloin Steak ☐ Filet Mignon ☐ New York Steak. All the Shadowbrook's steaks are choice, well-marbled, properly aged, and charcoal broiled.

Dinner includes: A huge salad with romaine lettuce, black olives, fresh mushrooms, cherry tomatoes, and green peppers, and main course with baked potato or herbed rice. **Prices:** Medium. **Basics:** 1750 Wharf Rd. (at Capitola Rd.), Capitola—3½ miles from Santa Cruz. Tel: (408) 475-1511. Hours: 5-10:30 pm Mon.-Sat.; 2-9 pm Sun. Reservations necessary. Cards: MC, V. Full bar. Parking lot.

Note: Capitola is a quaint town. It has some turn-of-the century buildings . . . Sausalito-style shops . . . a good beach . . . and a wooden railroad trestle bridge right out of a 1940 Hollywood western.

L'Escargot: Carmel
French/Romantic country inn atmosphere

A chef and a pharmacist both mix things together for a desired result, but only one of them has a degree on the wall that says he knows what he's doing. With a chef, you have to take his medicine before you find out if he's qualified for the job. But there are exceptions. At L'Escargot, chef Yvan Nopert's diplomas from European restaurant schools greet you as you enter. The display suggests that Yvan must have the equivalent of a Ph.D in food.

Yvan's cooking skills have helped him attract some admirers. When Yvan was chef at the Belgian Embassy in Washington, D.C., President Eisenhower came to dine; and at the restaurant Yvan now owns in Carmel, Elizabeth Taylor and Richard Burton dropped in for dinner. Many times. They liked L'Escargot's small size, its French country inn decor, its quiet clientele of everyday people, and most of all, they liked the richness of Yvan's chicken in a truffle-flecked cream sauce. Of course, when Elizabeth Taylor sat in Yvan's dining room, she tried to go unnoticed. Which is hard to do when you're wearing a diamond ring the size of a potato.

Menu Specialties: ☐ Chicken a la Creme (roasted chicken in a sauce made from the purest, freshest dairy cream, mushrooms, Périgord truffles, and Portuguese Madeira wine.) ☐ Pork Piquante (moist, tender slices of premium pork loin crowned with a distinctive brown sauce. The sauce has a gentle tartness that pleases and mystifies at the same time.) ☐ Bourride Seafood (fresh red snapper in a garlicky seafood sauce that's the color of a Mediterranean sunrise.)

Starters: Soupe de Tomates (tomato soup. Common, you say? Not this one. This herb-flavored soup is made from fresh tomatoes. In fact, the soup tastes so fresh, it's as if the chef hauled his stove out to the fields and cooked the tomatoes as they were picked off the vine.) **Prices:** Medium. **Basics:** Mission St., between 4th and 5th Ave., Carmel. Tel: (408) 624-4914. Hours: 6-9 pm Mon.-Sat. Closed Sun. (Note: also closed the entire month of Dec.) Reservations necessary. No cards. Wine and beer.

Nepenthe: Big Sur
American/Located on a cliff above the Pacific

At Nepenthe, they feature big, thick, juicy hamburgers with all the extras. "So what?" you say, "plenty of places offer the same thing." True. But one of the extras here is a sweeping view of the Big Sur coastline.

Nepenthe sits on an oak-shaded cliff, 808 feet above the Pacific Ocean. It's an impressive building of native redwood, glass, and adobe. Years ago, the place was owned by Orson Welles and Rita Hayworth. Outside, there's a large stone dining terrace—complete with canvas director's chairs, a huge brick fire pit, and, of course, a view of miles and miles of raging surf.

Nepenthe's impressive location and appearance bring to mind a line by George Bernard Shaw, the famous playwright. After William Randolph Hearst finished showing Shaw around his majestic San Simeon castle, Shaw remarked, "Bill, this is the way God would have done it, if He had your money."

Menu Specialty: □ The Ambrosiaburger (a hamburger with a pedigree. A thick ground steak patty on a French roll. Escorted by Nepenthe's mayonnaise sauce, red leaf lettuce, and kosher pickles. The hamburger also comes with a garbanzo and kidney bean salad in an herb-flavored dressing.), $4.00. Sure, that's expensive, but Nepenthe sits on expensive land. Remember, this is Big $ur. **Basics:** State Highway One, Big Sur—3 miles south of Big Sur State Park, 30 miles south of Carmel. Tel: (408) 667-2345. Hours: 11:30 am-9:30 pm daily. Cards: MC, V. Full bar. Parking lot.

Raffaello: Carmel
Northern Italian/A small place with quiet charm

The predominant style of Italian cooking in the United States belongs to the southern Italians who came here at the turn of the century. These immigrants were from the poorest section of Italy; consequently, their recipes called for inexpensive, starchy ingredients. Also, because of the abundance of olive trees in southern Italy, olive oil became the basic cooking medium. This might help explain why, at some Italian restaurants, it seems like Mama is in the back squirting on the olive oil with a firehose.

Raffaello is an Italian restaurant, but it's a "northern" Italian restaurant, and you'll discover that the cooking of northern Italy is different from that of the south. The lightness and complexity of northern Italian cooking almost elevates it to the level of French haute cuisine.

The cooking at Raffaello's is handled by Mrs. Amelia d'Agliano, who personally prepares the egg noodles for the tagliatelle alla Bolognese, and also personally makes sure that the brown truffle sauce for the veal Piedmontese is every bit as rich as it should be. Her son, Remo, acts as host, always seeing that every party in the small twelve-table dining room gets personal attention. Remo's family has been in the restaurant business in Italy for over 75 years, and Remo runs his restaurant like a man who's proud of his heritage. He even looks the part. With his handsome Italian features, gentle smile, and custom-tailored European suits, Remo truly looks like the Prince of Pasta.

Menu Specialties: □ Veal Piedmontese (tender white veal cloaked with fontina cheese and then topped with an Italian truffle sauce. Truffles are the Rolls Royce of the mushroom family, presently selling for $240 a pound.) □ Tagliatelle alla Bolognese (homemade egg noodles—each strand stamped with pride. First, in the kitchen, the pasta is tossed in butter. Then, it's brought to your table in a silver tureen and the waiter tosses it again in a rich Bolognese meat sauce.) □ Chicken alla Fiorentina (a butter-glazed breast of chicken layered with prosciutto ham and fontina cheese. Served on a bed of brandied mushroom sauce.) □ Cannelloni alla Raffaello (feather-light homemade pasta stuffed with specially roasted minced veal, and crowned with cheese and a fresh, herb-laced tomato sauce.)

Dinner includes . . . 3 courses: Soup (maybe a Stracciatella consomme with parmesan cheese), a fresh romaine salad, and main course with beautifully-handled, sauteed spinach. Dessert: Mussa di Fragole (an air-light mousse made with fresh strawberries and zinfandel wine); Spumoni (a rich, fruit-studded Italian ice cream that's personally made by Mrs. d'Agliano.) **Prices:** Medium. **Basics:** Mission St., between Ocean Ave. and 7th Ave., Carmel. Tel: (408) 624-1541. Hours: 6-10 pm Mon., Wed.-Sun. Closed Tues. Reservations necessary. Jackets requested. Cards: MC, V.

Clock Garden: Monterey
Creative Cooking/In a historical adobe building

There are restaurant suppliers who make fancy heat-and-serve frozen dishes which aren't too bad, but these convenience foods don't belong in a restaurant. It doesn't make much sense to go out for dinner tonight and get something that was cooked six months ago in Chicago. What we need are more places like the Clock Garden. They haven't forgotten that the classic definition of a restaurant is "a place where food is prepared." In the Clock's kitchen you can watch dishes like their Vallarta casserole being assembled from the bottom up: first a layer of veal, then a handful of mushrooms, a thin slice of smoky ham and Monterey Jack cheese, and finally four spoons of sour cream-celery sauce. When the casserole is finished it will share oven space with the Clock's pecan pies, and breast of chicken Del Sur.

The Clock Garden's food is enjoyable, and so are the surroundings. The Clock's white adobe building was once a carriage house, dating back to the 1890s. Today, the white stucco walls are covered with a rainbow of crepe paper collages and a collection of antique clocks in every conceivable size and shape. Outside, a tree-lined brick courtyard is used for lunches and Sunday brunch.

These dining areas are always filled with people. And they're here because of the high standards of the Clock Garden's kitchen. The Clock's chef truly believes that the only people with a good excuse for serving frozen food are the Eskimos.

Menu Specialties: □ Veal Vallarta □ Salmon Steak (fresh Monterey Bay salmon marinated in wine, olive oil, and herbs, and then broiled over charcoal.) □ Chicken Del Sur (a boned breast of chicken steamed in sauterne for one hour. Then placed in a casserole, topped with a sherry sauce and fresh sliced mushrooms, and browned in the oven.) □ Scallops del Suizo (scallops in a sauce that's rich with fresh cream, Swiss cheese, and bay shrimp.)

Dinner includes: Greek lemon soup, or a huge wedge of Salinas Valley lettuce with Green Goddess dressing, German black bread, and main course with sauteed zucchini. Dessert: Homemade pecan pie, Texas style. **Prices:** Medium to a step above medium. **Basics:** 565 Abrego St. (near Pearl, about nine blocks from Fisherman's Wharf), Monterey. Tel: (408) 375-6100. Hours: 11:30 am-2 pm Mon.-Fri.; 5:30-10 pm Mon.-Thurs., Sun.; 5:30-10:30 pm Fri., Sat. Reservations necessary. On Sunday brunch is served from 10:30 am-2 pm. All major cards. Full bar.

Whaling Station Inn: Monterey
Continental/In a fine old building on Cannery Row

Close Encounters of the Table Kind

An eerie glow filled the night as the giant saucer-shaped craft hovered above Russ Riera's office. Two shadowy figures with dark green skin and high-collared metallic uniforms descended from the ship.

It had worked. Along with the help of Stanford scientists, Riera, the author of this book, had made contact with a U.F.O. Standing before Riera were two aliens from outer space.

Riera came right to the point. "Listen," Riera began, "for years you guys have been visiting our planet, right? And every time the *National Enquirer* does an article about you fellows landing, where are you spotted? In a corn field. On a barren mountain top. In the middle of a dark forest. Never in a restaurant. Maybe you don't like to eat in strange places."

"Anyhow, as a local restaurant reviewer, I feel it's my duty to take you to one of our restaurants. After all, if you fellows from outer space keep on ignoring our food, it's going to give the restaurants on this planet a bad name."

Riera took his guests to the Whaling Station Inn—an attractive antique-filled restaurant located in a restored 1929 building on Cannery Row in Monterey. Although there were many things Riera liked at this restaurant, he decided to center the dinner around steak and seafood. "Very popular earth food," he told them. Riera ordered the Whaling Station's aged, oak-broiled New York steak, a combination of Monterey prawns, clams, and Eastern scallops on a bed of imported linguini pasta, and a cioppino made with fresh Dungeness crab.

Before these dishes arrived, they were served three other courses: a steamed Castroville artichoke with garlic mayonnaise, a rich soup, and a salad of fresh Salinas lettuce. Riera's guests were especially interested in the artichoke. They said it looked like the women back home.

After Riera and his party had left, their bus boy said to the waiter, "I think I've seen the fellow called Riera before, but who were those other two?"

"Tourists. They said they were just visiting the area," the waiter answered. "But I kinda figured that. The guy with four arms and six eyes kept asking me for a souvenir menu and the one with the silver helmet stole an ashtray."

Menu Specialties: ☐ Prawns, Clams, and Scallops with Linguini ☐ New York Steak (the steaks, each weighing one full pound, are selected for the Whaling Station by a special supplier, aged at least eighteen days, and broiled over oakwood.) ☐ Crab Cioppino (you're brought a tureen of fresh, cracked Dungeness crab in a fragrant broth of tomatoes, white wine, and fresh herbs, including basil and oregano that's grown especially for the restaurant by an Italian family in their backyard.) ☐ Veal Rollatine (veal stuffed with prosciutto ham, pine nuts and three kinds of cheese. Served with a light Marsala sauce.)

Dinner includes . . . 4 courses: Appetizer (a fresh steamed Castroville artichoke served with a great vinaigrette and garlic mayonnaise), soup (maybe cream of asparagus or a French-style seafood soup), salad, and main course with seasonal vegetables. **Prices:** Medium to a step above medium. **Basics:** 763 Wave St. (on Cannery Row), Monterey. Tel: (408) 373-3778. Hours: 5:30-10 pm daily. Reservations strongly suggested on weekends. All major cards. Full bar. Parking lot.

Fernand's: Carmel Valley
Continental/Chef 30 years behind the stove

New York Times food editor Craig Claiborne wanted a memorable meal. So he got one. On November 12, 1975. At Chez Denis in Paris. Dinner was 33 courses, lasted 4½ hours, and included 9 rare wines. One wine, a Madeira, was 140 years old. It was a meal that Craig Claiborne will never forget. And he'll also never forget the check— $4,000 for two.

You too can follow Claiborne's example and have a memorable meal. At Fernand's in the Carmel Valley. But you won't have to spend $4,000. Most of Fernand's dinners are priced around $7.50.

Fernand's gives you a number of memorable ways to go. On the small Continental menu there's fresh Monterey petrale sole Trouvillaise in a buttery herb sauce, tiny veal mignonnettes flavored with parmesan cheese and ham, and stuffed breast of capon in a velvet-smooth mushroom sauce. And each of these dishes is cooked by Fernand himself—a man who has 30 years of experience behind a stove.

Fernand's isn't a big restaurant. Fernand handles the kitchen, while his wife and one European waiter handle the modest, white-tableclothed dining room. With this kind of arrangement, things happen at Fernand's that don't usually happen at bigger restaurants. Like the time we overheard a lady loudly raining compliments on Fernand's food. A few moments later, Fernand marched from the kitchen, removed his tall white chef's hat, bent over, and kissed her cheek. Twice. Now that's being grateful.

Menu Specialties: ☐ Filet of Sole Trouvillaise (fresh petrale, last seen in the blue waters of Monterey Bay, and now appearing in a light yellow sea of butter, lemon juice, and herbs.) ☐ Veal Mignonnettes (tiny veal cutlets coated with a parmesan cheese-flavored batter and then sauteed with slender ribbons of ham.) ☐ Capon Lorraine (boned breast of capon stuffed with finely minced and seasoned chicken. Topped with a fresh mushroom-wine sauce.)

Dinner includes . . . 3 courses: Soup (maybe salmon chowder or cream of asparagus), salad (in a dressing flavored with tarragon Fernand grows himself), and main course with vegetable ratatouille and stuffed potato. **Prices:** Medium. **Basics:** 55 West Carmel Valley Rd. (near Carmel Valley Village), Carmel Valley—13 miles from Carmel. Tel: (408) 659-4766. Hours: 5:30-9:30 pm Tues.-Sat. Closed Sun., Mon. Reservations necessary on weekends. Cards: MC, V. Wine and beer.

Ledford House: Little River
Creative Cooking/Hillside house overlooking the Pacific

Barbara Mastin places a telephone call from the kitchen of her restaurant. "Hello, Mrs. Tomkins. Did that dill plant of yours sprout yet? Good. Could you pick me a basket? I'll send someone by to get it."

"Whew!" One of the Ledford House's waiters heaves a sigh of relief as he gently lowers a 40-pound Chinook salmon into the kitchen sink. His hobby of fishing is paying for itself. For the last three weeks, Barbara has been buying all the salmon he can catch.

After she's called several more people, Barbara reviews the list of foodstuffs her neighbors have promised to deliver and starts to map out her dinner menu. Tonight, she decides to take the dill and salmon and fuse them into a delicate soufflé with nantua sauce and shrimp butter. Lamb raised on a nearby Mendocino hillside will be used for the selle d'agneau nicoise—a saddle of lamb roasted with fresh herbs and served with a rich sauce made from mushrooms, sweet butter and Madeira wine. To start the meal, Barbara will serve a minestrone soup that sings with the flavor of just-picked vegetables. And to end the meal, she'll prepare a fresh fruit tart made with raspberries grown by a grandmother who lives near Willits.

This is the way Barbara Mastin operates. Her vegetables come from local farms, her fruit comes from local orchards, her meat comes from local ranches, and her seafood comes from the neighboring Pacific. You might say that Barbara and the countryside are partners. Every day Barbara goes through the same procedure. She calls around to see what's available, and then she plans her menu for the evening. And although this arrangement means her menu is constantly changing, you can be sure of one thing—whatever she prepares will be good.

Barbara's restaurant is located in a house which has some interesting historical wrinkles. Built in 1870 and later sold for $500 in gold, 2 cows, and 17 chickens, this small house has a dining room porch facing the Pacific, antiques from local attics, and a fireplace that's always lit at sunset. Barbara's waiters tie the whole package together. Occasionally, it's nice to be helped by someone who believes that a smile is the shortest distance between two people.

The Menu: We've seen Barbara's recipe file. It looks like the card catalog at the San Francisco Public Library. So, understandably, she has an ever-changing menu. But the following dishes are Barbara's favorites and they tend to appear often: ☐ Italian Lamb (thick chops cut from a rack of lamb and coated with a batter made from eggs and Asiago, an imported Italian cheese similar to parmesan. Then they're sauteed in butter and topped with Marsala sauce.) ☐ Salmon Steak (fresh salmon poached in a vintage French white wine, and then saddled with an herb-laced cream sauce. And the aroma of these herbs clearly announces that they are recent graduates of local gardens.) ☐ Veal Piedmontese (scallops of veal topped with imported fontina cheese and a brandied truffle sauce.)

Dinner includes . . . 3 courses: Soup (maybe Oriental snow pea soup or abalone chowder), homemade brioche rolls, salad (red leaf and butter lettuce in a dressing made from Gorgonzola, an Italian blue cheese), and main course with homemade fettucine pasta or vegetables Erma . . . Erma being the grandmother who raises them on a patch of land near Willits. Dessert: It varies . . . maybe chocolate-chestnut cake or fresh raspberry soufflé. **Prices:** A step above medium. **Basics:** State Highway One (next to Schoolhouse Creek Inn), Little River—4 miles south of Mendocino. Tel: (707) 937-0282. Hours: 6-10 pm Mon.-Sat. Closed Sun. (From Oct.-June they're also closed on Thurs.) Reservations necessary on weekends. No cards. Wine and beer.

Elk Cove Inn: Elk
Homecooking/Victorian mansion on coastal cliff

Dinner observer

"Quit playin' that organ, Mabel. Brother Elmo is ready to say a few words to the congregation."

"Thank you, brother Quincy. I'd like to start off by sayin' . . . brethren, take heed! 'Cause jes' last night I found me a couple of sinners. You see, I was drivin' down the Coast when I spotted this house on a cliff overlooking the ocean. Now mind you, it weren't jes' any house—it was one of them Victorian mansions like you see on the cover of them Gothic love novels I told you not to read. Hallelujah! I was curious, so I called my cousin Orville, who has a farm nearby, and asked him 'bout the place. Orville said a husband and wife lived in the place with their family. Said the house is so big, they rent out rooms for the weekend and the missus cooks rich meals for the guests and a few others who drop by.

Well, forgive me, Lord, but I yielded to temptation and snuck over there and took a peek in the window. Holy salvation, what I saw! There were two couples settin' at this table. I could hear 'em through the window. The fellas called themselves Riera and Smith. Said they was writin' a restaurant guide. A lie, brothers and sisters! A lie worthy of Satan himself! These fellas was gluttons, pure and simple. They sat there for almost two hours a slurpin' up split pea soup, a soppin' up the herb salad dressing with homemade brown bread, a gobblin' up some German meatballs, and finally stuffin' up their cheeks with Bavarian cream cake.

When these sinners got up to retire for the evening, I noticed that the ladies with 'em weren't wearing no rings. Oh, Lord, I couldn't help myself. I yelled through the window, you fellas are gonna burn in the eternal fires of Purgatory! Say hallelujah! Amen!

You folks out there in the congregation, raise your hands and show the Lord you've never spent a wicked evening like that.

Well, what you folks waitin' for? It's been twenty minutes now and I ain't seen no hands."

The Menu: This is a small operation. The couple running the Inn, Roger and Uta Noteware, cook and serve dinner with no extra help. Between overnight lodgers and drop-in guests, they can accommodate only 16 people a night. This means that reservations are a must.

Dinner is a set 4-course affair which changes nightly. Here are some dishes that the Noteware's frequently prepare. *Main Courses:* Rouladen (rolled steak filled with a spicy stuffing and cooked in a clove-accented wine sauce); Shrimp Veloute (moist shrimp in a silk-smooth, cream-rich white sauce); Beef Ragout (the meat is marinated in burgundy and herbs and then slowly cooked.) *Soup:* Maybe cheddar cheese soup, winter borsch or Indian curry lentil soup. *Salad:* Red leaf and limestone lettuce from the Noteware's garden plus sliced tomatoes in a dressing laced with herbs and spices.

The meal also includes—*Homemade Bread:* A crunchy, crusty whole wheat loaf baked by Uta: "I love making bread. It's good therapy." *Mendocino Vegetables:* Fresh from neighbor's gardens . . . maybe zucchini sauteed with butter and garlic or butternut squash with brown sugar. *Dessert:* Maybe Bavarian mocha cream cake or raspberry cream pudding. *Coffee:* Uta grinds her own French roast blend. And the coffee is made with water that's piped in from five natural springs. **Prices:** Medium.

Lodging: A room with a fireplace and an ocean view + use of a private beach + breakfast and dinner—$29 a day per person. It's a good value, especially when you consider what the price includes. We've been to hotels where all they give you for $29 is a chair in the lobby and a sleeping pill. Note: Rooms should be reserved at least two weeks in advance. **Basics:** State Highway One, Elk—15 miles south of the town of Mendocino. Tel: (707) 877-3321. Hours: One sitting at 7 pm Thurs.-Sun. Closed Mon.-Wed. Reservations necessary. No cards. Wine and beer.

Greenwood Cafe: Elk
American/Classic husband and wife operation, modest prices

Roadside refreshment is part of our American heritage. One hundred and fifty years ago, we had stagecoach stops along our wagon trails; today we have Denny's along our freeways.

The Greenwood Cafe is another member of this roadside group, but it's certainly no match for a Denny's. The Cafe's hand-carved wooden sign has none of the shouting power of a Denny's neon, and the Greenwood lacks the automation of a Denny's. You can't get your morning juice until Ebie Petty, the owner's wife, squeezes the oranges; you can't order French toast if Ebie hasn't baked some of the homemade bread she uses for the dish; and you can't get fish and chips unless Kendrick Petty has been able to locate some fresh lingcod and had enough time to peel the potatoes. You can't even get a cup of coffee without Ebie scooping up a handful of beans, with the warning, "I have to make this terrible noise," and grinding them on the spot.

The difference between a Denny's and the Greenwood Cafe was especially noticeable on our last visit. While we were sitting at the Greenwood's counter talking to Kendrick, a man with a Buffalo Bill mustache appeared in the doorway. As he unbuttoned his Cossack coat, his eyes began to light up like a busy switchboard and he sputtered, "I dreamed you had strawberry cream pie."

"Sorry," Ebie answered, "your dream is a week ahead of schedule."

That remark seemed to jog Kendrick's memory. "Almost forgot,"

Kendrick said, "I have to get some blackberries for Ebie's pie. Excuse me."

After Kendrick left, we finished our coffee and drove off. Two hundred yards down the road, we spotted Kendrick in an open field—picking blackberries. It's definitely a procedure a Denny's man would frown on.

Menu Specialties: *Breakfast:* French Toast (freshly-baked bread is used, and it's served with homemade marmalade), $1.50. The Kendrick Omelet (Kendrick gets his eggs from neighboring farms. And inside a Kendrick omelet you'll find Monterey Jack cheese, mushrooms, and asparagus tips from Kendrick's own garden.), $2.85.
Lunch: Soup (maybe curried split pea or corn chowder flavored with bacon), 80¢. Salad (homegrown romaine and Great Lakes lettuce laced with vegetables and marinated onions in a dressing flavored with homegrown sweet basil and tarragon. It seems that the only thing they don't grow is the plate.), $1.25. Sandwiches (such as bacon, avocado, and tomato, or grilled ham and cheddar cheese), $1.65-$2.45.
Dinner: The menu changes daily but may include fish & chips, a hearty pot roast, or sauteed chicken. Dinner is usually about $4.50—salad and vegetables included. Dessert: When they can't pick blackberries, it might be apple or peach pie. Desserts are 95¢. **Decor:** Lots of hand-finished wood was used to make the eight counter stools and nine tables in this small cafe. **Basics:** 5926 South Highway One, Elk—15 miles south of the town of Mendocino. Tel: (707) 877-9997. Hours: 9 am-9 pm Wed.-Sun. Closed Mon., Tues. (Note: the cafe is closed Dec.-Apr.) Cards: MC, V. Wine and beer.

The story of a Mendocino man

William Bennett and His Redwood Love Affair: The beauty of the Mendocino area is enough to make a person forget their troubles. And when William Bennett arrived here in 1893, he had something he wanted to forget. Bennett came to Mendocino brokenhearted. His bride-to-be back East had run away with another man. Bennett never got over it. He lived by himself in a huge, eight-room house at 809 Franklin Street in Fort Bragg.

Over the years, Bennett grew more and more lonely. Then one night, he decided to end his loneliness. He picked up a knife. And . . . by the end of the third day, he had carved himself a life-sized woman out of redwood. He fell in love and found happiness. Then over the next few years, he carved himself five daughters, two sons, and, eventually, a son-in-law. Sometimes, Bennett would invite the neighbors over for dinner—with all of his "family" present. Hmmm. For eight years William Bennett lived with a woman carved out of wood. Do you want our opinion? Bennett must have had a lot of trouble meeting girls.

231

Short Takes

Patisserie Boissiere
The best pastries on the Monterey Peninsula

At this pastry shop-cafe, decisions are hard to make. The Patisserie's owner, Pierre Boissiere, prepares twenty different kinds of pastry each day. Count 'em, folks. That's 36 million calories to choose from. But it's not just the variety of pastries that makes the choice difficult. The Patisserie's display cases are filled with masterworks. For example, Pierre's lemon cheesecake is three inches high and one of the best versions we've come across. In fact, we've had the cheesecake so many times, it's effected our teeth. Both of us have so many cavities, we talk with an echo. The cheesecake is $1.75, and the pastries are $1.50.

Basics: Mission St., between Ocean Ave. and 7th Ave., Carmel. Tel: (408) 624-5008. Hours: 10 am-9 pm Mon., Tues., Thurs.-Sun. Closed Wed.

And on the way to the coast . . .

The Round Up
Oak-barbecued spareribs, the aroma alone can stop a car

New Yorker magazine columnist Calvin Trillin has stated in print that Arthur Bryant's barbecue in Kansas City is "The Single Best Restaurant in the World." Now that's a man who likes barbecue. In any case, Mr. Bryant . . . meet Mr. Smalley, the owner of the Round Up restaurant in Salinas. He's after your title. At least as far as barbecued spareribs are concerned. If Calvin ever shows up in Salinas, Mr. Smalley is ready to give him some "real barbecue." And we're putting our money on the Round Up. Just think. Maybe some day the local Chamber of Commerce will be able to say that according to the *New Yorker*, the world's best restaurant is in Salinas.

The Round Up is located in a solidly-built, 1948-vintage house. Mr. Smalley, a gray-haired gentleman from Tuscaloosa, Alabama, arrives here at 7:30 a.m. each morning to start his oakwood fire. He then spends the day "smokin' ribs and makin' sauce." His barbecue sauce is excellent. The sauce contains 15 ingredients, but as Mr. Smalley explains with a thick down-home accent, "I never measure anything. Mah hands jes' know what to do by themselves." Barbecued Spareribs, $5.50. Dinner includes salad and a bowl of homemade chili.

Basics: 700 West Market St. (at Clark), Salinas. Tel: (408) 758-0511. Hours: 5-9 pm Wed.-Sun. Closed Mon., Tues. Reservations necessary. Cards: MC, V. Wine and beer.

WINE COUNTRY

Before the vineyard? I used to help this guy grow carrots.

Depot Hotel: Napa
Italian/The meal is big, the price is small

Some people say that overeating is criminal. Want to commit a felony? Order one of the Depot's 5-course Italian dinners. The meal begins with a bowl of bean-thickened minestrone and a basket of locally-baked sourdough bread. Then, you're served a tossed salad that's accompanied by a gang of appetizers: mortadella, marinated garbanzo and kidney beans, wine-cured salami, olives, and pepperoncini.

If you stopped eating at this point, it would be a simple misdemeanor. But no one does. Next comes a platter of homemade ravioli and some bullet-shaped rounds of malfatti—a dumpling-like spinach pasta. The Depot's original owner, Mama Tamburelli, introduced malfatti to Napa in 1925, and the Depot is still one of the only places that makes them. Although you may have an urge to hijack more than your fair share of malfatti from the platter, it might be wise to save your appetite. Shortly, the waitress is going to serve you the main course, some hand-cut fries, a vegetable, and dessert.

If overeating is criminal, the Depot's 5-course Italian dinner is certainly an example of organized crime. And since the Depot's dinners are around $6.25, it's . . . well . . . a steal.

Menu Specialties: □ Chicken Saute (the chicken slowly takes on the flavor of the onions, mushrooms, and tomatoes it's cooked with.) □ Veal Florentine (veal scallops topped with mozzarella cheese and prosciutto ham, breaded, and sauteed in olive oil.) □ Veal Scallopine (sauteed with fresh mushrooms and sherry.)

Dinner includes . . . 5 courses: Soup, salad and appetizers, pasta, main course with hand-cut fries and vegetable, coffee, and dessert. **Prices:** Inexpensive. **Decor:** The restaurant is located in a former railroad depot that's over 100 years old. Inside, there's a comfortable, homespun atmosphere. **Basics:** 806 4th St., Napa. (Once in Napa, travel north on Highway 29 until it becomes Soscol Ave. The Depot is located just before the intersection of Soscol Ave. and 3rd St.) Tel: (707) 255-9944. Hours: 5-9:30 pm Mon., Wed.-Sat.; 2-9 pm Sun. Closed Tues. No cards. Full bar. Parking lot.

Carriage House: Napa
Continental/New England-style building, moderate prices

The limestone caves of Beringer. The cellars of Charles Krug. The Inglenook vineyards. You've spent the afternoon wine-tasting. Now, it's time for dinner. And you're hoping to find a restaurant with some wine country atmosphere. Of course, you're also hoping that the place won't be expensive. No one likes to visit a restaurant where the prices work like a can of Drano on your wallet.

Well, relax. The Carriage House offers moderately priced 3-course dinners that are personally prepared by the two ladies who own the place. And the Carriage House also has lots of atmosphere. The restaurant is located in the former carriage house of the elegant Noyes mansion. Inside, there's a rustically romantic dining room that's softly-lit with real gas lanterns.

Now, imagine that there's a man and a woman sitting in this dining room. And imagine that one of these people is you. Tonight, you had the stuffed breast of chicken, and your partner had the crab Mornay. Now, imagine that dinner is over and you're holding hands, feeling romantic, and discussing dessert. What kind of dessert did you two decide to end the evening with? C'mon, use your imagination.

Menu Specialties: ☐ Chicken Cordon Bleu (boned breast of chicken stuffed with ham and cheese, and topped with a sherry cream sauce.) ☐ Beef Bourguignon (pieces of lean beef simmered for hours in a hearty burgundy wine sauce laced with fresh mushrooms, bacon, bay leaves, and thyme.) ☐ Prawns Brochette (large Gulf prawns are first allowed to soak in a special house marinade. Then they're skewered, gently grilled, and served with a spicy Piperade sauce.) □ Crab Mornay (Dungeness crab sauteed with sherry and mushrooms, and topped with Mornay sauce.)

Dinner includes . . . 3 courses: Soup (maybe cream of mushroom or Spanish white bean soup), salad (romaine and red leaf lettuce with black olives and a buttermilk-based blue cheese dressing), and main course with fresh vegetable (maybe green beans with bacon or a tomato stuffed with spinach). **Prices:** Medium. **Basics:** 1775 Clay St. (one block from the intersection of Jefferson and 1st St.), Napa. Tel: (707) 255-4744. Hours: 11:30 am-2:30 pm Mon.-Fri.; 5-9 pm Mon.-Sat. Closed Sun. All major cards. Full bar. Parking lot.

Jonesy's Steak House

Napa County Airport

Jonesy's sirloin club steak is this thick, weighs over a pound and costs $6.75

For years, it's been chef Hugh Jones' policy to charge reasonable prices for a dinner that includes a large romaine salad with a special blue cheese dressing and a big steak. And Jonesy has found that cutting a steak with a generous hand is good for business. "The size of my steaks keeps the customers talking," says Jonesy, "which means my place is always making new friends."

Jonesy's reputation rests not only on the size of his steaks but also on the way he selects and cooks them. To qualify for a vacancy on Jonesy's grill, the meat must be well-marbled, aged Kansas City beef with an outside rim of fat. Yes, fat. Jonesy believes that steak with some fat is more juicy and flavorful than totally lean beef.

When it comes to cooking the meat, Jonesy has some definite opinions: "Broiling isn't the way to go. Too many of the meat's valuable juices drip away." So, like a prison warden, Jonesy has come up with a method of preventing escapes—he's invented a special cooking process. After the steak is seasoned, he lays it on a hot grill. Then, he picks up a big rock. Is this a last minute attempt to tenderize the meat? Nope. Jonesy smiles and notes that he uses a rock for one reason: "These smooth rocks from the Sacramento River are just the right weight and size to keep my steaks firmly pressed against the grill." As the meat cooks, a crust forms on the surface. The crust acts as a wall to lock in all the steak's rich juices and also gives the meat a unique flavor edge.

Since Jonesy's is located at the Napa Airport, many of his customers fly to the restaurant. One of Jonesy's airborne customers is Arnold Palmer, who's so rich he flies his own twin-engine plane. Big deal, you say . . . lots of people fly twin-engine planes. In their living room?

Menu Specialties: □ Sirloin Club Steak □ New York Steak □ Filet Mignon. Dinner includes: The Jonesy salad bowl (a huge salad of crisp romaine, garbanzo beans, black olives, green onions, and croutons in one of the most unusual blue cheese dressings we've had. It's definitely a mop-up-every-drop dressing.), main course with potatoes Jonesy-style (hand-grated hash browns blanketed with cheese and a huge oval of red onion), and coffee. **Prices:** Medium. **Basics:** Napa County Airport (about one mile down Airport Rd. from the intersection of Highway 29 and Highway 12.) The airport is six miles south of Napa. Tel: (707) 224-2945. Hours: 10 am-9:30 pm Tues.-Sat.; 10 am-9 pm Sun. Closed Mon. Cards: MC, V. Full bar.

Au Relais: Sonoma
French/A wine country building of 1871 vintage

We may be tempting you to have an affair—with food. After trying Au Relais' salmon quenelles, you may get the urge to spend every weekend with this French dish. The quenelles tempt you to sneak away because they offer you something you may not be getting at home— delicate salmon dumplings poached in chablis and covered with a rich, brandy-kissed Nantua prawn sauce. Love at first bite.

Then there's the profiterole pastry puff . . . a dessert which woos you to stay just a little longer and taste its Grand Marnier cream filling and explore its fine topping of port-marinated strawberries.

The building where diners and food couple up for the weekend is a fine, time-mellowed structure that dates back to 1871. Inside, the walls are paneled in native redwood, and French windows overlook a garden where diners sit among passion flowers and bonsai oaks. Just the right atmosphere for an affair with food.

Unfortunately, every affair has its risks. Repeated weekend dates with Au Relais' rich food could cause some problems. For your waistline. After a few trips to the scale, one night you may be forced to tell your salmon quenelles, "I'm sorry, but we can't go on meeting like this."

Menu Specialties: □ Salmon Quenelles □ Chicken Berrichone (a half-chicken, mushrooms, and bacon are wedded to a rich, sherry-laced brown sauce. The chef handles the arrangements.) □ Noisette Beaulieu (a premium cut of lamb sauteed with sherry, fresh artichoke hearts, mushrooms, and black olives.) □ Prawns Provencale (prawns flambéed in Pernod liqueur and topped with a flavorful tomato sauce that trumpets its freshness.)

Dinner includes . . . 3 courses: Soup (maybe potato-leek or cream of broccoli), incredibly good French bread from the Sonoma French Bakery, salad (butter lettuce, tomatoes, watercress, and fresh green beans in a Caesar dressing), main course with two fresh vegetables, and coffee. Dessert: Profiterole. **Prices:** Medium to a step above medium. **Basics:** 691 Broadway (three blocks from Sonoma's historical town plaza), Sonoma. Tel: (707) 996-1031. Hours: 11 am-10 pm Mon., Wed.-Sun. Closed Tues. Reservations necessary on weekends. Cards: AE, MC, V. Full bar.

Cazadero Inn: Cazadero
Breakfast/Buttermilk hot cakes and homemade preserves

The autumn sun rising above our cabin had a "good morning" glow. The Russian River was waking up. And so were Margie and Lorraine—our roommates. After we were all awake, Margie looked the situation over and softly made a suggestion . . .

"Let's get some breakfast."

Before long, we were in Cazadero, a recluse of a town. Across from the lumber mill, we spotted our objective—a small cottage with cross-pane windows. We walked in and sat down at one of the redwood burl tables.

A minute later, a lady with a bright yellow apron and a hello-folks smile came out from the kitchen to greet us. "Watcha need?" she asked. Lorraine told her we wanted breakfast. "Well, honey," the lady said, "it's a little late, but I can still fix you up some buttermilk hot cakes topped with my boysenberry preserves. Got to hurry, though. I'm putting up seven quarts of raspberries today."

The old country breakfast may be an endangered species, but at least it's not extinct.

Menu Specialties: □ Give the Cazadero's owner, mama Banks, $2.75 and for breakfast she'll give you two large, fresh Petaluma eggs, some thick, hand-sliced bacon, crisp hash-browns made from potatoes mama peeled herself, plenty of rich coffee brewed with pure mountain water, and toast . . . which you can spread with something mighty special—mama's homemade preserves . . . wild blackberry, apricot, or plum butter. □ Mama's buttermilk hot cakes, $1.25. □ Mama, bless her soul, will also make your young'uns hot cakes that are shaped like a teddy bear, 75¢. **Basics:** 6115 Cazadero Highway, Cazadero—about 8½ miles from the Russian River at Monte Rio. Tel: (707) 632-5271. Hours: 9 am-8 pm daily. No cards.

L'Omelette: Forestville
French/City cooking at country prices

Forestville is a tiny farming community near the Russian River. Around Forestville you'll find the expected: apple orchards, blueberry fields, and vineyards. But in Forestville itself, you'll find the unexpected: a French chef who's cooked at Romanoff's of Nob Hill, and at the legendary Le Pavillon in New York—which, during its years in business, was often referred to as "the best French restaurant in America."

Chef Leon Arseguel came to Forestville to retire. He was 65 years old. But he and the kitchen had been friends for a long time. And breaking up was hard to do. So he decided to open a restaurant—a little place that's only open Friday, Saturday, and Sunday. Just so he and the kitchen could keep in touch.

L'Omelette's 3-course dinners are very moderately priced considering some of the elegant dishes that chef Arseguel offers . . . like his breast of capon Monte Carlo. The breast is marinated for one week in port wine; then, when it's served, it comes surrounded by a moat of rich white cream sauce, and topped with a halo of orange sauce and a fresh apricot slice. For us, this is what makes L'Omelette a real discovery. It's one of those rare places that offers city cooking at country prices.

Menu Specialties: ☐ Breast of Capon Monte Carlo ☐ Coquille of Seafood Riviera (shrimp, scallops, and fresh mushrooms in a deeply-flavored cream sauce that's made the long, hard way—the way Paris chefs have done it for the last 195 years. The base of the sauce comes from shrimp shells that have been simmered for their essence—much the same way beef bones are simmered to make a great bordelaise stock. The result? The flavor of the sauce glows with 4-star kilowattage.) ☐ Omelet Champignons (the omelet is a golden cloud of lightness filled with sauteed mushrooms and topped with a port wine sauce.)

Dinner includes . . . 3 courses: Soup (maybe puree of vegetable or split pea), salad tossed in a fine creamy house dressing, and main course with three vegetables (hopefully, one of them will be the chef's beautifully souffléed potatoes.) **Prices:** Inexpensive to medium. **Decor:** A small bistro with checkered tablecloths and a modest but friendly decor. **Basics:** 6685 Front St. (on Highway 116), Forestville—7½ miles from the Russian River at Guerneville. Tel: (707) 887-9945. Hours: 5:30-9:30 pm Fri.-Sun. Closed Mon.-Thurs. Reservations necessary. No cards. Wine and beer.

Union Hotel: Occidental
Italian/Endless meals in a tree-shaded town

When you finish one of the Union Hotel's meals, your belt feels like a boa constrictor. But at least this time, you'll have a solid excuse for overeating. Occidental's Union Hotel serves the largest dinner in California. It's a seemingly endless, multi-course feast. And the portions are so big, you begin to think you're at an Italian wedding. By the way, there are two other restaurants in Occidental that serve similar dinners, Fiori's and Negri's, but in our opinion the Union Hotel is the best of the three.

Occidental is an isolated town of 250 where restaurant seats outnumber residents five to one. But the room is needed. The town's chief industry is feeding people. Every weekend, this hamlet with pine-tree scented air is buried under an avalanche of hungry people. And one of the main things that has these people coming to Occidental is the bargain prices. Repeat bargain prices. At the Union Hotel, one of their huge dinners with chicken as a main course will cost you only $5; or you can have a thick 16-ounce steak on the dinner for $8.

The Union Hotel has been causing these population explosions since 1892. The oak floors of this dinosaur building have been worn thin from the friction of thousands of feet carrying overloaded stomachs. And from the start, the people in charge of these feasts have been Italian. But that shouldn't be any surprise. The Italians are usually the navigators when dinner starts drifting toward the Bay of Excess.

The Menu: A Union Hotel dinner goes like this . . . *First,* a metal cart is rolled out freighted with a mammoth tureen of minestrone, piles of crusty French bread, a giant salad of lettuce, beets, and green beans in a house Italian dressing, and bowls filled with miniature mountains of marinated kidney beans, garbanzo beans and vegetables giardiniera, and plates of Monterey Jack and salami . . . *Second,* a platter of the Union Hotel's homemade ravioli . . . *Third,* the main course—either fried chicken, roasted Long Island duck, or a 16-ounce steak. All main courses include roasted potatoes and the house specialty, zucchini frittella—a sort of Italian vegetable pancake . . . *Fourth,* a platter of apple fritters for dessert, and coffee. **Prices:** Inexpensive to medium.

Big Record Holder: If you think this is a lot of food, it only means one thing—you're no competition for Bozo Miller. He'd consider this dinner just a snack. According to the *Guinness Book of World Records,* Bozo, who has a 57-inch waistline, is the world's greatest eater. Bozo lives in the Bay Area and local restaurants know him well. Once, at a restaurant in Oakland, Bozo ate 324 ravioli, and at Trader Vic's in San Francisco, he sat down and finished off 27 chickens. Amazing? Not for Bozo Miller. He consumes up to 25,000 calories a day. **Basics:** Main St., Occidental—8 miles from the Russian River, 9 miles from Sebastopol. Tel: (707) 874-3662. Hours: 11:30 am-9 pm Mon.-Sat.; noon-9 pm Sun. Reservations necessary on weekends and every day during the summer. Cards: MC, V. Full bar.

Vast's: Sebastopol
American/Homecooking and modest prices on a genuine farm

At the Vast's restaurant you'll find the best turkey dinner in America. Yes, we realize this is a big statement to make, but we've done some research in this area. Although, we admit, it's been difficult. Some people are very uncooperative when we ring the doorbell during Thanksgiving and ask to sample their dinner.

Fred and Silvie Vast have an honest respect for the turkey. They raised turkeys for over twenty years. Then, in 1969, the Vasts decided to start a new business. They took a rustic old building on their farm, restored it, filled the place with antiques, and opened a restaurant. A barnyard where the turkeys used to walk around is now a parking lot.

Besides using premium turkeys, one of the main keys to the flavor of a Vast turkey is the cooking process. The Vasts have their own smokehouse on the farm; the turkeys are cooked over a very low heat for fourteen hours in this smokehouse. And each order of turkey comes with an old-fashioned sage stuffing, a rich gravy made from smokehouse pan drippings, and candied yams.

But it's not just the turkey that's enjoyable. So is the price. A Vast turkey dinner is $6.25, and that includes a long-simmered soup, salad, and seasonal vegetables that the Vasts grow themselves. Even the water is "homemade." Right. We said homemade water. The Vasts serve water from their own well.

The nature of the Vast's restaurant is evident as soon as the waitress brings you a basket of oven-fresh powder biscuits with quince jam. She gives you a shy smile, points out the window and says, "That's the quince tree they make the jam from."

Menu Specialties: □ Roast Turkey □ Smokehouse Ham (Fred Vast takes whole choice hams and slowly smokes them over smoldering oakwood for a full day. The hams are then sliced to order and served with a fresh pineapple-raisin sauce.) □ Chicken Silvie (Silvie Vast takes half of a plump, locally-raised chicken and sautees it with mushrooms, sherry, and a sprinkling of well-chosen herbs.)

Dinner includes . . . 3 courses: Soup (maybe lentil with bacon or turkey-vegetable soup), salad with a special house blue cheese dressing, and main course with homegrown vegetables and real mashed potatoes. **Prices:** Inexpensive to medium. **Basics:** 5186 Gravenstein Highway South, Sebastopol—on Highway 116, 3 miles from the intersection of Highways 101 and 116. Tel: (707) 795-4747. Hours: 6-9:30 pm Thurs.-Sun. Closed Mon.-Wed. Cards: MC, V. Wine and beer.

LAKE TAHOE

Chez Villaret: South Lake Tahoe
Continental/A small cottage shaded by pine trees

The most popular leisure-time activity is assumed to be golf or tennis. We don't agree. Judging from sheer numbers, the public's favorite participation sport is going to restaurants for a round of recreational eating. And Tahoe restaurants like Chez Villaret are where this sport is played the hardest.

Chez Villaret is housed in a pine-shaded cottage about six miles from the casinos. In the small, romantic dining room there are paisley-print drapes, white tablecloths, kerosene lanterns, and two friendly waiters; and in the kitchen, there is owner Ed Pevenage—a man who doesn't make any compromises when it comes to cooking.

At Chez Villaret, chef Pevenage's chicken Chambertin is marinated for three days in red wine, thyme, and bay leaves; the sauce for his veal chop contains $43-a-pound wild Morille mushrooms from France; and the pasta for his cannelloni is made on a special pasta-making machine imported from Italy. And although it takes hours, for dessert Ed makes Sicilian cassata cake soaked in Grand Marnier. It's a dessert that can put a smile on any recreational eater's face.

Recreational eating. What a great sport . . . one that's becoming more popular every day. Hmmm. Maybe Ed will let you trade in your tennis racket for a piece of cassata cake.

Menu Specialties: □ Chicken Chambertin (a roasted chicken topped with mushrooms—each piece bursting with the flavor of the spicy wine marinade it's been soaked in.) □ Cannelloni (homemade pasta stuffed with four different meats and spinach. Topped with white sauce, cheese, and diced tomatoes, and baked.) □ Veal Morilles (a beautifully white, beautifully tender veal chop in a buttery cream sauce with the hypnotizing flavor of wild Morille mushrooms.) □ Bouillabaisse Marseillaise (lobster, shrimp, red snapper, and scallops in a saffron and wine fragrant seafood stock.) Dishes include three vegetables (maybe zucchini ratatouille, Mornay-sauced cauliflower, and feather-light Dauphine potato balls.)

Starters: Salad Maison (butter lettuce, shrimp, peeled tomato quarters, and hard-boiled eggs in a French vinaigrette.) Dessert: Cassata cake. **Prices:** Medium. **Basics:** 536 Emerald Bay Rd. (one mile north of the intersection of Highway 50 and Highway 89; six miles from Harrah's), South Lake Tahoe. Tel: (916) 541-7868. Hours: 6-11 pm daily. Reservations suggested on weekends. Cards: MC, V. Wine and beer.

Squirrel's Nest: Homewood
Lunches/Outdoor dining and special desserts

God bless motherhood, little children—and the Squirrel's Nest. Yes folks, it's that good. In our opinion, the Squirrel's Nest serves the best lunches in Tahoe.

Your lunch could start with a 24-carat-rich oyster-spinach soup, or a farmer's vegetable soup with huge hunks of corn-on-the-cob floating in the flavorful liquid. When you finish the soup, you could try a moist turkey breast sandwich topped with melted Tillamook cheddar cheese, or a hot Eastern ham and Jack cheese sandwich on a French steak bun. Or you could order a Staunton salad, a Sierra mountain of fresh watermelon, cantaloupe, strawberries, nectarines, bananas . . . well, enough fruit to stock three fruit stands in Gilroy. Partnered with the salad is some homemade apricot bread.

Speaking of baked goods, nobody but *nobody* leaves the Squirrel's Nest without ordering dessert. Maybe you'll get to try their cream-filled bourbon cake, brandy pecan pie, or if you're really lucky, their black magic chocolate cake layered with cheesecake filling and topped with blueberries. You guessed it. The Squirrel's Nest is a major West Coast distributor of calories.

The Squirrel's Nest provides the perfect setting for a Tahoe lunch. All meals are served outdoors. You sit under towering redwood trees at hand-painted tables with Technicolor umbrellas. One round table is even painted to look like a huge watermelon slice. And strung between the redwoods are clotheslines holding everything from gilded cupids to a stuffed toy monkey wearing a cowboy hat. No question—this area looks like it was landscaped by Smokey the Bear and decorated by Alice in Wonderland.

The Menu: □ Giant Sandwiches (served with German potato salad, and huge hunks of watermelon, tomatoes, and cucumbers), $3.65 to $3.95. □ The Daily Soup (always homemade, always creative, always good), 85¢. □ The Staunton Salad, $3.85. □ The Daily Desserts (at least five oven-fresh cakes and pies to choose from. How sweet it is.), about $1.50. **Basics:** 5405 West Lake Blvd., Homewood—7 miles from Tahoe City, 25 miles from South Lake Tahoe. Tel: (916) 525-7944. Hours: Noon-4 pm daily, the last week of June through Labor Day. Closed the rest of the year. Reservations necessary. No cards. Wine and beer.

Le Petit Pier: Tahoe Vista
French/Small, romantic dining room overlooking the lake

Le Petit Pier is expensive. But at this restaurant, there's a reason. Le Petit attempts to give you the best, and the best is never cheap. The Pier has game pheasant flown in from the East Coast, imports Dover sole from England, and seasons their dishes with herbs imported from France. At the Pier, nothing is overlooked. We learned that the bread served here is baked locally from a recipe supplied by the Pier's owner, Jean Dufau. And what Jean can't get from somebody else, he gets himself. Jean sometimes drives to San Francisco to get fresh mussels. He makes the trip in one day—leaving at six in the morning and returning in time to cook dinner that evening.

Then there's the service. In the small dining room the Pier manages to fit in five waiters. But don't worry, you'll be able to see more than just the waiters. The restaurant has been built over the water, giving everyone a view of Lake Tahoe.

Food. Service. Location. When you put everything together, the Pier's prices seem justifiable—particularly when we all know that there are some "tables" in Tahoe where the only thing $30 buys you is the privilege to hold two cards for five seconds.

Menu Specialties: ☐ Dover Sole Hollandaise (imported from England and served with a well-made hollandaise sauce.) ☐ Pheasant Braise Forestiere (sauteed in butter, then flambéed in cognac, and finally covered with a rich brown sauce that contains a fortune in Morille mushrooms and black truffles. Serves two.) ☐ Medallions of Veal Normande (milk-fed veal in a fine sauce made with butter, shallots, fresh mushrooms, and Calvados, French applejack brandy.) ☐ Duckling Montmorency (a roasted duckling stuffed with orange wedges, flambéed tableside with Grand Marnier, and garnished with cherries.) Items above include soup (maybe cream of watercress and leek), and vegetable (maybe an artichoke bottom filled with fresh peas.) Starters: Clams Nicoise (fresh East Coast clams steamed with chablis, garlic, and tomatoes); Mushrooms Petit Cafe (marinated in olive oil, Pommerey mustard, and herbs imported from France); Heart of Romaine Salad (covered with a beautiful dressing that contains chunks of the real thing . . . the famous white cheese made in the aging caves cf Roquefort, France.) **Prices:** Expensive. **Basics:** 7252 North Lake Blvd., Tahoe Vista—9 miles from Tahoe City, 30 miles from Stateline. Tel: (916) 546-4464. Hours: 6-10 pm daily; closed Tuesday in the winter. Reservations necessary on weekends. Cards: AE, MC, V. Wine and beer.

GOLD COUNTRY

HAVE YOU EVER CONSIDERED JUMPING PROFESSIONALLY?

Included in This Section

Page 248
Big homecooked meals at bargain prices on a farm that
was once used as a setting for a Hollywood movie.

Page 249
A former boarding house for miners that offers
4-course Italian dinners for $5.25.

Page 250
Oak-barbecued spareribs and the biggest drinks west
of the Rockies in an old Wells Fargo bank.

Page 251
Romantic dinners in a classic gold rush building
by a mountain creek.

Paul's Boarding House: Buena Vista
American/Bargain priced meals down on the farm

Turn off the stove, Mama. Helen Kovacevich is preparing dinner tonight. And for less money than you can cook it yourself. You don't believe us? Pencil in hand, try to figure out how much it would cost to fix: a large tureen of fresh vegetable soup, a hearty beef stew, a mound of potato salad, a dish of well-seasoned Navy beans, a platter of baked ham, a crisp salad, a basket of fried chicken, and a whole lemon meringue pie. Oh, by the way, Mama, Helen serves seconds on everything—no extra charge. Keep this fact in mind as you work up your estimate.

While you're figuring up the food bill, Mama, we'll tell you a little about Paul's. It's located in a white farmhouse surrounded by five acres of green fields. During the Thirties, the biggest bootlegging still in California could be found three miles down the road. And in 1956, the land around Paul's was used as a setting for *Come Next Spring* starring Ann Sheridan and Walter Brennan.

Time's up, Mama. How much do you figure it would cost to duplicate the boarding house's eight-dish dinner? About $6 you say? Sorry, Mama, that figure is wrong. Helen, bless her soul, only charges $3.25 per person. Now, all you have to do is figure out how she does it. Excuse us, though, we're heading for Paul's.

The Menu: The meal we've described above is served on both Saturday and Sunday, and please note that Paul's is *only* open on these two days. **Prices:** Inexpensive. **Basics:** Camanche Park Rd., Buena Vista—41 miles from Sacramento, 36 miles from Stockton. (Once in the town of Buena Vista, drive west on Jackson Valley Rd. about one mile. Turn left onto Camanche Park Rd. Paul's is about half a mile down Camanche on the right-hand side of the road.) Tel: (209) 274-4084. Hours: 5:30-9 pm Sat.; 1:45-9 pm Sun. Closed Mon.-Fri. No cards. Wine and beer.

Buscaglia's: Jackson
Italian/Big dinners, the house policy since 1916

Beginning Instructions: Please step on a scale and weigh yourself. Now, get down off the scale and read this article.

At Buscaglia's, the fried chicken is $5.25, the veal valdostana is $5.85, and the steak parmigiana is $7.75. And these prices buy you a big dinner.

Since the day they opened in 1916 as a boarding house for miners, Buscaglia's has started off every meal with a family-style tureen of→

Minestrone Soup fortified with home-grown herbs and nuggets of potatoes and celery. The next course is a large bowl of→

Salad with a homemade red wine vinegar and olive oil dressing. Partnered with the salad is a plate of→

Antipasto: pepperoncini, marinated garbanzos, salami, and country-style pickles. After you've finished this plate you're ready for→

The Main Course, which could be fried chicken, veal valdostana, or steak parmigiana. Tagging along with the main course are two platters of→

Homemade Ravioli and Spaghetti both topped with a meaty tomato sauce spiced with rosemary and thyme. Finally, the parade of dishes ends as your waitress brings you a dish of→

Spumoni Ice Cream for dessert.

Ending Instructions: Step on the scale again. Doesn't the thought of all this food we've just talked about make you weigh a pound more?

Menu Specialties: ☐ Veal Valdostana (layered with prosciutto ham and Monterey Jack cheese, then baked in wine.) ☐ Fried Chicken (with a crispy, golden brown crust.) ☐ Steak Parmigiana (sirloin steak, Italian style. The steak is topped with melted cheese, mushrooms, and a marinara sauce.) Dinner includes . . . 4 courses: Soup, salad with antipasto, main course with vegetable, pasta, and dessert. **Prices:** Inexpensive to medium. **Basics:** 1218 Jackson Gate Rd., Jackson—48 miles from Sacramento, 43 miles from Stockton. Tel: (209) 223-9992. Hours: Noon-2 pm, 5-9:30 pm Mon., Thurs., Fri.; 1-10 pm Sat.; 1-9 pm Sun. Closed Tues., Wed. No cards. Full bar. Parking lot.

Poor Red's: El Dorado
Oak-Barbecued Spareribs/Small prices and giant drinks

Occasionally, we get three or four couples together and make the drive to El Dorado, an ancient little town eight miles from where gold was discovered. Our destination is Poor Red's—a sturdy old structure which probably hasn't had a major face lift since it was built by Wells Fargo in 1858.

Poor Red's bartender always greets us with a drawl that sounds like it came mail order from Rapid City, South Dakota. "Hi thar, did you know your date's legs are like clouds? Thar always partin'." Rather than get mad, we're always relieved to find that Poor Red's hasn't changed since our last visit.

Usually, there's about an hour's wait for a table. No problem. It gives us an excuse to bivouac at Poor Red's bar and consume a few liquid appetizers. Since we're familiar with Poor Red's pouring policies, we always order a Whiskey Sour, a Gold Cadillac, or some other drink that has to be mixed in a blender. The bartenders here have an unwritten policy that, when a customer orders a blended drink, he gets a cocktail glass and a water tumbler and a drink big enough *to fill both*. At Poor Red's there's so much alcohol on people's breath, even the air is 86 proof.

Sometime later, we halt our marathon drinking contest and stumble into the dining room. Everyone always orders Poor Red's backwoods specialty—spareribs barbecued over an open oakwood charcoal pit. And they're only $4.00 an order.

After dinner, it's back to the bar for more tall drinks and crude comments, although by this time our dates are usually making most of them.

Menu Specialties: ☐ Barbecued Spareribs (the ribs are cooked over oakwood charcoal. Red has a man who makes the charcoal just for him. It's a long process. To make the charcoal, oak logs are left to smolder for one week. Then, before Red cooks the ribs over this charcoal, he coats them with a special barbecue sauce made with 20 spices. It took Red 5 years of mixing, matching, and blending to find the right formula. Once, we asked him what was in it. His answer was, "It's . . . my . . . secret." We can't blame him. His secret sells 50 tons of ribs a year.) ☐ Barbecued Ham or Barbecued Chicken (both cooked like the ribs.)

Dinner includes: Salad, New Orleans rolls, and baked potato.
Prices: Inexpensive. **Basics:** Main St., El Dorado—a few miles off Highway 50 near Placerville. (Once in Placerville, take Highway 49 south and stay on it until you reach El Dorado, about 5½ miles.) Tel: (916) 622-2901. Hours: 11:30 am-2 pm, 5-11 pm Mon.-Sat.; 2-11 pm Sun. Cards: MC, V. Full bar.

Jack's Deer Creek: Nevada City
Continental/In a creekside, gold rush era building

The fortuneteller affair

A thick fog hung over the deserted alley and the wind made a low moaning sound as Russ Riera, the 34-year-old author of this book, entered the beaded curtain doorway of Madame Zenobia's. Although the room had the lighting of a dungeon, Riera spotted the gypsy fortuneteller immediately. The old lady's forearms were tattooed with astrological signs, and her massive, 350-pound frame was wrapped in yards of purple satin. Madame Zenobia looked like she'd be safe from advances even if she cooked naked in a lumber camp.

Riera sat down and began to explain his problem. "I've just finished checking out ten different restaurants. They were all terrible. Tell me, please, does the future look any better for me?"

"Well, my son, let's have a look," said Madame Zenobia gazing into her huge crystal ball. "Aha! I see something already. I see a charming three-story building . . . by a moss-rimmed mountain creek . . . a fine gold rush relic . . . an outdoor deck has been added on . . . inside there's small, romantic dining areas . . . comfortable chairs, flowers, oil paintings in antique frames . . . ahh, yes, I see you at a table with a woman . . ."

"A woman?" Riera interrupted.

"Shhh!" cautioned Madame Zenobia, "you'll break the spell." With her bowling-pin nose almost resting on the crystal ball, she continued, "I see two men running this restaurant . . . they have imagination when it comes to cooking . . . they change the menu every three months . . . the spirits say their food is good . . . well, I see the woman with you says the mushroom salad tonight is affecting her like an aphrodisiac . . ."

"Hey, what about this woman?" Riera asked.

Madame Zenobia looked up at Riera. Her raisin-black eyes were burning like two gas-range pilot lights. "Quiet, insolent one!" she roared and then resumed her chant delivery. "I see your dinner tonight . . . a rich shrimp bisque . . . a tender, generously stuffed Cornish game hen . . . fresh broccoli with cheddar cheese sauce . . . wait . . . oh, my . . . I see the woman rubbing your leg under the table . . ."

"Stop!" Riera shouted, "I *demand* to know. Who is this woman!"

Madame Zenobia suddenly sprang to her feet with a momentum that knocked over the tiny table and began chasing Riera around the room, leaving a trail of tarot cards and tea leaves. Finally, after a few minutes, Riera tripped over the crystal ball and she caught him. Squeezing Riera into a bearhug grip, Madame Zenobia whispered, "Me."

The Menu: This restaurant changes its menu every three months according to the season. Although only a fortuneteller can predict exactly what dishes each season will bring, these are some of the dishes that appear frequently: Cornish game hen with a chestnut stuffing; rack of lamb with mint sauce; pork chops with an apple-flecked stuffing; fettucine Alfredo (tender ribbons of pasta in a velvet-smooth sauce of pure cream, butter, and imported parmesan cheese); East Indian shrimp curry (shrimp sauteed in butter and white wine, topped with a curry sauce flavored with seven spices, and garnished with grapes and slices of peach and watermelon—a rollercoaster ride of flavors.)

Dinner includes . . . 3 courses: Soup (maybe shrimp bisque or a Spanish Christmas soup), salad (either a marinated mushroom salad or a fresh spinach salad laced with bacon), and main course with fresh vegetable (maybe broccoli with cheddar cheese sauce or locally-grown corn—which is picked at 3 and served at 6.) **Prices:** Medium.

A Note on Nevada City: After dinner, take a walk around town. Jack's is located in one of the most colorful and well-preserved towns in gold country. Nevada City looks exactly like those places you used to see in early TV westerns. The town will remind you of those innocent days when you never questioned how the Lone Ranger was able to buy silver bullets since he never had a job. **Basics:** 101 Broad St., Nevada City—18 miles from the junction of Highway 80 and Highway 174 at Colfax; 68 miles from Sacramento. Tel: (916) 265-5808. Hours: 11:30 am-2 pm Mon., Wed.-Fri.; 6-9 pm Mon., Wed.-Sun. Closed Tues. Reservations suggested on weekends. Cards: MC, V. Full bar.

Two More: *A restaurant on the Sacramento Delta and a restaurant in the San Joaquin Valley*

Al's Place: Locke
Steak/Old-time establishment in a unique Delta town

Al's looks like the kind of place that Charles Bronson would start a fight in. The paint is yellow and peeling. An ancient Acme Beer sign hangs on rusty hinges over the door. The floor creaks. On a shelf above the bar are a dusty stuffed ostrich and a barnacle-encrusted harpoon. And the dining room looks like a truck stop luncheonette. At most establishments all this would be called "a reason to remodel"; at Al's it's called atmosphere. Al's has been around since 1934. It's hard to say when it stopped being a saloon and became an institution.

No one really knows why Al came to this Delta town in the first place. Al was a full-blooded Italian, and Locke was an all-Chinese settlement that was built in 1912 by the Chinese who had once worked on the railroad gangs.

For years, Locke remained a peaceful, isolated settlement. But as Prohibition gained momentum, it was invaded by an assortment of tong gangsters, rum runners, and honky-tonk women. By the time Al arrived, the opium smoke was at smog level.

Today, Locke is quiet once again. The rum runners are gone, but the Chinese are still there. Many of them are descendants of the railroad workers who originally built the place. And over the years not much has changed. The town is a fascinating collection of rickety buildings and narrow alleyways. Locke is a rare sight—it's sort of an Old West town with a Chinese twist.

Al's Steak Dinner: Al's hasn't changed its menu since 1934. Only one item is served—New York steak. It's a thick, flavorful, 16-ounce steak topped with fresh mushrooms. The price is a reasonable $7.75 for the complete dinner, which includes a tossed green salad with blue cheese dressing, hand-cut fries, spaghetti in a meat sauce made with New York steak tips, and coffee. **Basics:** Main St. (just off Highway 160), Locke, Sacramento Delta—48 miles from Concord. Tel: (916) 776-1800. Hours: 11:30 am-2 pm, 5-10 pm daily. No cards. Full bar.

After Dinner: Have a drink at Foster's Big Horn—13 miles down the road from Al's. On the outside, Foster's looks like a small neighborhood bar. But wait 'til you open the door. Inside, you'll find one of the largest private collections of stuffed animal heads in the United States—252 trophies in all: tiger, rhinoceros, Congo buffalo, cheetah, elephant, and more. The place looks like Tarzan's living room. Foster was a big game hunter and, according to rumor, the Mafia offered him $1 million to move his collection to New York. Foster's: 143 Main St., Rio Vista. Tel: (707) 374-9993. Hours: 10 am-2 am Mon., Wed.-Sun. Closed Tues.

Imperial Dynasty: Hanford
French/Farm town Chinese chef who's cooked for presidents

If we had one last meal on earth, it would be hard deciding what to eat. We just hope that Richard Wing isn't busy that day. We might be asking him to do the cooking.

He certainly could handle the job. Wing has won the *Holiday* award every year since 1966; gourmet societies have traveled to Hanford, the small San Joaquin Valley farm town where Wing's restaurant is located, just to have dinner; and before he began creating dishes at the Imperial Dynasty, Wing cooked for Winston Churchill, Eisenhower, and Truman.

Wing's cooking career began while he was in the Army. In 1945, he became an aide to George C. Marshall, U.S. Army Chief of Staff and later Secretary of State. General Marshall quickly discovered that Wing was a kitchen talent. The General found out that his best strategy was to have Wing behind the stove whenever he entertained Churchill and other heads of state.

Wing traveled with Marshall for the next eleven years, constantly learning new techniques from chefs he met in France and other countries. When Marshall went to China, for example, to negotiate between the Nationalists and the Communists, Wing spent his time in Chiang Kai-shek's kitchen, comparing notes with Chiang's French chefs. The slogan "Join the Army and learn a skill," is certainly true in Wing's case.

After his tour of duty, Wing returned to Hanford's China Alley, where his family had run a noodle shop since 1883. Slowly, he expanded and remodeled the family business. Today, the job is complete. The restaurant resembles a Chinese art museum, and the crisscross of tunnels underneath the building, that were once hide-outs for tong gangsters, are now used to store Wing's $250,000 wine collection.

When Wing took over his family's restaurant, he also changed the menu. The place no longer offers Chinese noodles. The Imperial Dynasty's menu now features elegant French dishes, but since the site of the restaurant is a farming community, the prices are surprisingly moderate for the kind of dinners Wing offers. Another surprise is the flavor of Wing's dishes. The food can best be described as French cooking with a Chinese accent. Everyone from Wing's mother to Parisian chefs have contributed to Wing's cooking knowledge, and this varied background has produced some unique dishes.

Hold it. There's a catch. When Wing cooks for gourmet societies or private parties, he can turn out a constellation of star dishes. But the daily pace of a restaurant's kitchen somehow dilutes his skill. At the Imperial Dynasty, the food is just plain very, very good. Which is okay with us.

Menu Specialties: ☐ Tournedos of Beef Bordelaise (two tender medallions cut from the eye of the filet, and topped with Wing's bordelaise—a sauce made from French Bordeaux wine, butter, and a fantastically rich stock that takes 30 hours to make.) ☐ Roast Duckling Tangerine (a boned duckling is soaked in a citrus juice marinade, and then tumbled in Chinese water chestnut flour and partially steamed. Then, it's roasted until the skin is crackly-crisp and topped with a tangerine-flavored wine sauce.) ☐ Roast Rack of Lamb Oregano (the lamb is marinated in olive oil, brushed with sesame seed butter, dusted with Chinese Five-Spice powder, and partially baked. Then, it's glazed with a rich brown oregano-scented sauce.)

Dinner includes . . . 5 courses: Soup (maybe winter melon soup or Philadelphia pepper pot), salad, crab foo yung appetizer, main course with rice pilaf, coffee, and coconut ice cream. **Prices:** Medium to a step above medium. **Basics:** No. 2 China Alley (near North Green St., half a block off East 7th St.), Hanford—32 miles from Fresno. Tel: (209) 582-0196. Hours: 4:30-10:30 pm Tues.-Sun. Closed Mon. Reservations necessary. Cards: AE. Full bar.

Conversation Pieces

Facts that make interesting table talk

Two Rooms in One

In the 1890s, many of San Francisco's famous French restaurants, including Delmonico's, Marchand's, and Maison Dorée, had private upstairs dining rooms with locks on the doors. Behind those doors? In the typical room you'd find gilded mirrors, two plush velvet armchairs, and a table set with fine China and sterling silverware. And a few feet from the table, you'd find a canopied bed with a red satin bedspread. Back then, when people said it was a romantic restaurant, they meant it.

Since these restaurants also catered to the general public in their downstairs rooms, in order to prevent any gossip or scandal, the upstairs dining bedrooms could be reached by special entrances. One San Francisco restaurant, Blanco's, even went further than that to protect the privacy of its customers: it had a custom-designed elevator that was so large, a carriage and its passengers could be driven into the elevator from the street. When the elevator reached the second floor, a silent, formally-dressed waiter would help the passengers out of the carriage and lead them to one of Blanco's dining bedrooms.

Don't Break the Law

In California, it is illegal to sleep in a kitchen. In Oklahoma, it is against the law to take a bite out of someone else's hamburger. In Idaho, you're not allowed to buy a chicken after sundown unless you have the sheriff's permission. In Lexington, Kentucky, it is illegal to carry an ice cream cone in your back pocket. In Knoxville, Tennessee, it is against the law to lasso a fish. And in the town of Spades, Indiana, you're breaking the law if you shoot open a can of food.

Sea Power

Our Pacific Coast Dungeness crab would be no match for the boxing crabs of the Samoa Islands. Samoan crabs actually use their claws like fists. When faced with a natural enemy, these Samoan crabs spar, jump, and throw right and left jabs using their front claws as fists.

For boxing gloves, Samoan crabs grab sea anemones from behind and hold one in each claw. The anemones have powerful frontal stinging cells and Samoan crabs know that when they hit an opponent with one of these anemones, the stinging cells will discharge. A boxing crab. . .it's a promoter's dream. We can hear the foghorn-voiced fight announcer right now: "In this corner, weighing 216 pounds and wearing white trunks . . . Muhammad Ali! And in the opposing corner, weighing 15 ounces and wearing seaweed trunks . . ."

What's Up, Doc?

The hot dog was first introduced to America in 1904 at the St. Louis World's Fair. Twelve years later, a man named Nathan Handwerker decided to open a restaurant that specialized in this new food. Mr. Handwerker opened his first Nathan's hot dog stand in 1916 at Coney Island, New York. It was not an instant success. In fact, business was bad. The hot dog was still a relatively unknown food. People were very suspicious of a strangely-shaped sandwich that only cost a nickel.

Mr. Handwerker was a man with a problem. But Mr. Handwerker was also a man with a solution. He hired a group of serious-looking young men and dressed them in starched white coats. He then gave them stethoscopes and told them to make sure to have the stethoscope dangling out of the coat's front pocket. Nathan Handwerker now had himself a group of young men who looked like young doctors. When Handwerker hired them, he said the job would be easy. It was. To earn their wages, all these "young doctors" had to do was stand in front of Nathan's place and eat hot dogs. Before long, the word got around that doctors were eating at Nathan's and the place became jammed with customers. People figured that if doctors ate these nickel hot dog sandwiches, they had to be good for you. And today, Nathan's Inc. still runs the most popular chain of hot dog stands in America.

When the Cooking Begins, Chang Watches

As ancient custom dictates, near the stove in many homes in China there is a brightly colored picture of Chang Kung. And the Chinese have a lot of respect for this picture. Chang Kung is the Chinese Kitchen God. The Chinese believe that Chang watches over the family's activities in the kitchen and then reports to the Emperor of the Sky.

His departure on the 23rd of December is filled with ceremony. On this day each year, families start by taking the Kitchen God's picture off the wall. The lips of the Kitchen God are then rubbed with molasses. Why? The Chinese believe this will make him speak sweetly about the family. But those who have burned the chow mein or overcooked the rice must take more drastic measures. Unsure of what the Kitchen God will report, these kitchen sinners rub his lips with opium or dip his picture in wine, on the theory he won't be able to remember what he saw.

Once the picture has been properly prepared, it's placed on a small sedan chair made of straw and carried out to the street. With great ceremony, the picture is then set on fire. The Kitchen God ascends in a cloud of smoke accompanied by prayers, firecrackers, and incense. Seven days later, another picture of the Kitchen God is put on the wall.

Sourdough Safeguards

The most important ingredient in San Francisco sourdough bread is the starter dough. It's what gives San Francisco sourdough its special character. Bakers use starter dough like yeast. Each day, the baker takes a chunk from his batch of fermented starter dough and mixes it with flour, water, and salt to make the dough for his bread. Once the dough is made, a piece of this fresh dough is put back into the starter or "mother" batch to replenish it. At some local bakeries this process has been going on for over a hundred years.

One of these bakeries is Parisian. Their batch of starter dough dates back to 1853. And they consider it a valuable possession. According to Peter Kane, the vice president of Parisian, the starter dough for their bread is stored at a secret location. And only two employees know where it's kept. Each day, one of these men arrives at this private storage facility, picks up a huge chunk of starter dough, and brings it back to the bakery in a special unmarked vehicle.

The man who owns Boudin Bakery in San Francisco doesn't take any chances, either. When Gaspar Rivas, the 77-year-old owner of Boudin, decided to open a branch of his bakery in Chicago, he had a chunk of Boudin's starter transported to the San Francisco International Airport in a Loomis armored truck. And as an added precaution, Gaspar had the starter dough packed for flight in a locked strongbox, and had it insured for $500,000 by the Great American Insurance Company of San Francisco.

The Dishwasher Song

Little Richard has sold 18 million records and is considered one of the pioneers of rock 'n' roll. And like many singers, Little Richard's first song was the result of personal experience. The idea for the song came to him while he was working in the dish room of a restaurant.

In 1955, Little Richard was working as a dishwasher at a restaurant in Macon, Georgia. It was a tough job. Everyday, the waiters would throw stacks of dishes at him and then swear at him for not working fast enough. And Little Richard knew he'd be fired if he swore back. But he had another way of taking out his frustrations. Little Richard just pointed his finger at the waiters and wailed, "A wop bop a loo bop, a lop bam boom." After a few months of repeating this original curse, Little Richard decided to write a song called "Tutti-Frutti," using the "a wop bop" curse as part of the lyrics. The song ended up selling over a million records and turned Little Richard into a major rock star.

Moral: when you hear a dishwasher sing, you'd better listen—and take notes.

People Who Like Chicken

In the 17th century, King Louis XIV of France required noblemen to rise from their chairs and make a low bow whenever a platter of chicken passed on the way to the royal table. Today, chicken has even become a favorite of the FBI. A Chicago FBI agent, Thomas Green, recommends that kidnap victims eat fried chicken. Agent Green explained that after eating fried chicken, "You'll leave fingerprints all over, creating evidence which leads to the successful prosecution of the kidnappers."

Another admirer of the chicken is Hugh Hefner, the publisher of *Playboy* magazine. When Mr. Hefner dined at Maxim's in Paris, he ordered fried chicken. And Maxim's version passed Mr. Hefner's test. "It was delicious," Hefner said, "it tasted just like Colonel Sanders'."

But the people who had the highest regard for chicken were the farmers of La Grange, Texas, during the Depression. When the madam of La Grange's house of prostitution learned that the farmers were no longer dropping by because they were short on cash, she began to accept chickens as payment for her services. Before long, the madam had so many chickens, she decided to go into the poultry business, selling chickens from a stand behind the house.

Aztec Screenplay

The journals kept by Spanish conquistadores Bernal Díaz and Hernando Cortez that describe the Aztec empire they found in Mexico in the 16th century both agree on one point—dinner at Montezuma's was a big affair. Cortez was amazed at the feasts that were served to the Aztec emperor, later writing that the meals consisted of "all the products that could be found in his lands." Fresh food came in daily from all over the empire, brought by men who ran in relay until they reached the Aztec capital of Tenochtitlán.

As soon as the food for the daily feast was prepared, Montezuma would appear before his guests. And then he'd disappear. When Montezuma was ready to eat, screens were placed around him. According to Aztec law, no one was allowed to watch the emperor swallow his food. Only after Montezuma had finished his meal were the screens removed and the guests allowed to begin eating.

Play It Again, Oyster

In nineteenth century London, on Drury Lane, there was a modest restaurant owned by a retired sea captain named Pearkes. Business was never very good for Mr. Pearkes and to economize, he did most of the repair work himself.

It was repair work that kept him up late one night in 1840. Mr. Pearkes was upstairs fixing a broken table leg, when suddenly he heard a whistling noise in the kitchen. His heart started pounding. Mr. Pearkes was sure that thieves were coming to take what little money he had. He grabbed the broken table leg for protection and very quietly began to creep down the stairs. As he inched his way toward the kitchen, he heard the whistle again. It was coming from the larder room. Trembling, but determined to protect what was his, Mr. Pearkes crept over to the larder and flung open the door, ready to club the criminal inside. The room was empty. Yet, the whistling continued. The sound was coming from a barrel of oysters. One of the oysters in the barrel had a small hole in its upper shell. When it breathed, water was forced through the hole, causing the whistle.

Mr. Pearkes was no fool. The next morning, he renamed his restaurant "The Whistling Oyster," and put this musical shellfish on display. Within weeks, Mr. Pearkes' place became one of London's most well-known restaurants, attracting such guests as Charles Dickens and William Thackeray. Thackeray even left us with a record of the experience. After listening to the oyster, he later wrote that he found it "talented."

Coffee Divorces & The Coffee Patrol

History has been clear on what was the most popular drink among the Turks of the Ottoman empire during the 16th century—these people were serious coffee-drinkers. The Turks not only enjoyed coffee, they considered it a necessity of life. At Turkish wedding ceremonies, men vowed to provide coffee for their brides throughout their lives. If a man failed in this responsibility, his wife was allowed to ask for a divorce.

Not everyone in history had as high an opinion of coffee as the Turks. Frederick the Great of Prussia didn't like it at all. The king of his former German state felt that so much money was being paid to foreign coffee merchants, it was depriving the royal treasury of possible revenues. To discourage the German people from drinking coffee, Frederick issued a manifesto in 1777 which stated:

> . . . Everybody is using coffee. If possible, this must be prevented. My people must drink beer. His Majesty was brought up on beer, and so were his ancestors, and his officers. Many battles have been fought and won by soldiers nourished on beer; and the King does not believe that coffee-drinking soldiers can be depended upon. . . .

But the manifesto wasn't very effective. Stronger measures were needed. So Frederick issued an edict which forbid the roasting of coffee except in establishments licensed by the king. The catch was that coffee-roasting licenses were only granted to the nobility. And to prevent the common people from roasting coffee in secret, Frederick employed soldiers as "coffee sniffers." As military assignments go, this was easy duty. The soldiers were ordered to follow the aroma of roasting coffee through the city streets and report anyone who was roasting coffee without a license.

Monkey Business

In the southeastern province of Kiangsi, China, a deeply-flavored green tea grows that is called Wun Mo Chaah or "Cloud Mist"—a tea that's so rich, it's served in very small cups and sipped like a liqueur. The tea's character comes from being grown on cliffs of the highest mountains in the province. At these altitudes planting the tea is a dangerous job and harvesting it is almost an impossible "human" task. But that's okay. Because humans don't pick the tea. Cloud Mist tea is harvested by trained monkeys. The Chinese train monkeys to scale the cliffs, pluck the delicate tea leaves, put the leaves in baskets, and then bring the baskets down the mountain.

Recipes for Love

In some parts of Italy, unmarried girls would sometimes prepare a dish heavily spiced with basil—an herb the Italians feel symbolizes love. Then these maidens would put a pot of flowering basil in the kitchen window. This was a signal to their lovers that their parents were gone.

Of course, there have been women who've used a more direct approach. An ancient Persian recipe for dessert not only included eggs, honey, and spices, but also instructed the woman preparing it to throw her lover's pants into the pot. And German girls in the Middle Ages didn't take any chances at all. First, they would find a bin of wheat and roll around in it naked. Then, after the wheat was milled, they would bake some of it into bread for the man of their choice. German girls believed that men who ate a slice or two of this "wonder bread" would find them irresistible.

The Mutton Chops of Monte Carlo

In 1868, James Gordon Bennett, Jr. inherited the *New York Herald* from his father. At the time, the *Herald* was one of the most successful newspapers in the country, and although after Bennett took control, he spent the majority of his time in Europe, the paper continued to prosper. Bennett's income averaged, in today's dollars, about $6,000,000 a year.

Of course, a man with that kind of income needs a hobby. And Bennett had one—spending money. Especially when it came to food. For example, when Bennett had his giant steam yacht, the *Lysistrata,* built in 1900, he had them design a special padded room for a cow, so he could have fresh butter while at sea.

Yet this was nothing compared with what he once paid for a plate of Southdown mutton chops. Mutton chops were Bennett's favorite dish, and one of his favorite places to have them was a small, hillside restaurant overlooking Monte Carlo. He had lunch there often, always taking a table on the restaurant's terrace and always ordering the mutton chops. But one day Bennett visited the restaurant and found all of the tables on the terrace occupied by drinkers. The worried maitre'd asked if he'd like a table inside. "No!" Bennett replied. Bennett was a man who knew what he wanted, and at that moment he wanted mutton chops on the terrace. Spotting the owner, he called him over. Bennett came right to the point. He wanted to buy the restaurant. The owner could name his price, but the transaction had to be completed immediately. It was. A figure, in today's dollars, of $200,000 was agreed on and the restaurant changed hands.

Bennett's first function as the new owner was to have the drinkers moved inside. Then Bennett sat down on the terrace and had his mutton chops. It must have been an enjoyable lunch. Very enjoyable. As a tip, Bennett gave his waiter the deed of sale. The waiter was told the restaurant was his on one condition—he had to have mutton chops and the terrace available whenever Bennett paid the restaurant a visit. "Anything you say, Mr. Bennett," the waiter answered.

By chance, Bennett had picked the right man. The waiter's name was Ciro, and Ciro's of Monte Carlo was to become one of the world's most famous restaurants.

80 Proof American History

The next time you're passing by your favorite tavern, go in and have a drink. It's a patriotic thing to do. The tavern is a great American institution. Where did the Founding Fathers hold the first Continental Congress in 1774? At the City Tavern in Philadelphia. And down the road at the Indian Queen Tavern in Philadelphia, Thomas Jefferson wrote the first draft of the Declaration of Independence.

Taverns have also inspired other American writers. Francis Scott Key completed "The Star-Spangled Banner" at the Fountain Inn in Baltimore. In fact, taverns have served as a "cradle" of American history in more ways than one. The 8th President of the United States, Martin Van Buren, was born in a tavern in Kinderhook, New York. Our 16th President also had fond memories of a tavern. Abraham Lincoln was part owner of a tavern in New Salem, Illinois in 1832. So the next time your local tavern owner starts talking politics, listen to him—he might be President someday.

Chocolate Facials & Licorice Shoes

If you're tired of giving fruit-filled bonbons on Valentine's Day, the Astor Chocolate Corporation of New York has just what you're looking for. They'll make you a set of chocolate lollipops in the shape of your face. They cast a die from your photo and then make you 120 lollipops, the minimum order. The total cost is $140.

This may be a lot of money for lollipops, but it's relatively reasonable compared to what Charlie Chaplin had to spend for candy. In the 1925 silent-film classic, *The Gold Rush,* there was a scene where Charlie Chaplin had to eat one of his shoes. So he called the American Licorice Company of San Francisco and had them make him a "shoe." The licorice shoe cost $220, and it took Chaplin 30 takes to eat the thing. Chaplin hated licorice.

Two Ways to Save Money

Oil tycoon J. Paul Getty was considered one of the world's richest men—his fortune was estimated at anywhere between $2 billion and $4 billion. And Getty's wealth was no accident. The man was extremely careful with his money. Rather than pay the cover charge at an exclusive supper club, Getty once waited until the band finished playing before being seated.

William Randolph Hearst was another man who seemed to know the value of money. The Hearst castle at San Simeon cost $40 million, and Hearst's dinner guests at the castle included everyone from Greta Garbo to President Coolidge. But no matter who came to dinner, Hearst never violated one rule. At dinner parties, the Hearst staff was always instructed to set the table with paper napkins.

Bibliography

Beebe, Lucius. *The Big Spenders*. Doubleday and Co., Inc., 1966.

Bolitho, Hector, ed. *The Glorious Oyster*. Horizon Press, Inc., 1961.

Cohn, Nik. *Rock from the Beginning*. Stein and Day, 1969.

Edwords, Clarence E. *Bohemian San Francisco*. Paul Elder and Co., 1914.

Farga, Amando. *Eating in Mexico*. Mexican Restaurant Association, 1963.

Feng, Doreen Yen Hung. *The Joy of Chinese Cooking*. Faber and Faber, 1952.

Hendrickson, Robert. *Lewd Food*. Chilton Book Co., 1974.

Horizon Magazine, ed. *The Horizon Cookbook*. American Heritage Press, 1968.

Mario, Thomas. *Playboy's Gourmet*. Playboy Press, 1971.

McMahon, Ed. *Ed McMahon's Barside Companion*. Pocket Books, 1970.

Quimme, Peter. *The Signet Book of Coffee and Tea*. The New American Library, Inc., 1976.

Roate, Mettja C. *The New Hot Dog Cookbook*. Aspen Books, 1973.

Seuling, Barbara. *You Can't Eat Peanuts in Church and Other Little-Known Laws*. Doubleday and Co., Inc., 1976.

Sia, Mary. *Mary Sia's Chinese Cookbook*. University of Hawaii Press, 1956.

Stanford, Sally. *The Lady of the House*. G.P. Putnam's Sons, 1966.

Swanberg, W.A. *Citizen Hearst*. Charles Scribner's Sons, 1961.

Trager, James. *The Food Book*. Avon Books, 1972.

Tannahill, Reay. *Food in History*. Stein and Day, 1973.

Wason, Betty. *Cooks, Gluttons and Gourmets, a History of Cookery*. Doubleday and Co., Inc., 1962.

Give Us a Call
655-2068

If you have a question about a restaurant in San Francisco or the Bay Area, pick up your telephone and dial our number. The area code is 415. We just might have the information you're looking for. When to call? We'll be at the phone from 8:00 to 10:00 p.m. Thursday and 4:30 to 6:30 p.m. Saturday.

The Gift Department

Let's say you'd like to give your friend a gift. And you've narrowed it down to either a completely restored 1937 Cord roadster or a copy of this book. What's our advice? Be practical. Cars are too hard to gift-wrap. For a copy of *Two Hundred Good Restaurants* send a check to Moss Publications for $2.95. We pay postage and handling. Also, as a way of saying "thanks," your authors will personally autograph all mail order copies.

Mail your order to:

Moss Publications
P.O. Box 644
Berkeley, California 94701

Restaurants by Location

San Francisco

The East Bay

The Artists

Jim Parkinson, with the assistance of Jim Wasco, did the cover and all the artwork that introduced each section. Frank Ansley did the illustrations on pages 60, 78, 88, 136, 140, 196, and 264. Tom Cervenak did pages 124, 162, and 186. Leonard K. Jennings did page 170.

Photo Credits

Hugh Brown: 36, 46, 50, 57, 70, 90, 116, 128, 159, 168, 182.

Benny Benvenuti: 27. Don Wienecke: 83. Raymond Goyenchea: 101. Clare Bell: 118. Roy W. Blandin: 131. Jed Dugish: 139. Paul Williams: 146. Michael Francisco: 173. John Levin: 193. Tom Patterson: 218. David Sievert: 220. Dean Miles: 227. Linda Toronto: 235. Harry Marsden: 238. Karl Ferris: 271.

A Word of Thanks

A special note of thanks is due to Walt Perry, Francoise Meltzer, and author Riera's father, Russell D. Riera. Their help and interest in this book was greatly appreciated.

About the Authors

Russell S. Riera, the 34-year-old author of this book, enjoys writing about restaurants—Riera and food have been good friends for a long time. At the age of 12, he sold live crabs in front of his father's restaurant at San Francisco's Fisherman's Wharf. And years later, at Sacramento State University, he spent his summers working in casino restaurants in Lake Tahoe. Then, in 1967, Riera was drafted and sent to Qui Nhon, Vietnam. What kind of assignment did the U.S. Army give him? Food supply. Riera ended up as a Spec 5 in the First Logistical Command and was put in charge of shipping food supplies to 120,000 combat troops stationed outside Qui Nhon. Needless to say, Riera never forgot to ship the food.

For the last ten years, Riera has spent all of his time around restaurants in San Francisco and the Bay Area, both writing about them and working at them. And in 1972, while at Giovanni's, Riera co-authored a Bay Area guidebook, *The Good Time Manual*. It was a local best seller.

Riera has some definite plans for the future. Besides continuing his occupation as a food talent scout, Riera intends to put the recipes he's collected over the years to work. It'll be called Riera's restaurant.

The gravitational pull of good food has been a force Chris Smith has never been able to ignore. While he was in law school, Smith would round out a day of studying contracts and torts with a meal at a restaurant. From law school, Smith went on to work for the Lieutenant Governor of California and the Rand Corporation—all the while expanding his waistline and notebook as he discovered new places to eat. The first spin-off from this research was *The Good Time Manual*, which he co-authored with Russ Riera.

Inevitably, an author's first book sets the stage for his second. While he went on with his education by earning a master's degree in health services administration, Smith continued to knife, fork, and spoon his way through some of the Bay Area's best—and worst restaurants. As he currently pursues a career in the health care field, Smith's endless meal continues.

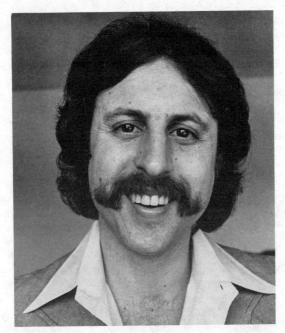

Russell S. Riera

Chris Smith